Survey of the
Old Testament

Survey of the Old Testament

by
Paul N. Benware

MOODY PRESS

CHICAGO

© 1988 by
PAUL N. BENWARE

Library of Congress Cataloging in Publication Data

Benware, Paul N., 1942-
    Survey of the Old Testament.

    (Everyman's Bible Commentary)
    Bibliography: p.
    1. Bible.   O.T.—Introductions.   I. Title.
II. Series.
BS1140.2.B45   1988   221.6'1   88-1770
ISBN 0-8024-2091-5

5 6 7 Printing/EP/Year 93 92 91

*To my Old Testament students
at Moody Bible Institute—
together pursuing the wisdom of God*

CONTENTS

Index of Graphics   9

Part 1: Introduction and Overview

1. Introduction to the Old Testament   12
2. Overview of the Old Testament   17

Part 2: The Foundational Books

3. Genesis   26
4. Exodus and Leviticus   49
5. Numbers and Deuteronomy   64
6. Joshua   77
7. Judges and Ruth   85
8. 1 Samuel   95
9. 2 Samuel   101
10. 1 Kings   106
11. 2 Kings   115
12. 1 and 2 Chronicles   121
13. Ezra and Esther   128
14. Nehemiah   137

Part 3: The Poetic Books

15. Hebrew Poetry   144
16. Job   147

17. Psalms   151
18. Proverbs   156
19. Ecclesiastes   159
20. Song of Solomon   163
21. Lamentations   166

Part 4: The Prophetic Books

22. God's Prophetic Messengers   170

Group 1: Prophecies During the Divided Kingdom

23. Obadiah   178
24. Joel   181
25. Jonah   184
26. Amos   187
27. Hosea   190
28. Isaiah   194
29. Micah   198

Group 2: Prophecies During the Single Kingdom

30. Nahum   202
31. Zephaniah   206
32. Jeremiah   209
33. Habakkuk   213

Group 3: Prophecies During the Exile

34. Daniel   218
35. Ezekiel   222

Group 4: Prophecies After the Exile

36. Haggai   228
37. Zechariah   231
38. Malachi   234

Notes on Special Topics

A. The Mosaic Authorship of the Pentateuch   238
B. Various Views of Origins   241
C. The Names of God in the Old Testament   244
D. The Date of the Exodus   248
E. Israel and the Nations   252
F. The Extermination of the Canaanites   263

Selected Bibliography   266

INDEX OF GRAPHICS

Order and Classification of the Books of the Old Testament 15-16
Eras of the Old Testament   22
Chronological Relationships of Old Testament Books   23
Abraham's Journeys   35
God's Covenants with Israel   41
The Chronology of the Patriarchs   44
The Family Tree of Abraham   45
Locations in Genesis   45
Chronology of Genesis and Exodus   49
The Chronology of the Life of Moses   51
The Plagues in Egypt   53
Israel's Journey to Sinai   55
The Plan of the Tabernacle   57
Plan of the Camp of Israel   66
Priestly Line in Israel   67

Israel's Complaints in the Wilderness	68
Boundaries of the Promised Land	76
The Three Major Campaigns of Joshua	81
Joshua's Central Campaign	82
Joshua's Southern Campaign	83
Timeline of Joshua and Judges	86
Chronology of Israel's Judges	87
Cycle of the Judges	89
Period of the Kingdoms	100
Davidic Covenant	104
Approximate Boundaries of the Two Kingdoms in the Days of the Divided Monarchy	111
A Comparison of the Two Kingdoms	114
Rulers in the Era of the Monarchy	120
Relationship of Samuel, Kings, and Chronicles	123
Comparison of Samuel, Kings, and Chronicles	123
The Period of Captivity in Babylon	124
The Babylonian Empire	125
The Chronology of the Restoration	129
The Gates, Walls, and Towers of Jerusalem	140
Dating the Writing of Job	148
Chronology of the Prophets of Israel and Judah	176
Prophecies During the Divided Kingdom	177
Prophecies During the Single Kingdom	201
The Last Days of the Kingdom of Judah	212
The Deportations of Judah: Beginnings of the Exile	216
Prophecies During the Exile	217
The Prophetic Calendar and Daniel's "Times of the Gentiles"	221
Prophecies After the Exile	227
The Chronology After the Exile	230
Israel and the Pharaohs	251
Nations Related to Israel	253
Israel's Near Neighbors	254
Israel's Distant Neighbors	258

Part 1

Introduction and Overview

1

INTRODUCTION TO THE OLD TESTAMENT

THE IMPORTANCE OF STUDYING THE OLD TESTAMENT

A person will never properly understand the New Testament Scriptures if the Old Testament Scriptures remain a mystery to him. Yet for the average Christian the pattern, unity, and progression of the Old Testament remain vague or unknown. Although almost everyone knows about Noah and the ark, Moses and the Red Sea, and numerous other stories found in the books of the Old Testament, the Old Testament itself often seems fragmented and is seen only as a loosely knit group of stories. But to understand God's ways and His purposes in this age, as well as His plans for the future ages, requires a clear comprehension of the Old Testament.

For example, there are about 350 direct quotes or clear allusions from the Old Testament found in the New Testament book of Revelation.[1] This amounts to about fifteen Old Testament references per chapter. It is no wonder that for many who do not have a good grip on the Old Testament, Revelation is essentially a closed book. Or who can really appreciate the apostle Paul's discussion about Israel in Romans 9-11 if there is no understanding of Genesis 12 and Jeremiah 31? Comprehending the Old Testament is crucial to understanding the New Testament.

Great doctrinal truths are developed in the Old Testament. For example, significant revelations concerning the attributes of God

1. Merrill C. Tenney, *Interpreting Revelation* (Grand Rapids: Eerdmans, 1957), pp. 101-16).

are recorded. The New Testament, of course, concerns itself with the Person of God, but it is the Old Testament that gives us our basic understanding of God's majesty, power, holiness, and sovereignty. His love, goodness, and wisdom are the subjects of many psalms and numerous prophetic declarations. What can rival Isaiah 40 on the greatness of God or Psalm 23 on the loving care of God?

Perhaps it is our lack of understanding of the Old Testament that has brought about a basic deficiency in our knowledge of God and, as a result, our walk with Him.

> The Church has surrendered her once lofty concept of God and has substituted for it one so low, so ignoble, as to be unworthy of thinking, worshiping men. . . . The low view of God entertained almost universally among Christians is the cause of a hundred lesser evils everywhere among us. A whole new philosophy of the Christian life has resulted from this one basic error in our religious thinking.[2]

After serious study of the Old Testament one is inclined to walk with more reverence before our majestic God.

So much foundational truth is found in the Old Testament—truth that the New Testament writers assume we know and understand. An almost endless list of doctrinal truths and meaningful facts could be given to validate the importance of the Old Testament to the New. Yet so often, students of the Scriptures wrestle with truth found in the books of the New Testament because they fail to recognize Old Testament background.

THE PURPOSE OF THIS SURVEY BOOK

The purpose of this study is to assist the Bible student in seeing the pattern, progression, and unity of the Old Testament Scriptures and to be able to think through the entire Old Testament. A person must see the "big picture," and then he can begin to relate the various parts to this comprehensive view. Also, it is the pur-

2. A. W. Tozer, *The Knowledge of the Holy* (New York: Harper and Row, 1961), p. 7.

pose of this book to develop the central, unifying theme of the Old Testament, which is God's covenant promises to the nation of Israel.

THE APPROACH OF THIS SURVEY BOOK

The Old Testament is made up of thirty-nine books. These books contain the history of the nation of Israel, the laws of God for Israel, insightful and inspiring poetry, and the messages of numerous prophets. To observe how these books relate to one another our study will begin with and will emphasize the eleven "foundational books." These eleven books develop the story line of the Old Testament. Since these foundational books form the chronological and historical basis for the other twenty-eight books, the great emphasis in this study of the Old Testament will be placed on them. Once we work our way through the foundational books, the other books will be linked to this historical base. This approach will aid in our awareness of the pattern and progression of the Old Testament Scriptures (see chart "Order and Classification of the Books of the Old Testament," pp. 15-16).

Another emphasis of this study will be to develop the central, unifying theme of the Old Testament, which is God's covenant promises to Abraham and his descendants. God's great covenant promises to Israel are the "glue" that holds the Old Testament together. In fact, the whole of the Bible is unified by God's covenant relationship with Israel, which also includes the Gentiles. It is unlikely that a full comprehension of the "New" covenant, based on the death of Jesus Christ, can exist without understanding its Old Testament context.

When the chronological framework is understood and the unifying theme is observed, the Old Testament makes sense. The fragmentation is gone, and the unity, pattern, and progression can be appreciated.

ORDER AND CLASSIFICATION OF THE BOOKS OF THE OLD TESTAMENT

THIS STUDY	STANDARD ENGLISH CLASSIFICATION	HEBREW CLASSIFICATION

Foundational Books
  Genesis
  Exodus
  Numbers
  Joshua
  Judges
  1 Samuel
  2 Samuel
  1 Kings
  2 Kings
  Ezra
  Nehemiah
	Books of the Law
	  Genesis
	  Exodus
	  Leviticus
	  Numbers
	  Deuteronomy
		The Law
		  Genesis
		  Exodus
		  Leviticus
		  Numbers
		  Deuteronomy

Complementation Books
  Leviticus
  Deuteronomy
  Ruth
  1 Chronicles
  2 Chronicles
  Esther
	Books of History
	  Joshua
	  Judges
	  Ruth
	  1 Samuel
	  2 Samuel
	  1 Kings
	  2 Kings
	  1 Chronicles
	  2 Chronicles
	  Ezra
	  Nehemiah
	  Esther
		The Former Prophets
		  Joshua
		  Judges
		  1 Samuel
		  2 Samuel
		  1 Kings
		  2 Kings

Books of Poetry/Wisdom
  Job
  Psalms
  Proverbs
  Ecclesiastes
  Song of Solomon
  Lamentations
	Books of Poetry/Wisdom
	  Job
	  Psalms
	  Proverbs
	  Ecclesiastes
	  Song of Solomon
		The Latter Prophets
		  Isaiah
		  Jeremiah
		  Ezekiel
		  Hosea
		  Joel
		  Amos
		  Obadiah
		  Jonah
		  Micah
		  Nahum
		  Habakkuk
		  Zephaniah
		  Haggai
		  Zechariah
		  Malachi

Prophets During the Divided Kingdom
  Obadiah
  Joel
  Jonah
  Amos
  Hosea
  Isaiah
  Micah
	The Major Prophets
	  Isaiah
	  Jeremiah
	  Lamentations
	  Ezekiel
	  Daniel	

(Continued next page)

THIS STUDY	STANDARD ENGLISH CLASSIFICATION	HEBREW CLASSIFICATION
Prophets During the Single Kingdom Nahum Zephaniah Jeremiah Habakkuk **Prophets During the Exile** Daniel Ezekiel **Prophets After the Exile** Haggai Zechariah Malachi	**The Minor Prophets** Hosea Joel Amos Obadiah Jonah Micah Nahum Habakkuk Zephaniah Haggai Zechariah Malachi	**The Writings** Psalms Job Proverbs Ruth Song of Solomon Ecclesiastes Lamentations Esther Daniel Ezra Nehemiah 1 Chronicles 2 Chronicles

2

OVERVIEW
OF THE OLD TESTAMENT

The Old Testament is the story of the nation of Israel, a nation unique and distinct from all the nations of the earth because God Himself entered into a covenant relationship with them. It is the story of a nation designed by God to bring glory to Himself and salvation to mankind—a story of the great spiritual victories and defeats of men and the amazing faithfulness and grace of God.

GOD'S DEALINGS WITH MANKIND

The Old Testament is divided into two distinct parts, each covering several thousand years of history. The first is Genesis 1-11 and is a record of God's dealings with mankind generally. During those years, there was no special group such as the church or the nation of Israel. God's dealings were with individuals. Since we do not know the exact date of the creation of the universe, we cannot say with certainty, as some do, that Genesis 1-11 covers two thousand years. It could be several thousand years more (but not millions or billions of years). Much is not recorded about these early years of man, but four important events are included—the creation account, the Fall of man, the great Flood of Noah's day, and the division of mankind at the Tower of Babel. These events are briefly recorded so that we understand where this material universe came from, where sin and evil came from, and why the world of mankind is so fragmented. But the first few thousand years of human history are passed over quickly in order to get to the main emphasis of the Old Testament, which is the selection of Israel as God's chosen nation.

GOD'S DEALINGS WITH ISRAEL

The second distinct part of the Old Testament covers about 2,000 years. This part begins with Genesis 12 and includes all the rest of the Old Testament. Genesis 12 is the cornerstone chapter of the Bible. It is here that God selects a man by the name of Abraham and enters into an eternal, unconditional covenant with him and his descendants. God made many promises to Abraham. These promises included personal blessings to Abraham and his descendants and blessings that would include all the rest of mankind.

THE ABRAHAMIC COVENANT

In this covenant, God promised that from Abraham He would make a great nation. The first four foundational books (Genesis, Exodus, Numbers, and Joshua) record the formation of the nation of Israel. In order to have a nation, three basic elements must be present—*people, law,* and *land.*

Genesis 12-50 records how God began to populate this new nation. In these chapters God's dealings with Abraham and his family make it abundantly clear to all that God is the giver of life and He guarantees the ''people element'' of a nation. When Genesis ends the nation has grown to about seventy-five people, which is not usually thought of as a ''great'' nation. But during the 275 years between Genesis and Exodus, a population explosion took place. By the Exodus, the nation's population had grown to more than 2 million. The *people* element of the nation was completed.

THE MOSAIC LAW

Next, in order to function as a legitimate nation, Israel needed a code of *laws* to live by. Israel had become enslaved to the Egyptians during the period between Genesis and Exodus, but was miraculously set free by God and His human leader Moses. After their mighty deliverance, recorded in the book of Exodus, the people of Israel journeyed to Mount Sinai, where they received their constitution, laws covering all aspects of life. They camped at Mount Sinai for about a year, receiving the law and constructing their portable worship center, the Tabernacle.

THE PROMISED LAND

When the year at Mount Sinai was completed, Israel left to possess the Promised Land, the land of Canaan. This land was part of the covenant God had made with Abraham about four hundred years before. With the taking of this *land,* the third and last element would be fulfilled, and Israel would begin her role as a "great" nation. However, the third foundational book, Numbers, records a terrible moment in Israel's history. At that time, Israel refused to believe and obey God, which kept her from possessing the land. Instead of living in Canaan, Israel wandered aimlessly in a wilderness region for almost forty years.

When that period of discipline was over, Israel headed to the east side of the Jordan River and prepared to cross into her land. It was at this time that Israel's great leader Moses died. Just before Moses' death, God chose Joshua to lead the nation. He led Israel across the river and into the land of the wicked Canaanites. He directed the armies of Israel in the destruction of the main strongholds of the Canaanites. This period of warfare lasted from five to seven years. With the breaking of Canaanite power, the people of Israel could lay claim to the entire land. Israel now had people, law, and a land. The period of the formation of the nation was over (see chart "Four Eras of Old Testament History," p. 22).

Joshua then divided the land, giving each of the twelve tribes of Israel a clearly delineated area. It was now the task of each individual tribe to complete the conquest of the land by eliminating every single Canaanite living in its tribal area. God had specifically commanded them not to intermarry with the Canaanites, not to make treaties with them, and not to allow any to live among them. Unfortunately, Israel once again chose not to obey.

THE NATIONAL RULERS

When Joshua died, Israel entered a new era in its national life. God did not replace Joshua with a new leader for His people. It was God's intention that the newly formed nation be a theocracy (God ruling) with no single human leader. God would govern through the law given at Sinai and through the priests as the interpreters and enforcers of the law. But the theocracy turned out to be a failure because Israel would not obey her own constitution. The fifth foundational book, Judges, records these years, known primarily for their defeat and failure. During the more than three hundred years of the theocracy, judges had to be raised up again and again in crisis situations. The judges would deliver Israel from her enemies and bring in a time of obedience and peace. But those times eventually gave way once again to sin, unbelief, and idolatry. Another judge would be raised up by God, and the cycle would repeat itself.

After three centuries of repeated failure, Israel demanded a human king. Even though this was a repudiation of God's rulership, He allowed Saul to become Israel's first king. With Saul's coronation Israel entered a third era in her history—the period of the monarchy. The next four foundational books (1 and 2 Samuel, 1 and 2 Kings) record the next 450 years of Israel's history. First and 2 Samuel tell the stories of Israel's first king, Saul, and Israel's greatest king, David. It was with King David that God made a marvelous covenant, much of which is fulfilled in David's "great son," the Lord Jesus Christ. David's son Solomon reigned after the death of David and was the third and last king to rule over all of Israel's twelve tribes.

THE DIVIDED NATION

Because of Solomon's sinful ways, God judged the family of David by dividing the nation into two separate kingdoms. The Northern Kingdom, Israel, consisted of ten tribes. The Southern Kingdom was called Judah and was made up of two tribes ruled by the family of David. For two centuries these two kingdoms co-existed, sometimes as friends and other times as foes. But the time of the divided kingdom came to an end when, because of sin and idolatry, the Northern Kingdom was destroyed by the nation of Assyria. The Southern Kingdom existed alone for more than one hundred years. It lasted longer because it was blessed with the presence of some godly kings. But, like the North, the Southern Kingdom went into idolatry. This time God used the nation of Babylon as His rod of discipline. Many people from the Southern Kingdom, including Daniel and Ezekiel, were deported from Judah to Babylonia. The nation lived in captivity for about seventy years.

THE PARTIAL RESTORATION

Finally, in fulfillment of His promise, God restored many of the people to their own land. The final period in the Old Testament history of Israel is recorded in Ezra and Nehemiah, the final two foundational books. This 150-year period focuses on both the political and spiritual restoration of Judah, and on several great men who were used in that restoration.

With the end of the book of Nehemiah, the story of the Old Testament comes to a close. Some four hundred years would go by before the Scriptures would pick up the story again. The years of silence would be broken by an angelic messenger, Gabriel, who would announce the birth of John the Baptist and the birth of Jesus the Messiah, the "great son" of David. God had not forgotten or gone back on His covenant promises to Abraham and his descendants.

This is a brief overview of the basic story of the Old Testament. Now our task is to look with greater care at each of the foundational books and then link to them the rest of the books of the Old Testament.

ERAS OF OLD TESTAMENT HISTORY

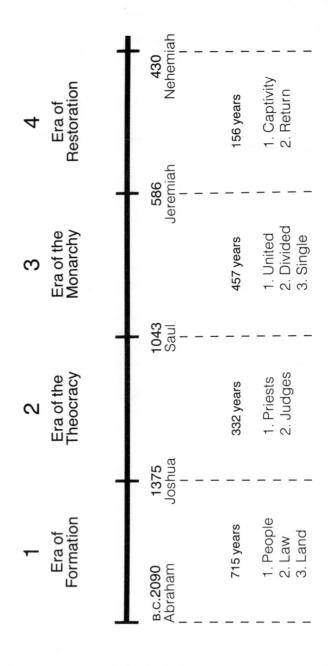

1	2	3	4
Era of Formation	Era of the Theocracy	Era of the Monarchy	Era of Restoration

B.C. 2090 Abraham — 1375 Joshua — 1043 Saul — 586 Jeremiah — 430 Nehemiah

715 years
1. People
2. Law
3. Land

332 years
1. Priests
2. Judges

457 years
1. United
2. Divided
3. Single

156 years
1. Captivity
2. Return

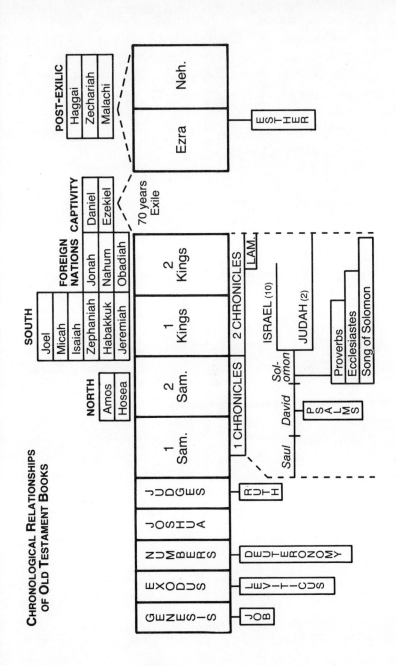

CHRONOLOGICAL RELATIONSHIPS
OF OLD TESTAMENT BOOKS

Part 2

The Foundational Books

3

GENESIS

INTRODUCTION TO GENESIS

A. AUTHORSHIP AND DATE OF GENESIS

The book of Genesis is part of the sacred Scriptures. Ultimately, therefore, God is the author and the source of all this recorded truth. Every Scripture is "God-breathed" (2 Tim. 3:16). But God did employ men to write down His message. Each human author used his own writing style, vocabulary, background, and personality as he wrote the truth of God. These men were "carried along" by the Holy Spirit of God in their efforts (2 Pet. 1:20-21), thus guaranteeing the accuracy and the authority of the writings. Genesis and the other Old Testament books are, therefore, documents with dual authorship—God's and man's.

Moses was the human author of Genesis and the other books of the Pentateuch. (*Pentateuch* is a Greek word commonly used for the first five books of the Old Testament.) These five "books of the Law" were written by Moses alone, with the exception of Deuteronomy 34, which records the death of Moses. (For a further discussion of the Mosaic authorship of Genesis and the rest of the Pentateuch, see Note A, "The Mosaic Authorship of the Pentateuch," p. 238.)

The writing of Genesis, and the rest of the Pentateuch, most likely took place after the Exodus and before Israel's entrance into the land of Canaan, probably during the days of Israel's forty-year wilderness wandering. This author holds to an early date for the Exodus (about 1445 B.C.) and so assigns the date for the writing of Genesis at about 1425 B.C.

B. PURPOSE OF GENESIS

Genesis is the book of beginnings. It was written, first, to tell us clearly and definitely that God created all things directly. The entire organized universe was brought into existence by the powerful, all-knowing, creator God. Second, Genesis was written to record the beginning of many other elements that exist in our world today. The beginnings of such important matters as marriage, languages, nations, sin, and worship are recorded. A third purpose of the book is to relate how Israel, through Abraham, was selected from among the peoples of the world to become God's chosen nation.

C. BASIC OUTLINE OF GENESIS

  I. God's Dealings with Mankind in General (chaps. 1-11)
   A. The Creation (1-2)
   B. The Fall of Man (3-5)
   C. The Flood (6-9)
   D. The Nations (10-11)
  II. God's Dealings with the Nation of Israel (chaps. 12-50)
   A. Abraham (12-23)
   B. Isaac (24-26)
   C. Jacob (27-36)
   D. Joseph (37-50)

D. IMPORTANT DATA ABOUT GENESIS

  1. Key Word: Beginnings
  2. Key Chapter: 12—The Abrahamic Covenant
  3. Key Verses: 12:1-3
  4. Key Characters: Adam, Eve, Noah, Abraham, Isaac, Jacob, Joseph
  5. Meaning of "Genesis": A Greek word that means "origin" or "beginning"
  6. Geography of Genesis: Ur, Canaan, Egypt

E.   SPECIAL CONSIDERATIONS ON GENESIS

1. Years Covered by Genesis

The total number of years covered in Genesis is uncertain because we do not know the time of creation. Genesis 12-50, from the call of Abraham to the death of Joseph, encompasses three hundred years. And we assign two thousand years to Genesis 1-11, so twenty-three hundred years is the estimate given for this study.

2. Background Points on Genesis

(a)   The Nature of Genesis

It is historically accurate. The book of Genesis records actual human history. It is not a book of legends or religious myths. Adam, Eve, Noah, and the rest were real people whose lives and experiences are accurately recorded. The Lord Jesus Christ and the apostles and other writers of the Bible believed in the historicity of Genesis. Genesis is quoted some sixty times in the New Testament in seventeen different books (such as Matt. 24:37; Luke 11:51; Rom. 5:14; 1 Tim. 2:13). Genesis is scientifically accurate. Genesis records the origin of all created life and matter. It tells of a worldwide flood and numerous miracles. In all cases, Genesis speaks truthfully and accurately. Although it does not use modern scientific terminology, it speaks correctly. God is the source of all truth, whether it has to do with spiritual law or natural law.

Furthermore, Genesis is characterized by supernaturalism. The reader of Genesis is immediately confronted with the issue of supernaturalism as he opens to chapter 1. And in the rest of Genesis, God steps in on occasion and temporarily suspends natural law. This, of course, poses no problem to the believer who understands that God is personally involved with both His creation and His people.

(b)   The Emphasis of Genesis

It is clear that the emphasis of Genesis is on God's covenant with Abraham and the initial outworking of that covenant relationship. The focus of thirty-nine chapters in Genesis is on four men—Abraham, Isaac, Jacob, and Joseph. By way of contrast, only two chapters are devoted to the creation of the entire universe, and only nine chapters are given over to man's earliest history. The first eleven chapters cover two thousand or more years, whereas the remaining thirty-nine chapters focus on three hundred years of history.

A Summary of Genesis

I. God's Dealings with Mankind in General (chaps. 1-11)

A. The Creation (1-2)

These two chapters affirm the fact of a special creation by God. Moses, in simple, nonscientific terms, states that God supernaturally created all things in the universe. He did not use any preexistent matter, but created the earth and the universe out of nothing (see Heb. 11:3). These two chapters answer the two key questions involving origins—the origin of the material universe and the origin of man. (For a discussion of the basic theories of origins, see Note B, "Various Views on Origins," p. 241.)

1. The Days of Creation (1:1-31)

The opening statement in 1:1 is critical to our understanding of the creation account. This first verse summarizes the creation account to follow by declaring that God created the entire organized universe and everything in it ("heavens and earth"). The New Testament gives additional light by revealing that the Creator is the Triune God—Father, Son, and Holy Spirit (John 1:3; Col. 1:16 with Job 33:4; Ps. 33:6). The word used for "created" is the Hebrew word *bara*, which strongly supports the idea of the ex nihilo ("out of nothing") creation. Moses could have selected no better word than *bara* to express the idea of an extraordinary activity by God.[1] God simply called the universe into existence.

All of this activity took place "in the beginning," which refers to the creation week and not to billions of years in the past.

"'Beginning' refers to the commencement of time in our universe and demonstrates that the matter of the universe had a definite origin; it is not eternal and did not start itself."[2]

Furthermore, Exodus 20:11 and 31:17 help define the "beginning" by defining the chronological limits of creation as being within a six-day period.[3]

---

1. Edward J. Young, *Studies in Genesis One* (Nutley, N.J.: Presbyterian and Reformed, 1964), p. 6.
2. Howard F. Vos, *Genesis* (Chicago: Moody, 1982), p. 10.
3. Weston W. Fields, *Unformed and Unfilled* (Nutley, N.J.: Presbyterian and Reformed, 1976), pp. 162-63.

So with this simple but profound declaration, Moses states that there is a God, He is powerful, and He is greater than His creation. The implications of this first verse in the Old Testament are great. Since God is the one and only Creator, He has the power and the right to do what He chooses with His creation. He deserves to be honored and worshiped by His creatures (see Rev. 4:11). Unregenerate men, however, willfully resist acknowledging the great Creator God.

(a) Day 1: The creation of light (1:2-5)

God created the material earth on the first day (1:1). The earth had no distinct features such as mountains or continents, however. At this point it was unfinished and was uninhabited and empty ("formless and void").[4] It awaited God's creative activity.[5]

The creation of light was the next act of God, making a separation between darkness and light. God created a light source, which was not the sun, in order to temporarily mark off the day-night cycle, as the earth rotated on its axis. The sun was created on the fourth day, after the creation of the earth. Perhaps this was to speak out against the future pagan worship of the "creator" sun, the false religious science of astrology, and the evolutionary idea of the earth's coming from the sun.

Although there is no specific statement in Genesis 1 on the subject of angelic beings, they may have been created on the first day as part of the creation of the heavens and the earth (Ps. 148:2-5; Job 38:7).

(b) Day 2: The creation of the upper and lower waters (1:6-8)

By elevating some of the waters that were on the earth to a region above the earth, God created the earth's atmosphere. Some believe that these upper waters were ordinary rain clouds.[6] Others believe that they formed a large vapor canopy that surrounded the earth, providing a "greenhouse" effect on the earth. This view also sees the upper waters as a great source of water for the Flood of Noah's day.[7]

---

4. John C. Whitcomb, *The Early Earth,* rev. ed. (Grand Rapids: Baker, 1986), p. 56.
5. Ibid., p. 146, and Fields, *Unformed,* p. 87.
6. Vos, *Genesis,* p. 14.
7. John C. Whitcomb and Henry M. Morris, *The Genesis Flood* (Philadelphia: Presbyterian and Reformed, 1961), p. 243.

(c)   Day 3: The creation of plants (1:9-13)

God spoke and great areas of land suddenly appeared from beneath the lower waters. The earth, which had a cool crust, now had mountains, plains, and ocean basins. God then called trees and vegetation into existence. They were created full grown with the capacity to reproduce after their own kind.

(d)   Day 4: The creation of the sun, moon, and stars (1:14-19)

Evidently the sun, moon, and stars were actually created on the fourth day and did not simply "appear." These luminaries were designed to give light to the earth and to function as a calendar for the earth, marking off days, months, years, and seasons. The sun and moon are "great lights" in the sense that this is the way they appear to those on the earth. It is the "language of appearance."

(e)   Day 5: The creation of birds and all marine life (1:20-23)

All water creatures came into being on this day, leaving no room in the biblical text for evolution with its gradual development from single-celled, marine organisms.

(f)   Day 6: The creation of land animals, reptiles, man (1:24-31)

After creating the animals, reptiles, and insects that would live on the earth, God turned His attention to the crown of creation, man. Only man would be created in the "image of God," which has reference to moral and spiritual likeness. Only man would be a "person," possessing intellect, emotions, and a will. Man was made to be "king of the earth" with authority to rule and to subdue the rest of creation.

When the creation week was completed, God's verdict was that it was all excellent (1:31).

2.   The Creation of Man (2:1-25)

Genesis 2 is a further development of part of day six. It is simply giving greater attention to the creation of man. It is not, as some have suggested, a separate and different creation narrative.

(a)   The Sabbath (2:1-3)

God set the seventh day apart, though there is no evidence that He commanded men to observe the Sabbath before the days of Moses (Ex. 16:23; 20:8-11; 31:12-17).

     (b)   Additional information (2:4-6)

This section probably refers to special types of vegetation that needed Adam's care.

     (c)   The creation of Adam (2:7-9)

Adam was created suddenly and supernaturally from the dust of the ground. After he was created, God placed him into the Garden of Eden. Also God placed two trees with special powers into the Garden—the tree of life and the tree of the knowledge of good and evil.

     (d)   The Garden of Eden (2:10-17)

Eden was a small area of the planet and would become the place where man's moral test would take place.

     (e)   The creation of Eve and the beginning of marriage (2:18-25)

Before Eve's creation, all Adam's relationships were vertical —to God above him and to the animals below him. Adam was "alone." In order to clarify this to Adam, God paraded the basic species of animals past Adam. Adam named them but in the process realized that he had no one as a "complement" to him. God gave Adam his needed helper by creating Eve. God did not create Eve from the dust of the ground, but from one of Adam's ribs to emphasize their oneness. Significant, foundational truths for marriage are found in this section.

  B. The Fall of Man (3-5)

    1. The Entrance of Sin (3:1-24)

The "very good" state of creation did not last for long. Satan, who may not have fallen very long before this, tempted Eve by casting doubt on the word of God and the goodness of God. She was deceived and took the fruit from the tree of the knowledge of good and evil (the experiential knowledge of moral good and evil). Adam was not deceived (1 Tim. 2:14) but nevertheless took of the fruit and sinned against God. This willful act brought about immediate spiritual death (Rom. 5:12-19) and many years later physical death. Adam and Eve were removed from Eden and faced a world cursed by God. And now God's great work of redemption had to begin.

2. The Story of Cain and Abel (4:1-25)

The effect of sin was seen early in the human experience as Cain murdered his brother Abel, and an apparent division between the godly and the ungodly appeared.

3. The Descendants of Adam (5:1-32)

Genesis 5 is given to take us quickly from the days of Adam to the times of Noah. This chapter also shows the fulfillment of the curse (2:17) of death on man because of sin.

C. The Flood (6-9)

1. The Catastrophe (6:1–8:19)

By the days of Noah, mankind had degenerated completely, and the world had become a terrible place to live (Gen. 6:5, 11, 13). Sin had gripped man so completely that only Noah was said to be righteous (Gen. 6:9; Heb. 11:7). God declared that He would destroy the world with a flood of water (6:17). Noah was ordered to build an ark to save all air-breathing creatures. This barge-like structure was about 450 feet long, 75 feet wide, and 45 feet high. It had three decks, giving it about 95,700 square feet of space.[8] It had plenty of room to handle its live cargo.

The Flood that came 120 years after God's pronouncement of judgment on mankind was universal. This is seen in the use of global terms such as "all" and "every" in describing the destruction of those days. The fact that the Flood lasted for more than a year (something not true of local floods) indicates that Noah's Flood engulfed the whole earth. Furthermore, the statement of Genesis that all the high mountains were covered by more than twenty feet of water dictates a flood that is not confined to a local area (7:19-20). Even the building of an ark at all and the gathering of animals to it makes little sense unless the Flood was worldwide.[9] Psalm 104:1-9 speaks of worldwide, catastrophic geologic activity during the time of the Flood.[10] All of these factors point to the Flood as a supernatural judgment of universal scope.

8. Ibid., p. 10.
9. Ibid., pp. 1-35.
10. David Barker, "The Waters of the Earth: An Exegetical Study of Psalm 104:1-9," *Grace Theological Journal* 7, no. 1 (Spring 1986): 57-80.

    2. Noah and His Family (8:20–9:28)

The Flood did not solve man's sin problem, though it did deal with a crisis of wickedness and reveal the power, holiness, and grace of God. When Noah and his family departed from the ark, a new era began, and God gave them some new guidelines. Commonly referred to as the ''Noahic covenant,'' these guidelines included the following: man was to spread out over the whole earth; man could now eat meat; man had the right to execute murderers; and man would now be instinctively feared by animals (9:1-7). God promised He would never again destroy the world by water, and He gave the rainbow as a sign of this covenant (9:12-15).

 D. The Nations (10-11)

    1. The Ancient Families (10:1-32)

This chapter is a partial record of the development of the human race through the sons of Noah. There is an emphasis on the Canaanites and their land, since Moses wanted to link all this information to God's promise to bless Israel as a nation in the Promised Land of Canaan.[11] The family of Shem is mentioned last in the account because the rest of the Old Testament is the story of Abraham, a descendant of Shem.

    2. The Tower of Babel (11:1-32)

The incident at the Tower of Babel explains how the human race became so divided when it had all descended from one man and his family. Chapter 11 chronologically precedes chapter 10. In spite of God's command to spread out over the earth (9:1-7), man chose to disobey and to congregate together (11:4). Foreseeing the resulting wickedness, God intervened with a unique act of judgment. He brought total chaos and confusion to man by causing the people at Babel (''confusion'') to begin speaking separate and distinct languages. The result was a dispersion of the human race to separate geographic areas.[12] This event marks the origin of the different human languages and, perhaps, the beginning of distinct racial groups.

---

11. Allen P. Ross, ''The Table of Nations in Genesis 10—Its Content,'' *Bibliotheca Sacra* 138 (January-March 1981): 22-34.
12. Allen P. Ross, ''The Dispersion of the Nations in Genesis 11:1-9,'' *Bibliotheca Sacra* 139 (April-June 1981): 119-33.

The chapter ends (11:10-32) by giving the generations of Shem leading up to the man Abraham. Some two thousand years of the early history of man have been sketched, and now Moses is ready to record the call of Abraham. With Abraham's call, the second major division of the Old Testament is opened.

II. God's Dealings with the Nation of Israel (chaps. 12-50)
    A. Abraham (12-23)
        1. The Call of Abraham (12:1-9)

These verses record the second call of Abraham (Abram). God first called Abraham when he lived in Ur of the Chaldees (Gen. 11:31; Acts 7:2-4). Abraham and several family members departed Ur and traveled to Haran, which was located in the northern part of the Fertile Crescent. After several years there and after the death of Terah, his father, Abraham left Haran. He evidently did not know exactly where God was leading him (Heb. 11:8) but knew enough to head for Canaan. God confirmed His covenant when Abraham arrived in Canaan at the age of seventy-five. This covenant is the cornerstone of the Old Testament. Without an understanding of the Abrahamic Covenant, there will be little understanding of the purposes and plans of God.

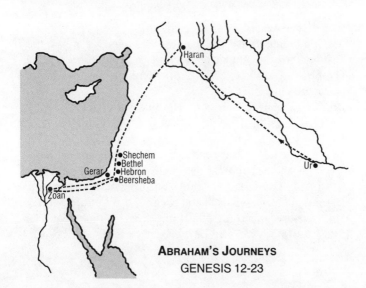

ABRAHAM'S JOURNEYS
GENESIS 12-23

THE ABRAHAMIC COVENANT

The idea of a covenant between individuals was dominant in the life of the ancient Near East. It is often seen in the Old Testament. Covenants made between men (e.g. Gen. 21:32), between groups (e.g. 1 Sam. 11:1), and between nations (e.g. Ex. 23:32) were common. A covenant was an agreement between two parties that bound them together with common interests and responsibilities. It was most serious and sacred to enter into a covenant. And covenants usually included blessings and cursings; blessings upon the one who fulfilled his part in the covenant and cursings on the one who broke his oath.

When God made a covenant with Abraham, therefore, it was not a strange or unusual event. Granted, one did not usually enter into a covenant with the almighty God. But Abraham would be thoroughly familiar with the idea of a covenant and the making of a covenant. The record of the covenant made with Abraham is found in Genesis 12:1-3; 13:14-17; 15:1-21; 17:1-22; and 22:15-18.

A. THE BASIC PROVISIONS OF THE ABRAHAMIC COVENANT

1. Personal Blessing for Abraham

God promised that Abraham would be the father of a great nation, have a multitude of descendants, and prosper materially (Gen. 12:2; 13:16; 15:5; 17:6). These promises to Abraham have been literally fulfilled.

2. Blessing to Abraham's Descendants

This aspect of the covenant does not apply to all of Abraham's physical descendants, but only to those who came through the line of Isaac and Jacob. This Covenant was passed on from Abraham to Isaac only and then to Jacob (Gen. 26:3-6; 28:13-14; 35:9-12). As with Abraham, these descendants are promised greatness as a nation (Gen. 12:2; 13:16; 15:5). Also, they were guaranteed the land of Canaan as their own (Gen. 12:7; 13:15-17; 15:7-8; 17:8). The area was described generally in Genesis 15:18 as extending from the river of Egypt to the Euphrates River. More exact boundaries would be given later as Israel actually prepared to possess the land of promise. This aspect of the Abrahamic Covenant has not yet been fulfilled.

3. Universal Blessing

The covenant also looked beyond the line of Abraham to include all mankind; "And in you all the families of the earth shall be blessed" (Gen. 12:3). It was not God's intention to isolate Israel from the nations, but rather that Israel would be a worldwide blessing (Gen. 18:18; 22:17-18; 26:3-4; 28:13-14). The ultimate fulfillment of this part of the covenant will be in "the seed" of Abraham, the Lord Jesus Christ (Gal. 3:16). This aspect of the covenant has been, is being, and will be fulfilled.

B. THE NATURE OF THE ABRAHAMIC COVENANT

1. It Is an Everlasting Covenant

Several times God declared that this covenant was to be everlasting (Gen. 13:15; 17:7-8,13,19). No time limit was placed on this covenant relationship. Israel was to remain a nation forever and would remain in their relationship with the Lord (Jer. 31:36).

2. It Is an Unconditional Covenant

Nearly all covenants made between men or nations were conditional in character; that is, certain conditions had to be fulfilled by one participant in the covenant before the other participant was obligated to do his part. For example, in the Mosaic Covenant God promised to bless Israel, *if* she obeyed His commandments.

The Abrahamic Covenant, however, was unconditional. God committed Himself to do certain things for Abraham and the nation that would come from him. Failure or unbelief on Abraham's or Israel's part would not set aside this covenant. This is an extremely critical point in interpreting numerous passages of Scripture that have to do with Israel's possession of the land of Canaan, her continuance as a nation, the reign of her Messiah on the earth, and her future redemption. The unconditional character of this covenant is undoubtedly one of the most important keys in Bible interpretation.

One view is that the Abrahamic Covenant had no conditions attached to it except the original one, that Abraham must leave his homeland of Ur of the Chaldees and go to the land of Canaan. Once he did that the covenant was unconditional.

> It is important to observe the relation of obedience to this covenant program. Whether God would institute a covenant program with Abraham or not depended upon Abraham's act of obedience in leaving the land. When once this act was accomplished, and Abraham did obey God, God instituted an irrevocable, unconditional program.[13]

> Except for the original condition of leaving his homeland and going to the promised land, the covenant is made with no conditions whatever. It is rather a prophetic declaration of God of what will certainly come to pass, and is no more conditional than any other announced plan of God which depends upon God's sovereignty for its fulfillment.[14]

This position properly emphasizes the unconditional nature of the Abrahamic Covenant and puts one on solid ground for interpreting the rest of the Old Testament.

Another view that also correctly underscores the unconditional character of the covenant states that the word from God to Abraham, "Go forth from your country" (Gen. 12:1), is not a condition, but is rather an invitation.

> This imperative is followed by two imperfects and then a series of cohortative imperfects in verses 2-3. But does a command amount to a formal condition on the divine intention to bless? . . . the accent of the passage was on the co-

---

13. J. Dwight Pentecost, *Things to Come* (Grand Rapids: Dunham, 1964), p. 74.
14. John F. Walvoord, *The Millennial Kingdom* (Findlay, Ohio: Dunham, 1963), p. 150.

> hortatives which emphasized intentionality rather than obligation. . . . The summons to "go," then, was an invitation to receive the gift of promise by faith.[15]

This position suggests that there was not an "original" condition to the Abrahamic Covenant. In either view, the proper emphasis is on the unconditionality of the covenant.

As the Abrahamic Covenant was repeated and enlarged, there were no conditions attached to it. After repeating the promise to Abraham in Genesis 13, God confirms His promise in Genesis 15, when He alone passes between the pieces of the sacrificial animals. Later (Gen. 17), God commanded that circumcision be part of the covenant—not as a condition, but rather as a "sign." When the covenant was confirmed to Isaac and then to Jacob, no conditions were attached. As time went on, even when Israel was unfaithful to the covenant, God remained faithful (Jer. 31:36). The writers of the New Testament also saw the covenant as based on God's promises and not subject to change (Heb. 6:13-18; Gal. 3:15-18).

One additional point must be made. The eventual complete fulfillment of the Abrahamic Covenant depended on God, and not on Abraham, Isaac, Jacob, or the nation of Israel. But the sins of these men and the unbelief of Israel did have significance. Although their failure would never negate the covenant, it would affect their own blessing and could even temporarily hinder the program of God.[16] Examples of such failures and their consequences are found scattered throughout the Old Testament. So even though the Abrahamic Covenant had no conditions attached to it, unbelief on the part of its recipients could, and often did, remove them from the place of favor and blessing. They would be "a mere transmitter of the blessing without personally inheriting any of its gifts directly."[17]

15. Walter C. Kaiser, *Toward an Old Testament Theology* (Grand Rapids: Zondervan, 1981), p. 93.
16. Walvoord, *Millennial Kingdom,* pp. 150-52.
17. Kaiser, *Old Testament Theology,* p. 94.

C. THE ABRAHAMIC COVENANT AND THE OTHER BIBLICAL COVE-
  NANTS

The first three covenants given below are enlargements of
the Abrahamic Covenant, and, as such, are also eternal and unconditional. These "sub-covenants" further define the provisions originally given to Abraham.

  1. The Palestinian Covenant

This covenant focused on Israel's right to the land of Canaan. God had promised Abraham that the land was his "forever" (Gen. 13:15; 17:8). The Palestinian Covenant confirmed
that the title deed did belong to Israel. But it also made clear
that even though they owned the land, they could be removed
from it because of sin. The covenant also promised that, in the
future, Israel would be converted and restored to the land. (See
Deut. 30:4-10; Lev. 26:14, 32-42; Num. 34:1-12; Ezek.
36:24-36.)

  2. The Davidic Covenant

This covenant develops the original promises having to do
with dynasty, nation, and throne. The promises of the seed of
Abraham were developed in the Davidic Covenant. (See 2 Sam.
7:11-16; Ps. 89:3-36; Jer. 33:14-22.)

  3. The New Covenant

This covenant focuses on the spiritual blessing and redemption of Israel. It goes beyond Israel, however, and includes the
Gentiles as well; "in you all the families of the earth shall be
blessed" (Gen. 12:3). (See Jer. 31:31-40; Luke 22:20; Heb.
8:6-13.)

  4. The Mosaic Covenant

This is a conditional covenant made between God and Israel
at Mount Sinai. It is not a part of the Abrahamic Covenant. It
was a conditional covenant and was designed to be temporary.

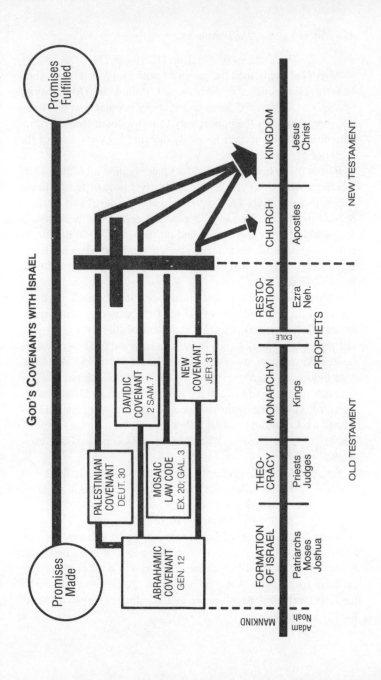

GOD'S COVENANTS WITH ISRAEL

Promises Made

Promises Fulfilled

ABRAHAMIC COVENANT GEN. 12

PALESTINIAN COVENANT DEUT. 30

MOSAIC LAW CODE EX. 20; GAL. 3

DAVIDIC COVENANT 2 SAM. 7

NEW COVENANT JER. 31

MANKIND — Adam Noah

FORMATION OF ISRAEL — Patriarchs Moses Joshua

THEO-CRACY — Priests Judges

MONARCHY — Kings

PROPHETS — EXILE

RESTO-RATION — Ezra Neh.

CHURCH — Apostles

KINGDOM — Jesus Christ

OLD TESTAMENT

NEW TESTAMENT

2. The Testings of Abraham (12:10–15:21)

After God confirmed the covenant with him in Canaan, Abraham traveled around the southern part of the land. (Archaeology reveals that southern Canaan was sparsely populated at this time, allowing Abraham the opportunity to move about freely.) Abraham built altars wherever he went, showing his awareness of the presence of God.

Before much time had elapsed a severe famine hit Canaan, and Abraham went to Egypt. It was evidently a time of failure in the life of this patriarch. (A "patriarch" was the legal and spiritual head of the family. He had great power over his clan, but also was responsible for the well-being and protection of all in his family unit.) Abraham did not evidence faith in the Lord when he fled to Egypt, nor when he had Sarah, his wife, lie about their relationship (12:10-20).

Returning from Egypt, Abraham separated himself from his nephew Lot, renewed his faith in the Lord at Bethel, and experienced material prosperity from the hand of the Lord (13:1-18). His prosperity was also seen in the large number of servants in his household (perhaps more than 1,000 based on 14:14). As Abraham evidenced a growing faith in the Lord (as exhibited in the courageous rescue of Lot and the paying of tithes to Melchizedek, 14:1-24), God once again revealed Himself to Abraham and affirmed the Covenant (15:1-21). (For a further discussion on the titles of God, see Note C, "The Names of God in the Old Testament," p. 244.)

Yet, in all the blessings of God on their lives, Abraham and Sarah were still childless, and God's promise of making a great nation out of him seemed remote.

3. The Sons of Abraham (16:1–22:24)

When Abraham entered Canaan originally, he was seventy-five years old and Sarah was sixty-five. But now ten years had gone by, and they were still childless. Sensing the need to solve this problem themselves, Abraham and Sarah resorted to a custom of the time, and Sarah gave her personal handmaid, Hagar, to Abraham as a concubine.

> According to the Nuzi tablets, ancient Hurrian cuneiform documents dealing with custom and law of this period, the action of Abram and his wife in this respect was perfectly legitimate. Any children born of this proxy arrangement would be considered legal heirs of the husband unless and until children should be born of the wife herself.[18]

Out of this union a son was born who was called Ishmael (16:15-16). Abraham loved this boy and desired that God would accept him as the son of the covenant (17:18-19). God rejected his petition but informed Abraham that it was Sarah who would bear the son of the covenant. God fulfilled His promise when Abraham was 100 years old. Sarah did indeed bear a son when she was 90 (21:1-5). This miraculous birth was designed to inform everyone that God was in charge of making a great nation from Abraham. He was going to populate this new nation.

A few years later, Abraham's faith was given its greatest test when God told him to sacrifice his son Isaac (22:1-19). Abraham believed that Isaac was God's choice to be the recipient of the Covenant. Faced with the command to kill Isaac, Abraham concluded that God would have to raise Isaac from the dead, since he was the one and only covenant son (Heb. 11:17-19). God honored Abraham for this act of faith and also provided a sacrifice on that occasion. It is worth noting that the geographic location for this drama of sacrifice, Mount Moriah, was the same spot where two thousand years later God would sacrifice His Son, Jesus, for the sins of the world (Gen. 22:2; 2 Chron. 3:1).

4. The Last Years of Abraham (23:1-20; 25:1-8)

God blessed and prospered Abraham in the years that followed. After the death of Sarah, Abraham did marry again. By his wife Keturah, he had other sons. But Isaac, and only Isaac, was the one to whom the covenant was passed on.

---

18. Eugene H. Merrill, *An Historical Survey of the Old Testament* (Grand Rapids: Baker, 1980), p. 76.

THE CHRONOLOGY OF THE PATRIARCHS

This chronology is based upon several key verses that assign specific lengths of time between important Old Testament events. These verses are 1 Kings 6:1 and Exodus 12:40. If these verses are taken at face value, then the list given below is relatively accurate.

	DATE B.C.	AGE OF THE PATRIARCH	SCRIPTURE IN GENESIS	EVENT IN GENESIS
A	2165	—	11:26	Abraham born in Ur
B	2090	75	12:4	Abraham enters Canaan
R	2079	86	16: 5	Ishmael born to Hagar
A	2065	100	21:2	Isaac born to Sarah
H	2050	115	22:6	Isaac taken to Mt. Moriah
A	2028	137	23:1	Sarah dies at age 127
M	2025	140	25:20	Abraham sees Isaac married
	1990	175	25:7	The death of Abraham
I	2065	—	21:2	Isaac born to Sarah
S	2025	40	25:20	Isaac marries Rebekah
A	2005	60	25:24	Esau and Jacob born to
A				Isaac
C	1928	137	27:1	Isaac deceived by Jacob
	1885	180	35:28	The death of Isaac
	2005	—	25:24	Jacob born to Isaac
J	1928	77	28:2	Jacob steals the blessing
A	1921	84	29:32	Reuben born–Jacob's first
C	1908	97	35:1	Jacob returns to Bethel
O	1875	130	46:5	Jacob moves to Egypt with
B				family
	1858	147	47:28	The death of Jacob
J	1914	—	30:22·	Joseph born to Rachel
O	1897	17	37:2	Joseph sold by his brothers
S	1884	30	41:46	Joseph made second ruler
E				in Egypt
P	1858	56	47:28	Blessing given—Jacob dies
H	1804	110	50:26	The death of Joseph

THE FAMILY TREE OF ABRAHAM

Terah

Haran   Nahor   **Sarah--ABRAHAM**

Lot   Milcah   Hagar   Keturah

Bethuel   Ishmael   6 Sons

Laban   **Rebekah--ISAAC**

JACOB   Esau

Leah ----   **(Zilpah)**   **Rachel**   **(Bilhah)**

1. REUBEN	7. GAD	11. JOSEPH	5. DAN
2. SIMEON	8. ASHER	12. BENJAMIN	6. NAPHTALI
3. LEVI			
4. JUDAH			
9. ISSACHAR			
10. ZEBULUN			
(Dinah)			

LOCATIONS IN GENESIS

A. THE FOUR PATRIARCHS

Abraham	— 11:26, 29; 12-25
Isaac	— 17:19; 21:3; 22:2; 24:62; 27; 35:28
Jacob	— 25:26; 27-35; 42-49
Joseph	— 30:24; 37-50

B. WIVES AND CHILDREN OF THE PATRIARCHS

12 Sons	— 29:31-35; 30:5-13; 30:17-24; 35:16
Dinah	— 34
Esau	— 25:25; 26:34; 27; 33:4; 36:1
Hagar	— 16:1; 21:14
Ishmael	— 16:11-15; 17:20; 21:9; 25:9-12
Keturah	— 25:1-6
Leah	— 29:16
Rachel	— 29:6-16; 35:16
Rebekah	— 22:23; 24:15
Sarah	— 11:29; 16:1; 17:15; 18:9; 20:12; 21:3; 23:2

C. OTHER RELATIVES IN THE FAMILY TREE

Bethuel	— 22:23; 24:15, 50
Haran	— 11:26-28
Laban	— 24:29; 28:5
Lot	— 11:26; 12:4; 13:5; 14:12; 19:1
Milcah	— 11:29; 22:20
Nahor	— 11:26-29; 22:20
Terah	— 11:26, 31

B. Isaac (24-26)

The story of Isaac is told briefly. He was the son of a famous father and the father of a famous son, Jacob. The emphasis of the Genesis story remains on populating the "great nation," and Isaac is a part of that story.

Isaac was married to Rebekah. Abraham had sent his trusted servant to Haran, where much of the family still lived, to get a wife for Isaac (24:1-67). Rebekah agreed to travel to Canaan and marry Isaac. Isaac and Rebekah were faced with that agonizing issue of childlessness. For twenty years no child was born to them. It was not until Isaac sought the Lord in the matter that the issue changed. God was in charge of populating this nation. Isaac and Rebekah had twins who were named Jacob and Esau (25:19-34). God selected Jacob to be the one who would receive the blessings of the covenant.

C. Jacob (27-36)

The "birthright" belonged to the oldest son in that society. In the case of Jacob and Esau, who were twins, Esau received the "birthright" because he was born moments before Jacob. There were benefits to possessing the birthright, such as having precedence over the other children, receiving a double share of the inheritance, and becoming head of the clan at the father's death (Gen. 43:33; Deut. 21:7; 1 Chron. 5:1). However, the benefits could be lost through some offense, traded, or negated by the father's last will. This last will was called the "blessing" and was actually more important than the "birthright" since the rights of the oldest son might be modified or even canceled. The "blessing" pronounced by the father was legally binding.

In the story of Jacob, he was able to obtain the birthright by trading with hungry Esau for some food. Because of this act, Esau not only lost his birthright but is called a "profane" person by the Scriptures (Heb. 12:16). Evidently Esau assumed that since he was the favorite of his father, Isaac, he would receive all the possessions and favors he wanted when his father gave the "blessing." He was probably correct in his thinking. However, Jacob deceived Isaac and took the blessing for himself (Gen. 27:1-45).

In an essentially nonliterate society, oral transactions were extremely important; and the oral blessing had the force of a legally-binding oral will, as texts from the Mesopotamian city of Nuzi demonstrate. The binding character of the blessing is clear because Esau did not argue for a transfer of the blessing to him just because a mistake had been made. He merely asked for some additional blessing.[19]

In order to avoid the wrath of his brother, Esau, Jacob fled to Haran to the house of his uncle, Laban. Here Jacob stayed for twenty years. Through a series of schemes and circumstances, Jacob accumulated a great deal of wealth as well as two wives, two concubines, and eleven sons (28:1–31:55). When Jacob returned to Canaan, after the twenty years in Haran, a twelfth son was born to him. These twelve sons of Jacob were to become the foundation stones of the nation that God was building.

Jacob was known for his scheming and deceit. But upon his return to Canaan, he met the Lord in a unique way (32:1-32). After this encounter he was a different man, transformed by God. Jacob (meaning "supplanter") had his name changed to Israel (meaning "having power with God").

Jacob settled in southern Canaan, and the story of God's making a "great nation" continued with the focus shifting away from Jacob to Joseph, his eleventh son.

D. Joseph (37-50)

Jacob made the fundamental mistake of openly showing favoritism toward Joseph. This generated the envy and hatred of Joseph's older brothers. They plotted to kill Joseph, but later changed their minds and sold their seventeen-year-old brother to a caravan that was headed for Egypt. The brothers then deceived their father, Jacob, into believing that Joseph had been killed by wild animals.

Through an amazing set of circumstances that were directed by the Lord, Joseph (now thirty years old, 41:46) became the second most powerful ruler in the land of Egypt. All this was part of God's plan for preserving His nation.

19. Vos, *Genesis,* p. 105.

A severe famine hit Egypt and Canaan, forcing the sons of Jacob to leave Canaan and come to Egypt to buy food that was available there. After discovering that his brothers had changed, Joseph revealed himself to his amazed brothers. What followed was a grand family reunion in Egypt. Jacob and all the other members of the family came to live in Egypt, under the protective care of Joseph. The "nation" now had a population of about seventy-five (46:27).

Egypt now became the protector of the infant nation. God was placing His baby nation into the incubator of Egypt until it was grown up enough to fend for itself. Egypt protected Israel in three ways. First, it protected Israel physically. Although the Egyptian army was unaware of it, they were guarding Israel against countless kings and robber bands that could have wiped out this young nation in a matter of hours. Second, Egypt shielded Israel morally. Although Egypt may not have been known for its righteousness, it was superior to the wicked Canaanites. By removing Israel from the degrading influence of these perverse Canaanite people, God was preserving His people from moral failure, which surely would have come if they had been left in Canaan. Third, Egypt secured Israel's racial purity. Israel would certainly have intermarried with the Canaanites (as Genesis 34 reveals), but they would not intermarry with the Egyptians. The Egyptians looked down on the Israelites because of their occupation of shepherding (46:34), and this was a key factor in keeping these two peoples apart.

Genesis ends with Israel safely inside the protective boundaries of Egypt. The nation has no land, no law, and only seventy-five people. But God is at work, and He will bring to pass His promise to Abraham, "And I will make you a great nation."

4

EXODUS AND LEVITICUS

EXODUS

INTRODUCTION TO EXODUS

A. AUTHORSHIP AND DATE OF EXODUS

Moses wrote the book of Exodus as well as the other books of the Pentateuch. Since Exodus is a record of Israel's departure from Egypt (about 1445 B.C.), this book was most likely written about 1425 B.C. (For a further discussion of the date of Israel's exodus out of Egypt, see Note D, "The Date of Exodus," p. 248.)

B. PURPOSE OF EXODUS

Exodus continues the story of God's dealings with the descendants of Abraham. It picks up the history of the people of Israel after a silent period of 275 years. During this lengthy period two significant things happened. First, Israel's population, which was about seventy-five at the end of Genesis, grew to about 2.5 million. And second, the people of Israel became enslaved to the Egyptians.

CHRONOLOGY OF GENESIS AND EXODUS

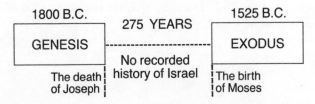

Exodus also records the giving of the law at Mount Sinai. The "constitution" given to Israel marks the second significant step in the process of becoming God's great nation. But before Israel could receive her new law code, God had to redeem His slave people out of the bondage of Egypt with a display of awesome power.

C. BASIC OUTLINE OF EXODUS

    I. The Journey from Egypt to Mount Sinai (chaps. 1-18)
        A. Events Leading Up to the Exodus from Egypt (1-14)
        B. The Journey to Mount Sinai (15-18)
    II. The Giving of the Law at Mount Sinai (chaps. 19-40)
        A. The Preparation for the Giving of the Law (19)
        B. The Giving of the Ten Commandments (20)
        C. The Giving of the Civil Laws (21-24)
        D. The Tabernacle and Its Service (25-40)

D. IMPORTANT DATA ABOUT EXODUS

    1. Key Word: Redemption
    2. Key Chapters: 12—The "exodus" out of Egypt; 20—The giving of the law
    3. Key Verses: 3:7-8; 15:13
    4. Key Characters: Moses, Aaron, Joshua, and Pharaoh
    5. Meaning of "Exodus": A Greek word that means "exit" or "departure"
    6. Geography of Exodus: Egypt, the wilderness, Mount Sinai

E. SPECIAL CONSIDERATIONS ON EXODUS

    1. Years Covered by Exodus

Technically the book of Exodus covers about eighty years, from the birth of Moses to the arrival of Israel at Mount Sinai. The emphasis of the book, however, is on the two-year period of Israel's departure from Egypt.

THE CHRONOLOGY OF THE LIFE OF MOSES

1525	1485	1445	1405
Moses in Pharaoh's Court	Moses in Exile in Midian	Moses with Israel in the Wilderness	
40 years	40 years	40 years	

2. Background Points on Exodus

(a) The Importance of Exodus

Practically every book in the Old Testament makes some reference back to this book, referring to the Exodus, the mighty miracles of God in the release of His people from slavery, or the law that was given at Mount Sinai. This book is also important historically. It records those early days of Israel as a fledgling nation, the receiving of its constitution and the origins of many religious customs and practices of Israel. Exodus has importance spiritually because there is much in the experiences of Israel that corresponds to our own Christian lives. Many principles of the spiritual life are played out in the successes and failures of the nation.

(b) Some Important Background Scriptures

In Genesis 15:13-14, the enslavement and residence in Egypt was foretold. These years in Egypt were all part of God's purposes for Israel, and they did not catch God off-guard. Genesis 50:24-26 records the last words of Joseph and his testimony to God's future deliverance. The bones of Joseph evidently became a visible reminder that God was going to fulfill His promises (see Ex. 13:19 and Heb. 11:22). Stephen's sermon in Acts 7:20-36 and the record found in Hebrews 11:23-29 give some insights and analysis not found in Exodus itself.

A SUMMARY OF EXODUS

I. The Journey from Egypt to Mount Sinai (chaps. 1-18)

A. Events Leading Up to the Exodus from Egypt (1-14)

1. Israel in Egyptian Bondage (1:1–6:30)

The historical silence of 275 years is broken in chapter 1 when Moses relates two important facts. First, the nation experienced a tremendous growth (1:7), and second, the nation fell out of favor with the rulers and into slavery (1:8-11). There is much debate over who these oppressors of Israel were. Some argue persuasively that those who put Israel into slavery were a largely Semitic people known as the Hyksos,[1] whereas others present strong evidence that the oppressors were native Egyptians.[2] Whichever group it was, Israel became the target of oppression and brutality. It was into that setting of slavery that God's deliverer Moses was born (2:1-9). Through some God-directed circumstances, Moses spent the first forty years of his life enjoying the palace life of Egypt (2:11 with Acts 7:23). But because of his own impulsive, violent actions Moses was forced to escape from Egypt to the land of Midian, where he spent the next forty years of his life tending flocks (2:11-22).

When Moses was eighty years old (7:7), God's time for redeeming His people out of slavery came. God "remembered" His covenant with Abraham (2:24) and called Moses to be His man to confront Pharaoh, king of Egypt. Though Moses was reluctant to be the leader and gave numerous objections to God (see 3:11; 3:13; 4:1; 4:10; 4:13), he nevertheless was used mightily by God in delivering Israel. Since Pharaoh was not willing to release Israel, God employed a series of miraculous plagues on Egypt to accomplish His purposes.

2. The Plagues of God on Egypt (7:1–11:10)

When confronted by Moses to release Israel, Pharaoh arrogantly challenged God (5:2). The ten plagues that followed and the incident at the Red Sea answered that challenge and educated Pharaoh on the subject of "who is the Lord?" But these miraculous deeds also instructed the people of Israel (8:22).

The plagues were essentially a contest between the true and living God of Israel and the whole multitude of false gods that were the objects of Egyptian worship (Ex. 12:12; Num. 33:4). Although God used natural phenomena, such as hail and frogs, these plagues were still supernatural. The supernatural character of the plagues

1. John J. Davis, *Moses and the Gods of Egypt* (Winona Lake: BMH Books, 1971), pp. 45-48.
2. Eugene Merrill, *An Historical Survey of the Old Testament* (Grand Rapids: Baker, 1980), pp. 101-2.

THE PLAGUES IN EGYPT

SCRIPTURE	PLAGUE	ISRAEL EXEMPT?	EGYPTIAN GODS INVOLVED
1. 7:14-25	Nile River to blood	No	Hapi—spirit of the Nile Khnum—guardian of the Nile
2. 8:1-15	Frogs	No	Heqt—form of a frog Hapi—spirit of Nile
3. 8:16-19	Swarms of lice/gnats	No	Uncertain; perhaps attack on Egyptian priests
4. 8:20-32	Flies	Yes	Uatchit—a god who manifested himself as a fly
5. 9:1-7	Disease on the cattle	Yes	Apis bull revered Sacred bulls and cows Ptah, Mnevis, Hathor
6. 9:8-11	Boils/sores on man and animal	Yes	Sekhmet—goddess with power to heal Serapis—healing god
7. 9:12-35	Destruction of crops and cattle by hail	Yes	Seth—protector of crops Nut—sky goddess
8. 10:1-20	Destruction of crops by locust	Yes	Isis—goddess of life Seth—protector of crops
9. 10:21-29	Darkness	Yes	Re—sun god Atum—god of setting sun. Amon-Re.
10. 11:1-10	Death of the first-born	Yes—if blood properly applied	Osiris—giver of life Pharaoh also was considered deity

is seen in that they were predicted ahead of time, they were extraordinarily intense, and they discriminated between Israel and Egypt (from the fourth plague onward). The plagues, which may have lasted about nine months from start to finish, devastated both the people and the land of Egypt (see Ps. 78:44-51; 105:26-38). With the climactic, terrible plague of the death of the firstborn (11:1-5), God broke the grip of the oppressors and led His people out of slavery.

3. The Institution of the Passover (12:1–13:16)

God gave to Israel a new calendar based on this meaningful event. The Passover sacrifice beautifully pictured the Lord Jesus Christ, our Passover (1 Cor. 5:7). Israel had to use a lamb that was in the prime of life and had no blemish (John 1:29; Acts 2:22, 27). The perfect lamb had to be slain, the blood shed (Heb. 9:28), and the blood applied (John 3:36). Doing these things would save a person from judgment (John 5:24). As a result of the Passover, all the firstborn in Israel now belonged to the Lord (13:1-16; Num. 3:44-45).

4. The Destruction of the Egyptian Army (13:17–14:31)

When Pharaoh saw that the Israelites had actually left the land, his hardened, sinful heart drove him to go after them. Trapped between the Red Sea and the oncoming Egyptian army, Israel seemed doomed. But God performed one of the great miracles of the Old Testament by parting the waters of the Red Sea and allowing His people to escape. God then destroyed the Egyptian army, which had ventured in after Israel (14:21-31). Deliverance was complete.

B. The Journey to Mount Sinai (15-18)

The spectacular and timely deliverance at the Red Sea brought forth praise from the lips of Moses and the people (15:1-21). But after only three days into the journey Israel began to grumble about their situation; in this case the lack of water. This was the first of many times Israel would complain.

The journey to Mount Sinai took about three months. Moses recorded four places where Israel stopped along the way. At Marah (15:22-26), bitter waters were miraculously made drinkable. At the oasis of Elim they rested (15:27). Next, Israel journeyed into the Wilderness of Sin (16:1-36) where God met their need for food by supernaturally supplying manna (16:31). This supplying of manna for food on a daily basis would last for forty years. Rephidim was the fourth stop recorded by Moses. It was here that God met the need for water by bringing water from out of a rock. Also at Rephidim, Joshua is mentioned for the first time as he led the people of Israel in their first military battle as a nation, a victory over the army of the Amalekites. God proved again and again during the three-month trek to Mount Sinai that He would care for His people.

ISRAEL'S JOURNEY TO SINAI

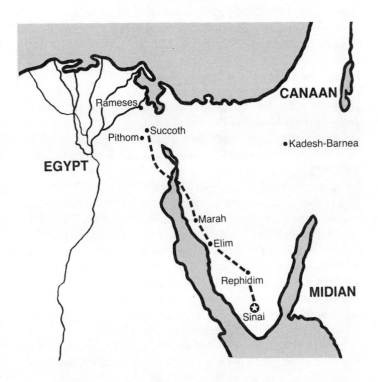

II. The Giving of the Law at Mount Sinai (chaps. 19-40)

    A. The Preparation for the Giving of the Law (19-25)

The area around Mount Sinai was familiar to Moses. It was there that he had been caring for his flock when God confronted him at the burning bush (3:1-6). Mount Sinai (or Horeb, as it is also called, Ex. 3:1; 19:11; Deut. 4:10) was to be the place where Israel would meet God and receive the law (3:12). But before the law was actually given, Israel had to commit herself to obeying it (19:5-8). Four different times in chapter 19, Moses went up and down the mountain, communicating God's words to the people and the people's words to God (19:3, 8, 20, 24). Once the people agreed to this conditional covenant (19:8), and once they cleansed themselves (19:10), God came down upon the mountain to give them some of their "constitution." He demonstrated great power in order that the people might fear Him and understand the seriousness of their commitment (see Ex. 19:16; 20:20; Heb. 12:18).

    B. The Giving of the Ten Commandments (20)

Before one law was given, God made clear that He had the right to regulate Israel's living since He was the one who had delivered her out of slavery (20:2).

The Ten Commandments do not constitute the whole of the law. These ten laws reflect spiritual and moral principles upon which the hundreds of laws in the Mosaic law code rest. There are more than six hundred other laws in Israel's constitution. The first four of the Ten Commandments stress man's relationship to God, and the last six emphasize man's relationship to man. These laws revealed God's holiness and the resulting standards for His people.

    C. The Giving of the Civil Laws (21-24)

These laws revealed God's great concern about the details of life; that nothing was outside of His interest and involvement. Included in this section are laws governing slavery (21:1-11); personal injury laws (21:12-36); property laws (22:1-15); morality, finances, and offerings (22:16-21); laws covering civil obligations (23:1-19); and ceremonial laws (23:10-19). These laws do not give a complete ethical code; that is, not every possible circumstance or issue was dealt with. These laws did, however, give examples from which application to life situations was to be made.

Later on, God would establish the priests to settle disputes by interpreting and applying the law (Deut. 17:8-13).

    D. The Tabernacle and Its Service (25-40)

        1. Preparing for Construction of the Tabernacle (25:1–31:18)

Two important events were to take place at Mount Sinai. First was the giving of the law, and second was the building of the Tabernacle. The Tabernacle was the portable worship center of Israel. Here Israel would be able to come to sacrifice and worship and have fellowship with God. Later, when Israel lived permanently in their land, the Tabernacle would be replaced by the Temple, a permanent structure in the city of Jerusalem. But for about 450 years the Tabernacle would be the central place for Israel's worship of the Lord.

At Mount Sinai, the detailed Tabernacle plans were given to Moses (25:40). The Tabernacle was to be surrounded with an outer court. The Tabernacle itself (the tent-like structure) would have two areas; the holy place and the holy of holies. Several altars and pieces of furniture were part of the plan. The Tabernacle had to be built just right, down to the last detail, because it was a picture of the person and redemptive work of Jesus Christ (Heb. 9:8-12).

THE PLAN OF THE TABERNACLE

A - Brazen Altar
B - Laver
C - Altar of Incense
D - Table of Bread
E - Candlestick
F - Ark of the Covenant
G - The Holy Place
H - The Holy of Holies

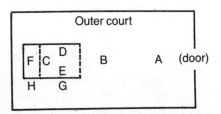

2. The Incident of the Golden Calf (32:1–34:35)

One of the greatest problems Israel would deal with in the days ahead was idolatry. The first two of the Ten Commandments warned against it. Yet, when Moses went up on the mountain for about six weeks, leaving his brother Aaron in charge (24:14), the law was quickly forgotten. In spite of the law and in spite of the awesome power of the Lord God in His total conquest of the gods of Egypt, Israel fell quickly into idolatry and the immorality that accompanied it. Aaron made a golden calf, and the people worshiped it. When Moses came down off the mountain, he disciplined the people for God and interceded with God for the people. Thousands died because of this event (32:28), and the matter was soon settled. But the incident was an ominous indicator of what lay ahead for the nation.

3. The Construction of the Tabernacle (35:1–40:38)

The construction of the Tabernacle was to be financed by a free-will offering from the people (25:2; 36:5-7). More than enough was received, and the materials were given to two men, Bezalel and Oholiab (31:2-6), who were to actually put the Tabernacle together. These men were blessed with great skill and wisdom from God. When the Tabernacle and its furnishings were complete, the glory of God filled the structure. God had taken up residence among His people (40:34-38). Now that the Tabernacle was built and the law was given, it was time to leave Mount Sinai and journey to Canaan, the land of promise. The nation had people, and they now had their constitution. Only the possessing of the land remained to make them a great nation. (For further discussion of God's revelation of Himself to Israel, see Note C, "The Names of God in the Old Testament," p. 244.)

LEVITICUS

The book of Leviticus complements Exodus; it does not advance the story of the Old Testament, although there is a brief historical portion in it (chaps. 8-10). Along with Exodus, Leviticus records the law code of Israel, which Moses received from the Lord at Mount Sinai. While he was inside the newly completed

Tabernacle, Moses received the detailed laws of Leviticus that related to the sacrifices, the priesthood, the feast days, and other matters. Leviticus teaches that the way to God is through sacrifice and that one must be holy to walk with God. The book of Leviticus had special relevance to the priests, giving them a manual by which to guide Israel.

INTRODUCTION TO LEVITICUS

A. AUTHORSHIP AND DATE OF LEVITICUS

Moses wrote the book of Leviticus about one year after the exodus from Egypt. Therefore, a date of 1444 B.C. would be fairly accurate.

B. PURPOSE OF LEVITICUS

The purpose of Leviticus is twofold: (1) to teach the nation of Israel the way to God, and (2) to teach them how to walk with God. This book was given to direct Israel to live as a holy nation in fellowship with a holy God. It was part of a code of law for the total well-being of the nation. For believers today the book gives insight into approaching God in worship and the need for holy living.

C. BASIC OUTLINE OF LEVITICUS

  I. The Way to God Is Through Sacrifice (chaps. 1-10)
    A. The Offerings and Their Regulations (1-7)
    B. The Consecration and Duties of the Priests (8-10)
  II. Israel's Walk with God in Fellowship (chaps. 11-27)
    A. The Daily Lives of God's People (11-22)
    B. The Festivals of God's People (23-25)
    C. Promises and Warnings to God's People (26-27)

D. IMPORTANT DATA ABOUT LEVITICUS

  1. Key Words: Holy and holiness; clean and unclean; atonement
  2. Key Chapter: 11—The requirement to be holy

3. Key Verses: 11:44—the command to be holy because the Lord is holy; 17:11—the need to shed blood to cover sin
4. Key Characters: Moses, Aaron, the sons of Aaron
5. Meaning of "Leviticus": Describes the book as directions for the rituals associated with the Levitical priesthood
6. Geography of Leviticus: The region of Mount Sinai

E.   SPECIAL CONSIDERATIONS ON LEVITICUS

The discussion under this same heading for Exodus applies to Leviticus as well.

A SUMMARY OF LEVITICUS

I. The Way to God Is Through Sacrifice (chaps. 1-10)
   A. The Offerings and Their Regulations (1-7)

Once the Tabernacle was completed, offerings became part of the daily life of Israel. Since God was holy and Israel was sinful, it was necessary to make atonement ("a covering") for sin through the sacrifice of animals. This section records the different kinds of offerings that were part of Israel's worship experience.

   1. The Burnt Offering (1:1-17)

This offering was the most common of the sacrifices and was to atone for the sin of the individual. The law demanded that the worshiper bring an unblemished male to be sacrificed, since that was considered the most valuable kind of offering. There was some flexibility on which kind of animal could be brought, depending on the financial condition of the person involved. He was to bring a bullock unless he was poor, and then a dove or pigeon would suffice (1:5, 14). When the offering was brought to the door of the Tabernacle, the priests followed the divinely revealed procedure.

> The offerer was to bring the animal to the priest in the courtyard surrounding the Tabernacle. Before killing the animal the offerer was to place his hand on its head, identifying it as his substitute. After it was killed, the priest was to sprinkle its blood on all sides of the altar. The offerer then had to skin the animal and chop it in pieces in preparation for the sacrifice.

The entire animal except the skin, which was given to the priest, was burned on the altar.[22]

2. The Meal Offering (2:1-16)

This offering was flour or grain. Though detail is lacking, it was evidently to express thankfulness and dedication to God.

3. The Peace Offering (3:1-17)

This voluntary offering provided the Israelites an opportunity to express their desire to fellowship with the Lord. An unblemished male or female from the flocks or herds could be used. The offerer received part of the sacrificed animal to enjoy as a festive meal.

4. The Sin Offering (4:1–5:13)

The main purpose of this offering was to deal with a situation where purification was needed. It was employed at the dedication of the Tabernacle to purify the altar (9:8 11); it was part of the annual Day of Atonement (16:11-14); and it was used for other purification needs (5:1-13).

5. The Trespass Offering (5:14–6:7)

If an individual violated the law by taking something that belonged to the Lord (such as the tithe) or man (such as property), he was required to bring a ram without blemish as a sacrifice. This offering was to be accompanied by proper restitution.

6. The Laws Regulating the Offerings (6:8–7:38)

The offerings are given again with regulations on the way they were to be presented.

B. The Consecration and Duties of the Priests (8-10)

When the Tabernacle was finally completed, Aaron and his sons were anointed (set apart) as priests by Moses (8:1-36). This act of consecration took one week and was followed immediately by a special time for setting apart Aaron as the high priest of Israel (9:1-24). But in these days of dedication two of Aaron's sons, Nadab and Abihu, were struck dead by the Lord at the Tabernacle. They had offered "strange fire before the Lord" (10:1). This may refer to fire unauthorized by Aaron or Moses, or perhaps it may have some connection to heathen practices they were using. Whatever it was, they had violated God's instructions. It has been

22. Samuel J. Schultz, *Leviticus* (Chicago: Moody, 1983), p. 54.

suggested also that they may have been drunk, since Aaron was warned immediately about drinking wine or strong drink (10:9).

II. Israel's Walk with God in Fellowship (11-27)
  A. The Daily Lives of God's People (11-22)
  In this section instruction is given on how Israel could be holy in their daily practices and so live in fellowship with the Lord, who is holy (11:44; 19:2). Great emphasis is placed on what was "clean" and what was "unclean." Something "clean" was thought to be pure. God wanted His people to be separated from physical and spiritual pollution.

  The law spoke to every area of life. God was interested in the total well-being of His nation. What Israel ate mattered to Him (compare 11:1-47 with Deut. 14:3-21). Distinction was made between clean animals that could be eaten and unclean animals that were not to be part of their diet. (Some animals were identified as unclean because they were disease carriers, whereas others may have been so designated because of their associations with pagan worship.)

  Regulations were given to govern activity at the birth of a child, and so the rites of purification and circumcision were given (12:1-8). God gave detailed instructions for identifying and dealing with a variety of skin diseases, a sort of medical handbook for the priests (13:1–15:33). God was equally precise on what constituted sinful sexual practices (18:1-30) and what God expected from them in their relationships with their neighbors (19:1-37).

  Specific guidelines were given for the Day of Atonement, that day when national sin was atoned for (16:1-34). On this day only Israel's high priest would enter the holy of holies with the blood of a sacrificed bullock. He would sprinkle the blood on the mercy seat (the lid of the Ark of the Covenant; Ex. 25:17-22) first for himself and then return later with blood for the people's sin.
  B. The Festivals of God's People (23-25)
  The Sabbath was the key assembly of Israel. Every seventh day was a sacred day of rest and worship (23:1-4). The Sabbath was a sign of the Mosaic Covenant and a constant reminder to Israel of their special relationship with God (Ex. 31:13-17). However, seven feasts were to be part of Israel's annual life.

1. The Spring Festivals (23:5-22)

The Passover was the most important of all the festivals, marking the start of the year and reminding Israel of God's deliverance from Egypt. *Unleavened Bread* reminded them of their deliverance from slavery and *Firstfruits* celebrated God's goodness. *Pentecost* (Weeks) celebrated the harvest.

2. The Fall Festivals (23:23-44)

The *Feast of Trumpets* was a solemn assembly in which sacrifice and offering were the priorities. The *Day of Atonement* was the day the nation's sins were atoned for. *Tabernacles* was the joyous festival that recalled God's deliverance from Egypt and provision in the wilderness.

3. The Sabbath Year and Year of Jubilee (24:1–25:55)

Every seventh year the land of Israel was to be given rest and to lie fallow. This was not only good agricultural procedure, but was also a test of Israel's faith and obedience. All Hebrew slaves were to be set free as well. Every fifty years was the Year of Jubilee. During this year, which began on the Day of Atonement, all land was to be at rest, and all land that had been sold was to be returned to its original owner (so keeping the land perpetually within the original tribe that owned it).

C. Promises and Warnings to God's People (26-27)

This section is particularly important because it details the steps of discipline God would take against Israel if they disobeyed Him. Chapter 26 provides the backdrop for many of God's future dealings with Israel and the messages of the prophets.

5

NUMBERS AND DEUTERONOMY

NUMBERS

INTRODUCTION TO NUMBERS

A. AUTHORSHIP AND DATE OF NUMBERS

Moses wrote the book of Numbers as an eyewitness to the
events recorded in it. Numbers concludes with Israel ready to enter and conquer Canaan. Since this conquest began just after Moses' death in 1405, a date of about 1406 B.C. is given.

B. PURPOSE OF NUMBERS

Numbers was written to record Israel's history from their departure from Mount Sinai to their arrival in Moab on the east side
of the Jordan River. Numbers continues the account of God's
faithfulness in making of Abraham a "great nation." The land of
Canaan would be Israel's in spite of this record of unbelief and
unfaithfulness on Israel's part.

C. BASIC OUTLINE OF NUMBERS

    I. The Journey from Sinai to Kadesh-Barnea (chaps. 1-12)
       A. The Preparation for the Journey (1-9)
       B. The Journey to Kadesh-Barnea (10-12)
   II. Israel in the Wilderness—the Time of Transition (13-19)
       A. The Crisis of Unbelief at Kadesh-Barnea (13-14)
       B. Laws After the Crisis (15)
       C. The Great Rebellion of Korah (16)
       D. The Aftermath of the Rebellion (17-19)

III. The Journey from Kadesh-Barnea to Moab (20-36)
  A. Incidents on the Way to Moab (20-21)
  B. The Incident with the Prophet Balaam (22-25)
  C. The New Numbering of the People of Israel (26-27)
  D. The New Instructing of Israel (28-36)

D. IMPORTANT DATA ABOUT NUMBERS

  1. Key Word: Wandering
  2. Key Chapter: 14—Unbelief at Kadesh-Barnea
  3. Key Verses: 14:26-32
  4. Key Characters: Moses, Aaron, Joshua, Caleb, Korah, and Balaam
  5. Meaning of "Numbers": Title of this book reflects the two times when a census was taken of Israel
  6. Geography of Numbers: Mount Sinai, the wilderness, Kadesh-Barnea, the plains of Moab

E. SPECIAL CONSIDERATIONS ON NUMBERS

  1. Years Covered by Numbers

The Book of Numbers covers a period of forty years. However, very little information is actually recorded for most of that time. Much of the forty years was spent in aimless wandering.

  2. Background Points on Numbers

In order to move several million people (with their belongings and livestock) from Mount Sinai to Canaan, certain organizational steps had to be taken. Israel was arranged by tribes around the Tabernacle, which was at the center of the camp. There was a fixed marching and camping order. Each tribe knew when to leave as the nation broke camp and marched, and where to set up camp when the march ended. The tribe of Levi (with its subdivisions of Merari, Gershon, and Kohath) camped nearest the Tabernacle. The other tribes camped around the Tabernacle to the four points of the compass. On each side there was one "standard bearer" tribe along with two other tribes. As it turned out, the nation learned the marching and camping order very well, since they spent forty years doing it.

PLAN OF THE CAMP OF ISRAEL

```
                    ★DAN                              ↑
                                                      N
           Asher              Naphtali
  Benjamin            Merari            Issachar
                              Moses
  ★EPHRAIM   Gershon  [TAB.]  Aaron     ★JUDAH
                              Priests
  Manasseh            Kohath           Zebulun
           Gad               Simeon
                    ★REUBEN
```

"M i x e d   M u l t i t u d e s"

ORDER OF DEPARTURE:

1. The Ark, Moses, Aaron
2. Judah and tribes
3. Gershon and Merari
4. Reuben and tribes
5. Kohath
6. Ephraim and tribes
7. Dan and tribes
8. The "Mixed Multitude"

A SUMMARY OF NUMBERS

I. The Journey from Sinai to Kadesh-Barnea (chaps. 1-12)

  A. The Preparation for the Journey (1-9)

   1. The First Numbering of the People (1:1–4:49)

After spending about a year at Mount Sinai, the nation of Israel was ready to conquer Canaan. Since Israel was going to have to fight against the nations in Canaan it was necessary to discover how many Israelites were able to go to war (1:3). The total number of men who were at least twenty years old and capable of fighting was 603,550 (1:46). All the tribes except Levi were counted. The Levites were not numbered because they were not to go to war (1:47).

The tribe of Levi was selected by God to be those special people to care for the Tabernacle and assist in the worship of the Lord (1:50-53). At the time of the tenth plague on Egypt when God preserved the firstborn of Israel, the Lord declared that the firstborn belonged to Him (Ex. 13:2). Now, the Levites were to belong to God in a special way (Num. 3:11-13, 45). All the firstborn had to be redeemed with a special price paid to the priests and Levites (18:16-17).

PRIESTLY LINE IN ISRAEL

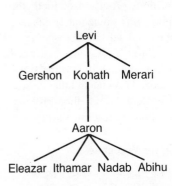

Levites were descendants of Jacob's third son, Levi (Gen. 46). Levi had three sons: Gershon, Kohath, and Merari (Num. 3:17). Sometimes men were identified by these sons (e.g. Gershonites). Aaron was a descendant of Levi's son Kohath. The priestly line came only from Aaron. Therefore, all priests were Levites, but very few Levites were priests. In the days of King David, the priesthood was divided into twenty-four groups—sixteen from the line of Eleazar and eight from the line of Ithamar (1 Chron. 24).

2. The Instructing of the People (5:1–9:23)

Once again the Israelites were reminded that they were to be clean because God dwelt among them. Emphasis was made on the need to be separate from that which was unclean and to be holy unto the Lord.

B. The Journey to Kadesh-Barnea (10-12)

1. The First Stage of the Journey (10:1-36)

The Israelites finally left Mount Sinai (10:11). On the journey, the people would be guided not only by the pillar of cloud (9:15-23), but also by the sounding of silver trumpets (10:2-9). In this way more than 2 million people would know when to leave, when to set up camp, when to go to war, and when to assemble together.

2. Rebellion Against Moses (11:1–12:16)

Although the Lord had graciously cared for Israel for more than a year, they repeatedly murmured and complained against His provisions for them. Complaining is an attack on the love and character of God and is viewed very seriously by God (cf. 1 Cor. 10:5-11). And Israel paid a high price for her ungrateful spirit.

The trouble recorded here probably began with complaints from the non-Israelites on the outskirts of the camp (11:4). The complaint was against God's miraculous provision of food, the manna (11:6). This rebellious attitude was immediately judged. Later, the attitude of insubordination moved closer to home as Moses' own sister, Miriam, and his brother, Aaron, challenged Moses' authority (12:1). God moved immediately into the situation, making clear that Moses was indeed special and that he was Israel's leader (12:6-8). But these incidents of rebellion revealed an attitude that caused Israel's great failure at Kadesh-Barnea.

ISRAEL'S COMPLAINTS IN THE WILDERNESS

SCRIP-TURE	ISRAEL'S COMPLAINT	MOSES' RESPONSE	GOD'S RESPONSE
Ex. 14:11	Grumbled at the sight of Pharaoh's army	Encouraged Israel to trust God	Delivered Israel
Ex. 15:24	Grumbled about the bitter water	Cried out to God	"Healed" the water
Ex. 16:2	Grumbled about the lack of food	Rebuked Israel	Supplied manna
Ex. 17:2	Grumbled about the lack of water	Prayed to the Lord	Water from the rock
Num. 11:1	Grumbled about God's provision of food	Anger and prayer	Judgment
Num. 14:2	Grumbled about Moses' leadership. Can't possess Canaan	Pled with Israel, prayed to the Lord	Judgment
Num. 16:2	Grumbled about Moses' leadership	Rebuked and prayed	Judgment
Num. 16:41	Grumbled about Moses	Prayed	Judgment
Num. 20:2	Grumbled about Moses and a lack of water	Rebuked Israel Struck rock	Supplied water
Num. 21:4	Grumbled about Moses and the manna	No response	Judgment

II. Israel in the Wilderness—the Time of Transition (chaps. 13-19)

    A. The Crisis of Unbelief at Kadesh-Barnea (13-14)

When Israel arrived at Kadesh-Barnea, twelve spies were sent into the land of Canaan to observe the conditions of the land and the people. Deuteronomy 1:22 makes clear that the people, not God, originated the idea of sending these spies into the land. After spending forty days in Canaan (13:25), they all returned with glowing reports on the fertility of the land (13:27). They agreed that the peoples of Canaan were mighty, living in fortified cities. But ten of the spies discouraged the people of Israel by declaring that it was impossible to possess the land. Only two spies, Joshua and Caleb, encouraged the people by reminding them that God would give them the land (13:30; 14:8). But the people, who had repeatedly doubted God's love and had complained against Him, responded in fear and unbelief. They spoke against the Lord Himself (14:3) as well as against Moses (14:2). They intended to kill Moses and return to Egypt (14:4, 10). The rebellion did not succeed, but because of their blatant unbelief, God declared that the rebels would not enter the Promised Land. Israel as a result would spend forty years aimlessly wandering in the wilderness until that generation died (14:23, 27-35). That generation lost the blessing of God, but they did not destroy His purpose of making Israel a "great nation" (Gen. 12:3).

    B. Laws After the Crisis (15)

Once again Israel was reminded to be holy (15:40). And again Israel was given information about making offerings for sin.

    C. The Great Rebellion of Korah (16)

This challenging of Moses' leadership was particularly critical because it was a rebellion by leaders. Motivated by jealousy, Korah (a Levite) and 250 important leaders in Israel openly challenged Moses' authority. In response, Moses correctly noted that this rebellion was really a challenge against God, since God Himself had clearly placed Moses in this postion (16:11). God immediately judged the rebels by having the earth open up and killing them (16:31-35). Though the hand of God was obvious in the matter, the attitude of many in Israel was still evil and rebellious (16:41).

D. The Aftermath of the Rebellion (17-19)

Because of the challenging of His leaders, God confirmed that the priesthood did in fact belong to Aaron and his family (17:1-13). Additional information is given regarding the provisions for the priests (18:1-32).

III. The Journey from Kadesh-Barnea to Moab (chaps. 20-36)

A. Incidents on the Way to Moab (20-21)

After the years of discipline were over, God brought Israel back to the place of their failure (Kadesh-Barnea) to begin again. Both Miriam and Aaron died at this time (20:1, 28). Aaron's son Eleazar became the new high priest of Israel.

Failure was still to be associated with Kadesh-Barnea. To provide water for Israel, God commanded Moses to speak to a rock and water would come out. But in the presence of the people, Moses disobeyed God, striking the rock in his anger instead of speaking to it (20:10-11). Because of this disobedience, God would not allow Moses to enter Canaan (20:12).

When Israel finally arrived on the east side of the Jordan River, they were met by hostile peoples. In the days that followed, Israel defeated Sihon, king of the Amorites (21:21-25), and Og, king of Bashan (21:33-35). Much of the east side of the Jordan, therefore, fell under Israelite control.

B. The Incident with the Prophet Balaam (22-25)

When Balak, the king of Moab, saw Israel easily defeat the other kings of the area, he realized that he had no hope of a military victory over Israel. He therefore hired a pagan prophet by the name of Balaam, promising great reward if he would pronounce a curse on Israel. But when God appeared to Balaam and warned him not to do so, Balaam was afraid and refused to curse Israel. But Balaam wanted the wealth offered by King Balak, and, instead of cursing Israel, he counseled Balak to get Israel involved in the degraded fertility religion of Baal. Such involvement would bring the wrath of the Lord on Israel, and Balak could watch Israel's God destroy His own people. The plan partially worked (25:1-9; 31:16). For his evil counsel, Balaam was later executed by Israel (31:8). Balaam is used by Bible writers as a negative example of one who was both covetous and a compromiser (cf. 2 Pet. 2:15; Jude 11; Rev. 2:14).

C. The New Numbering of the People of Israel (26-27)

As Israel readied to enter Canaan and fight, it was necessary again to take a census to determine the size of the army. The total in this census was 601,730, several thousand less than the first census. Normally a significant increase would have been expected, but the judgments of the forty years in the wilderness had had their effect.

D. The New Instructing of Israel (28-36)

Three noteworthy events took place at this point. First, Joshua was selected by God to be Israel's next leader (27:18-23). Joshua was publicly commissioned so there would be no power struggle at the death of Moses. Second, the tribes of Reuben, Gad, and half of the tribe of Manasseh requested and were granted permission to settle on the east side of the Jordan River (32:1-33). This territory was not part of the land area given Israel under the Abrahamic Covenant. Third, Moses set aside six "cities of refuge" (35:1-34). These cities were places where those who were guilty of accidently killing another person could be protected.

With the ending of the book of Numbers, Israel is poised and ready to possess the land of promise. The next foundational book, Joshua, records the taking of the land. (For further discussion on the foreign nations with whom Israel had dealings, see Note E, "Israel and the Nations," p. 252.)

DEUTERONOMY

The book of Deuteronomy complements Numbers; it does not advance the story of the Old Testament. The messages of this book were given by Moses as Israel camped in the Plains of Moab. Moses was about to die, and a new generation in Israel (which was not born until after Israel left Mount Sinai) needed some special instruction in the law of God. So these words of Moses were a needed reminder to all Israel, although they were particularly important to the new generation.

INTRODUCTION TO DEUTERONOMY

A. AUTHORSHIP AND DATE OF DEUTERONOMY

Most likely Moses wrote the book of Deuteronomy about the same time as Numbers. Therefore, a date of 1405 B.C. is given for Deuteronomy.

B. PURPOSE OF DEUTERONOMY

The main purpose of the book is to remind Israel of their special relationship to God. They were the covenant people and were to obey His laws. Israel was reminded in Deuteronomy of the privileged position that they had and the resulting responsibility to serve God faithfully and to be holy. In these messages Moses pled with the people to obey the commandments. His pleas to the nation were based on several facts: (1) God's goodness to them in the past (4:32-40); (2) God's goodness to them in the recent wilderness experience (29:5-9); (3) Israel's responsibility to be a good testimony to the nations of the earth (4:6-7); (4) God's love had been poured out on them (7:7-11); (5) God's sure promise of blessing (7:12-14); and (6) God's warnings of certain judgment for disobedience (29:24-28).

C. BASIC OUTLINE OF DEUTERONOMY

    I. Moses Reviews Israel's Journey from Sinai to the Plains of Moab (chaps. 1-4)
    II. Moses Reviews and Expands the Law for the New Generation (chaps. 4-26)
    III. Moses Reviews Israel's Covenant Relationship with God (chaps. 27-30)
    IV. The Final Ministry of Moses (chaps. 31-34)

D. IMPORTANT DATA ABOUT DEUTERONOMY

    1. Key Words: Observe, do, keep, and obey
    2. Key Chapter: 8—Exhortation to obey and keep the covenant with God

3. Key Verses: 10:12-13—A reminder to fear, love, and obey
the Lord God
4. Key Characters: Moses and Joshua
5. Meaning of "Deuteronomy": "deuter" = second ; "no-
mos" = law; a second giving of the law
6. Geography of Deuteronomy: The plains of Moab, east of
the Jordan River

E. SPECIAL CONSIDERATIONS ON DEUTERONOMY

The discussion under this same heading for Numbers applies to
Deuteronomy as well.

A SUMMARY OF DEUTERONOMY

I. Moses Reviews Israel's Journey from Sinai to the Plains of
Moab (chaps. 1-4)

To the new generation Moses gave the authoritative account of
Israel's recent history. Beginning at Mount Sinai and concluding
with the arrival in the Plains of Moab, Moses spoke of God's
great power and faithfulness as well as Israel's unbelief and failure. He reminded Israel of God's provision and protection. He
also reminded them that the way to blessing is through obedience.

II. Moses Reviews and Expands the Law for the New Generation (chaps. 4-26)

The majority of the book falls in this section. It deals with some
highly significant matters that will greatly affect the well-being of
the nation in the days ahead.

Absolutely essential to Israel's well-being was their knowledge
of God's law (their constitution). The priests and Levites functioned as teachers of this law. But even more significant than the
instructions by these men were the teachings of the parents. Parents were to be the key in the communication of God's truth from
generation to generation (6:1-9). Parents were to teach their children to fear the Lord and to love the Lord (6:2, 5, 12). They were
to be diligent in this task. Later on, parents in Israel would violate
this instruction with the result that whole generations would grow
up not "knowing the Lord" (Judg. 2:10).

Another vital issue given by Moses in this message concerned Israel's relationship to the Canaanites (7:1-6). Two critical orders were given. First, Israel was to destroy utterly and completely every Canaanite in the land, making no treaty of any kind with them. (For a further discussion of this radical invasion policy, see Note F, "The Extermination of the Canaanites," p. 263.) Second, there was to be no intermarriage with the Canaanites. During the several years that it would take to conquer Canaan, intermarriage would have been a possibility. But intermarriage would bring idolatry with it. As it turned out, both of these orders were violated numerous times by Israel, and the results were tragic (Judg. 1:28; 2:11-12).

In this message, Moses also revealed a unique fact about the Promised Land (11:10-17), which would be referred to again and again by the prophets of Israel. This land could not be irrigated like the land of Egypt. With the Jordan River hundreds of feet below sea level, it was not a source of water for crops or grazing areas. This land would be totally dependent on the rains. God promised that if Israel obeyed Him, He would always bring rain for her crops and cattle. He would withhold rain only if Israel was disobedient to His law. Therefore, drought (with the eventual famine) was a spiritual issue in Israel and was designed to be a clear, visible indicator that God was displeased because of her disobedience (e.g., see Joel 2:10-12; Hag. 2:11; Jer. 14:1).

Other subjects discussed by Moses in this message included the absolute necessity of removing all idolatry from Canaan (chap. 12), the great faithfulness of God (8-9), the matter of divorce (24), the positions of the prophets (13-18) and the kings (17), and additional information on Israel's relationships with foreign nations (20).

III. Moses Reviews Israel's Covenant Relationship with God (chaps. 27-30)

Since the covenant made at Mount Sinai was a "conditional covenant," there were blessings and curses attached to it. Curses were given for breaking the law and blessings were given for being obedient to it (chaps. 27-28). Extremely significant in this section is the discussion of the Palestinian Covenant, which is a subdivision of the unconditional Abrahamic Covenant. The Palestinian Covenant gave the "title deed" of Canaan to the nation of Israel. It was and always would be Israel's land. The borders of the land were defined in the law. However, Israel's sin and disobedience would affect this covenant. Although disobedience would not annul the covenant, Israel could lose their right to live on the land. But it was also clear that in the future, Israel would be converted and restored to the land (see Gen. 17:7-8, 13:14-17; Deut. 28:63-68, 30:1-10; Lev. 26:32-33; Ezek. 36:24-29, 37:11-14, 34:11-31; Rom. 11:26-27).

IV. The Final Ministry of Moses (chaps. 31-34)

After Moses communicated the needed information to the new generation, he knew it was his time to die (31:2). Joshua would now take over and lead the people (31:14, 23). Moses finished his literary task (31:24-26), blessed the people (33:1), and climbed Mount Nebo to see the land of promise (34:1-4). Moses then died, and the nation of Israel entered a new phase in its national life. Joshua and the people readied themselves for entering and conquering Canaan.

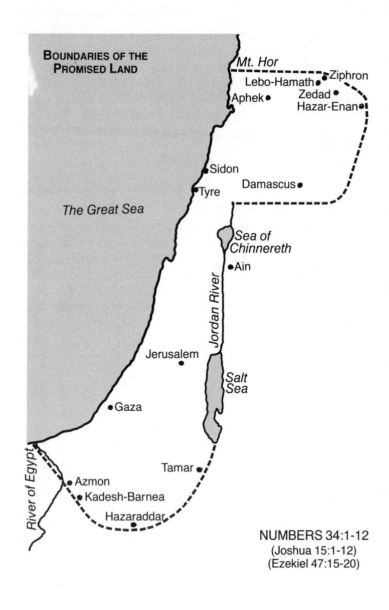

BOUNDARIES OF THE
PROMISED LAND

Mt. Hor

Ziphron

Lebo-Hamath

Aphek

Zedad

Hazar-Enan

Sidon

Damascus

Tyre

The Great Sea

Sea of
Chinnereth

Ain

Jordan River

Jerusalem

Salt
Sea

Gaza

Tamar

River of Egypt

Azmon

Kadesh-Barnea

Hazaraddar

NUMBERS 34:1-12
(Joshua 15:1-12)
(Ezekiel 47:15-20)

6

JOSHUA

Introduction to Joshua

A. AUTHORSHIP AND DATE OF JOSHUA

Among conservative scholars opinion is divided on the authorship of this book. Jewish tradition assigns the book to Joshua. It is
clear that Joshua did write some things found in this book (cf.
18:9; 24:26). The author was surely an eyewitness of these
events, as the details given reflect a precise knowledge of events
(for example, 3:14-17; 4:19-20; 5:1-12; 6:12-15). Furthermore,
the author was living at the time of these events because of certain
statements made, such as that Rahab was still living (6:25). It is
clear that a few verses would not have been written by Joshua
(24:29-30; 24:31-33). But these verses could have been added to
Joshua's writings by another without greatly affecting the authorship of Joshua. Although there is some debate on this matter, this
study assigns the authorship to Joshua with a date of about 1390
B.C.

B. PURPOSE OF JOSHUA

The purpose of Joshua is to record the conquest of the land of
Canaan by Israel and therefore show the faithfulness of God in
making of Abraham "a great nation."

C.   BASIC OUTLINE OF JOSHUA

    I. Possessing the Land (chaps. 1-12)
      A. The Entrance into Canaan (1-5)
      B. The Conquering of Canaan (6-12)
    II. Dividing the Land (chaps. 13-24)
      A. The Inheritances of the Tribes (13-22)
      B. The Last Messages of Joshua (23-24)

D.   IMPORTANT DATA ABOUT JOSHUA

    1. Key Word: Victory
    2. Key Chapter: 6—The beginning of the conquest
    3. Key Verses: 1:5-8; 21:43-45; 24:15
    4. Key Characters: Joshua and Caleb
    5. Meaning of "Joshua": Title reflects the key figure of the book
    6. Geography of Joshua: The plains of Moab, Gilgal, and Canaan

E.   SPECIAL CONSIDERATIONS ON JOSHUA

    1. Years Covered by Joshua

The book of Joshua covers about thirty years of Israel's history. However, the emphasis is on the five to seven years (based on the testimony of Caleb, 14:6-11) of Joshua's military activities. After the conclusion of the conquest of Canaan by Joshua, the eighty-five-year-old Caleb recalled that he was forty years old when he went and spied out the land in the days of Moses (Num. 13:6). Out of the forty-five years that followed that event (between the ages of forty and eighty-five), thirty-eight or thirty-nine of those years were spent wandering in the wilderness, leaving five to seven years for the conquest under Joshua.

    2. Background Points on Joshua
      (a) Joshua's Assigned Tasks

The first task given to Joshua was to destroy Canaanite power in the land. Strong, fortified cities and the key Canaanite kings were the targets of Joshua. Joshua would not have had time to search out every single Canaanite in the land and destroy him. But he faithfully destroyed the key cities. On both the east and the west side of the Jordan River Joshua destroyed a total of thirty-one kings (12:24). Joshua's second responsibility was to divide up the land among the tribes of Israel. Once the land was parceled out among the tribes, it became the responsibility of each individual tribe to enter its territory and eliminate all the Canaanites left there. Joshua obeyed the Lord and completed his assigned tasks. Unfortunately, as history reveals, Israel did not.

  (b) Israel's Foreign Policy

In Deuteronomy 7 and 20, Israel's relationships with other nations are detailed. Israel could enter into restricted treaties with nations who lived outside the boundaries of the land given in the covenant. But nations inside of those boundaries were to be totally destroyed, and no treaties or covenants could be made with them. (See Note F, "The Extermination of the Canaanites," p. 263.)

A Summary of Joshua

I. Possessing the Land (chaps. 1-12)
  A. The Entrance into Canaan (1-5)

God is never thwarted by the death of His servants. Although the death of Moses must have been a depressing event to Joshua and Israel, God immediately appeared to Joshua, bringing encouragement to him (1:5). Joshua was guaranteed of God's presence and blessing (1:1-9).

In preparation for entering Canaan, two men were sent into the area near Jericho to spy it out. When the mission of the spies was discovered by the Canaanites, they were protected by a prostitute named Rahab. Rahab not only protected them but also greatly encouraged them by revealing that the mighty peoples of Canaan were absolutely terrified by Israel's presence on the east side of Jordan (2:8-11). This fulfilled God's promise to bring great fear on the people of the land (cf. Deut. 2:25; 11:25). When Jericho was destroyed, the believing Rahab was spared (6:17, 25). She would later marry a prince of the tribe of Judah and become an ancestor of Jesus Christ (Num. 7:12; 1 Chron. 2:10-15; Matt. 1:4-

6). Rahab is an Old Testament illustration of the marvelous grace of God.

As Israel prepared to cross the Jordan River, God gave specific instructions that the Ark of the Covenant was to lead the people (a visible reminder that God keeps His covenants). The crossing of the Jordan River was an event to parallel the Red Sea crossing (3:5, 7). When the sandals of the priests carrying the Ark touched the water, the waters were immediately stopped and Israel crossed over on dry ground (3:14-17). After crossing the Jordan, Israel camped at Gilgal. Gilgal would be the base camp for Joshua, the people, and the army for several years.

Fear gripped the Canaanites in an even greater way after this supernaturally aided crossing (5:1). On the west side of the Jordan, several events took place before the conquest actually began. First, it was necessary to circumcise the males of Israel (5:2-9). Circumcision was the external sign of the Abrahamic Covenant, which the man of Israel bore on his body (Gen. 17:9-14; Acts 7:8). Also, Israel celebrated her first Passover in the new land and witnessed the end of the provision of manna (5:10-12). And finally, in preparation for the conquest, Joshua met the real commander of Israel's army, the Lord Himself (5:13-15).

B. The Conquering of Canaan (6-12)

These chapters give a greatly condensed account of the conquering of Canaan. During the next five to seven years Joshua would attack and defeat Canaanite strongholds, go back to rest at Gilgal, and then return to battle again. The conquest of Canaan took place in three stages. First, the conquest of central Canaan took place, which included such cities as Jericho and Ai. Second came the southern campaign, which brought about the defeat of such cities as Jerusalem and Hebron. Finally, the northern campaign centered on the Canaanite fortress city of Hazor.

1. The Victory in Central Canaan (6:1–8:35)

Though they were assured of victory in their battles, Israel had to obey God. The battle of Jericho was not won in the conventional way. It was won by doing it God's way. Jericho was a kind of "firstfruits" of the whole land and thus belonged to God (6:18-

THE THREE MAJOR CAMPAIGNS OF JOSHUA

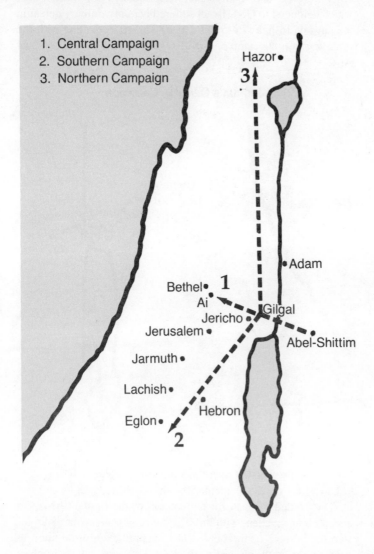

1. Central Campaign
2. Southern Campaign
3. Northern Campaign

Hazor •

Adam •

Bethel •   **1**
Ai •   Gilgal
Jericho •
Jerusalem •   Abel-Shittim
Jarmuth •
Lachish •
Eglon •   Hebron   **2**

3

19). Normally the spoils of war went to the people, but not in this case. Because one man, Achan, appropriated for himself that which belonged to God, Israel suffered her only military defeat in the days of Joshua (7:4-5, 11-13, 20-21). After dealing with the issue of sin in the camp of Israel, Joshua and the people defeated Ai.

JOSHUA'S CENTRAL CAMPAIGN

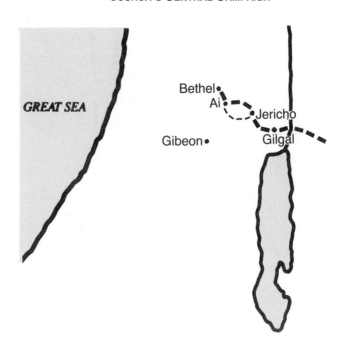

2. The Victory over the Southern Kings (9:1–10:43)

Unfortunately the incident at Ai was not the only failure of Israel. They failed to "ask for the counsel of the Lord" (9:14) and ended up in covenant with the Gibeonites, a people who lived inside the borders of the land. But God used even that failure to open up the southern part of the land. City after city fell before Joshua and the Israelites (10:1-43).

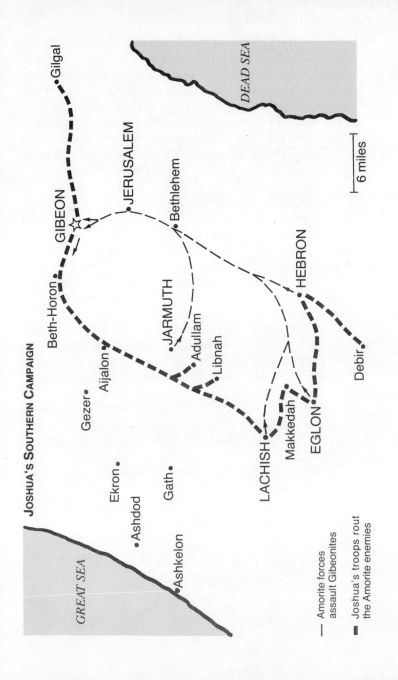

JOSHUA'S SOUTHERN CAMPAIGN

GREAT SEA

Ashkelon

Ashdod
Ekron

Gath

Gezer

Aijalon

Beth-Horon

GIBEON

JERUSALEM

Bethlehem

Gilgal

DEAD SEA

6 miles

JARMUTH

Adullam

Libnah

LACHISH

Makkedah

EGLON

HEBRON

Debir

— Amorite forces assault Gibeonites

■ Joshua's troops rout the Amorite enemies

3. The Victory over the Northern Kings (11:1–12:24)

In order to repel Israel, the remnants of the south along with mighty kings of the north formed an alliance to face Joshua. Joshua had never faced such a formidable army (11:4-5). But God encouraged Joshua, and a great victory was given to Israel (11:6-8).

The book then gives a summary of the conquests on both sides of the Jordan (12:1-24), noting that much territory still needed to be conquered (by the individual tribes, after the dividing up of the land, 13:1).

II. Dividing the Land (13-24)

A. The Inheritances of the Tribes (13-22)

Dividing up the land would be done by the casting of lots (Num. 26:52-55; 33:54-55). And the size of the tribe would also be a consideration. Historically the dividing of the land occurred in three steps. First was the distribution of the land on the east side of Jordan under the direction of Moses (Reuben, Gad, and half of Manasseh). The second step in the distribution of the land took place at Gilgal with Joshua in charge (15:1–17:13). Judah, Ephraim, and the other half of Manasseh received their land at this time. The third step in land distribution took place at Shiloh, after Joshua set up the Tabernacle there. The seven remaining tribes received their territories at this time (18:11–19:48). It should be noted that the tribe of Joseph received a double portion of the land, as the possessor of the birthright (1 Chron. 5:1-2). The double portion of the land is identified by Joseph's two sons, Ephraim and Manasseh.

B. The Last Messages of Joshua (23-24)

Before his death, Joshua exhorted the people to faithfully serve the Lord and to be obedient to His commands. As long as Joshua was alive Israel remained faithful to the Lord.

7

JUDGES AND RUTH

JUDGES

INTRODUCTION TO JUDGES

A. AUTHORSHIP AND DATE OF JUDGES

Unlike many of the books of the New Testament, which identify the author at the beginning of the letter, Old Testament authors are not so easily identified. Jewish and Christian tradition assign the book of Judges to Samuel, though there is some lack of certainty. Several times in the book the phrase "there was no king in Israel" is used. This suggests that the author was writing in a time when there *was* a king in Israel and was informing his readers of that important fact. The book also says that the Jebusites still were in control of Jerusalem (1:21), a situation that changed when David became king and removed them (2 Sam. 5:6). These statements, therefore, point to the real possibility that Judges was written during the monarchy, but before the days of David. The reign of Saul is the best estimate, and Samuel would fit very well. The authorship of Judges is assigned to Samuel, and the date of writing would then be about 1000 B.C.

B. PURPOSE OF JUDGES

Judges was written to record the experiences of Israel during the era of the theocracy. The book sets forth great failures of Israel during this period.

C. BASIC OUTLINE OF JUDGES

    I. The Record of Incomplete Obedience (chaps. 1-3)
    II. The Judges of Israel (chaps. 3-16)
    III. Illustrations from the Era of the Judges (chaps. 17-21)

D. IMPORTANT DATA ABOUT JUDGES

    1. Key Word: Defeat
    2. Key Chapter: 2—Gives the "cycle of the judges"
    3. Key Verses: 2:11-19; 17:6; 21:25
    4. Key Characters: Gideon, Samson, and Jephthah
    5. Meaning of "Judges": Title reflects the key office in this period of Israel's history
    6. Geography of Judges: Various locations within Israel

E. SPECIAL CONSIDERATIONS ON JUDGES

    1. Years Covered by Judges

The actual length of time for the period of the judges (the "era of the theocracy") is 332 years. The book of Judges is actually less than that, since two of the men who served as judges are found in the book of 1 Samuel. One of the chronological problems in the Old Testament is associated with the book of Judges. When the total number of years given for the length of judgeships and of the years of oppression by foreign nations is added up, the figure is 407 years (75 more years than is available in Israel's history). The solution to this problem is accounted for by noting that there were overlaps in the judgeships; that is, more than one judge ruled at a time.[1]

TIMELINE OF JOSHUA AND JUDGES

JOSHUA	"ELDERS"	JUDGES	
1405	1390	1375--------332 years--------1043	
Entering of Canaan	Death of Joshua (?)	Israel's First Apostasy	Saul Becomes King

---

1. Leon Wood, *Distressing Days of the Judges* (Grand Rapids: Zondervan, 1975), p. 10.

CHRONOLOGY OF ISRAEL'S JUDGES

JUDGE	SCRIP-TURE	NATION WHO OPPRESSED THEM	YEARS	YEARS OF PEACE AFTER DELIVERANCE
OTHNIEL	3:9-11	MESOPOTAMIA	8	40
EHUD	3:12-30	MOABITES	18	80
SHAMGAR	3:31	PHILISTINES	?	?
DEBORAH (Barak)	4:4–5:3	CANAANITES	20	40
GIDEON	6:1–8:35	MIDIANITES	7	40
TOLA	10:1, 2	?	?	23
JAIR	10:3-5	?	?	22
JEPHTHAH	11:1–12:7	AMMONITES	18	6
IBZAN	12:8-10	?	?	7
ELON	12:11, 12	?	?	10
ABDON	12:13-15	?	?	8
SAMSON	13:1–16:31	PHILISTINES	40	20
ELI	1 Samuel	PHILISTINES	—	—
SAMUEL	1 Samuel	PHILISTINES	—	—

2. Background Points on Judges

    (a) The Concept of the Theocracy

Before Moses died, Joshua was selected by God to be Israel's leader. But no provision was made for a leader when Joshua died. Why? Because it was not God's intention to have His nation ruled by one man. Such leaders were necessary in the era when the nation was being formed (see chart "Eras of Old Testament History," p. 22.) But once Israel had their "people," "law," and "land," God Himself was to be their supreme ruler (a "theocracy"). This was the ideal form of government for Israel and one that would bring the finest blessings and greatest satisfaction. (A monarchy or other form of government would be "second best.") In the theocracy, the people would live under God's law with the priests being those who taught and administered God's law. A theocracy is the highest and best form of government, and one day it will reinstituted with the Lord Jesus Christ as supreme ruler.

(b)   The Position of the Judge

The judges appeared as significant people during the theocracy period. But they came on the scene only because of sin and failure. They were, in a sense, unnecessary to the theocracy. Judges were introduced when it became necessary to rescue Israel from bad situations—situations brought about because of Israel's sin. The judges' basic responsibilities were to deliver Israel from foreign oppressors and to curtail sin in Israel.

Judges were not like the kings who appeared later in Israel's history. They had less power than the kings (for example, judges could not tax people or keep a standing army). They governed much smaller geographic areas, often including the territories of just a few tribes. And, unlike the kings, their position of rulership was not passed on to their descendants.

(c)   Key Background Scriptures

Deuteronomy 7:1-4 commanded Israel to exterminate the Canaanites in the land and to refrain from any intermarriage with them. It was the violation of these commands that became the source of Israel's trouble in the theocracy. *Psalm 106:34-39* is a "divine commentary" on the era of the judges. It reveals the depths of Israel's sin, which included terrible immorality and human sacrifice. *Joshua 24:29-31* gives insight into how quickly Israel departed from the Lord after the death of Joshua. Israel served the Lord only in those few years that followed Joshua's death when the "elders" who served with Joshua were still alive.

(d)   The Cycle of the Judges

The era of the theocracy is clearly summarized in Judges 2:11-19. This "cycle" is repeated again and again during the 332 years of the theocracy.

CYCLE OF THE JUDGES

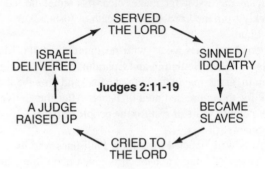

A SUMMARY OF JUDGES

I. The Record of Incomplete Obedience (chaps. 1-3)

In the days immediately after Joshua's military victories, Israel continued to obediently win battles over the Canaanites. But soon the Scripture text begins to record that the tribes "did not drive out the Canaanites who were living" in such and such an area (1:21, 27, 29-33). Instead, dominant Israel forced the Canaanites to serve them (1:28) in direct violation of God's command (Deut. 7:1). This disobedience was the seed that would bring forth a harvest of trouble for Israel.

II. The Judges of Israel (chaps. 3-16)

The book of Judges records seven apostasies of the nation of Israel during the theocracy. (An "apostasy" is a deliberate, knowledgeable turning away from the Lord.) In each of these cases Israel became enslaved to a foreign power, repented, and was delivered by a judge. Although much could be said about most of the judges, we will make only a brief summary statement. (For additional details about each judge, see the chart "The Chronology of Israel's Judges," p. 87.)

A. Othniel

He was the younger brother (or nephew) of the famous Caleb. Othniel was already known as a heroic individual, having taken part in the conquering of Canaan (Josh. 15:15-20). The presence of Othniel as the first judge makes clear that Israel did indeed depart quickly from the Lord after the death of Joshua.

B. Ehud

After enjoying forty years with no oppression, the Moabites subjugated some of Benjamin and Ephraim. Ehud, a leading man of Benjamin, assassinated the king of Moab and brought about deliverance for the oppressed area of Israel. After this deliverance, there were eighty years of rest for the people of Israel.

C. Shamgar

His efforts were directed toward the Philistines who lived southwest of Israel. Although not much is given about him, he must have been important in his day to be mentioned in the Scriptures.

D. Deborah (and Barak)

Deborah, a prophetess of God, was the judge, and Barak, an experienced general from the tribe of Naphtali, was the deliverer. Evidently God gave Barak victory over the iron chariots of the oppressing Canaanites by causing a heavy rain to make the battlefield muddy, thus bogging down the chariots (5:21).

E. Gideon

After convincing Gideon through the use of three supernatural signs (6:21; 6:36; 7:15), God used him to deliver Israel from the Midianites. The battle itself evidenced God's working on Israel's behalf (7:19-22).

F. Tola

G. Jair

These two were probably contemporary judges; Tola served west of the Jordan, and Jair on the east side.

H. Jephthah

He liberated Israel from the Ammonites. But the fame of this judge comes from a vow he made to God before the battle. He promised to sacrifice to God the first thing that came out of his house upon returning from battle. The first thing to come from his house was his only child, a daughter. The normal reading of the text indicates that he did indeed sacrifice her—something God would never approve (note Ps. 106:37).

I. Ibzan

    J. Elon

    K. Abdon

These three judges served in different areas of Israel. They were probably contemporaries of one another and perhaps served alongside Jephthah.

    L. Samson

He was clearly not of the spiritual quality of a Daniel or a Joshua. But God gave Samson unusual strength in order to cause the oppressing Philistines great problems and make it impossible for them to overrun Israel.

III. Illustrations from the Era of the Judges (chaps. 17-21)

The events recorded in these chapters transpired at different times during the era of the theocracy. These accounts were selected to represent and illustrate the major sins of this era. They are not the only sins or necessarily the worst sins of this time. The religious apostasy (chaps. 17-18) occurred fairly early in the period of the judges. Baal worship was the primary sin of Israel, but not the only one. The worship of Baal precipitated many other sins. The moral degeneracy and the political anarchy (chaps. 19-21) show how far away from the "constitution" Israel did go. The immorality and disregard for human life illustrate the basic weakness of the theocracy—sinful man.

RUTH

This book complements Judges. The setting of Ruth is in the era of the judges (1:1). The book does not advance the history of Israel, but it does illustrate life in the days of the judges.

INTRODUCTION TO RUTH

A. AUTHORSHIP AND DATE OF RUTH

The Jewish Talmud claims that Samuel wrote the book, but the author is unknown. It was not written prior to the time of David, since he is mentioned in 4:22. Since David is mentioned, but David's son Solomon is not mentioned, it has led some to assume that it was written before Solomon's time. Samuel could have written the book. If he did, a date of about 1000 B.C. would be given.

B. PURPOSE OF RUTH

One purpose of the book is to reveal that there were godly people during the era of the theocracy. Even though the nation found itself in deep apostasy, there were people in Israel who loved and obeyed the Lord God of Israel. In the book of Judges Israel forsakes the Lord and turns to idols, whereas in the book of Ruth one Gentile woman turns from her idols to serve the living and true God. Another purpose of the book is to reveal something of the family line of Israel's greatest king, David.

C. BASIC OUTLINE OF RUTH

    I. Ruth's Decision to Follow Naomi (chap. 1)
    II. Ruth's Faithfulness to Naomi (chap. 2)
   III. Ruth's Claim upon Boaz (chap. 3)
   IV. Ruth's Redemption by Boaz (chap. 4)

D. IMPORTANT DATA ABOUT RUTH

   1. Key Words: Kinsman and redeemer (based on Lev. 25:25, 47-79; Deut. 25:5-6)
   2. Key Chapter: 4—The family line of David
   3. Key Verses: 1:15-16; 4:10
   4. Key Characters: Ruth, Naomi, and Boaz
   5. Meaning of "Ruth": Obviously the name of the central character of the book
   6. Geography of Ruth: Tribal area of Benjamin and the country of Moab

E. SPECIAL CONSIDERATIONS ON RUTH

The discussion under this same heading for Judges applies to Ruth as well. Leviticus 25:25 and 47-49 teach the concept of the "kinsman redeemer" that is important as background for the story of Ruth.

A SUMMARY OF RUTH

I. Ruth's Decision to Follow Naomi (chap. 1)

The story begins by noting that famine had hit the land of Israel, which also indicates that the people were living in sin and disobedience (cf. Deut. 11:13-17). It also suggests that Israel was either in or heading into a time of foreign oppression. A family of Israel moved to Moab to try to avoid the famine. While in Moab the two sons married Moabite women, something expressly forbidden in the law (cf. Deut. 7:3; 23:3). Eventually the two sons died, as did the father, leaving three widows to face life alone. When news came that the famine was over (some judge had evidently delivered a repentant Israel), the mother, Naomi, decided to return home. Ruth, one of her daughters-in-law, insisted on going with her.

II. Ruth's Faithfulness to Naomi (chap. 2)

Ruth volunteered to care for the needs of Naomi by going into the fields and gleaning. Under the law (Lev. 19:9-10) the poor could enter fields, orchards, and vineyards and pick up leftover fruit or grain in order to provide food to meet their needs. It was a humbling task, but Ruth was willing to do it and in so doing put herself in the place for great blessing. Boaz was the owner of the field in which Ruth was gleaning. Boaz had heard of the godliness of Ruth (2:12 with Deut. 32:11) and her devotion to Naomi. He responded by allowing her to take home an unusual amount of grain (2:15-16, 19). Boaz's godliness and devotion to the Lord is seen in his obedience to the command to let people glean in his fields. (In light of the past famine, there would be a tendency to be grasping and to hoard all one could.)

III. Ruth's Claim upon Boaz (chap. 3)

To understand the story of Ruth, two customs of Israel must be kept in mind: (1) No land could be sold in perpetuity, that is, sold and kept forever by another. God did not want land falling into the hands of a few or passing to another tribe. (2) A male heir had to carry on the family line.

In the law a man was to be a "kinsman-redeemer" when it was necessary to buy back the inheritance of a poor relative, or to buy back a person from slavery, or to build the family of a deceased relative.

Acting on Naomi's instructions, Ruth went to Boaz and claimed his protection, since he was a near relative of Naomi. Boaz was willing (and anxious) to do this, but there existed a relative who was closer to Naomi than he.

IV. Ruth's Redemption by Boaz (chap. 4)

Going to the gate of the city (where public transactions were carried out), Boaz took the necessary legal steps to care for the matter. In the end, Boaz married Ruth, and they had a son whom they named Obed. Obed was the grandfather of David the king.

8

1 SAMUEL

INTRODUCTION TO 1 SAMUEL

A. AUTHORSHIP AND DATE OF 1 SAMUEL

The books of 1 and 2 Samuel, originally one book, were divided into the present two books in the third century B.C. The Jewish Talmud states that Samuel wrote part of the book (1 Samuel 1-24) and that Nathan and Gad composed the rest (cf. 1 Chronicles 29:29). The idea of there being several authors does not detract from the unity of the books or from the doctrine of inspiration.[1] For this study, a date of 975 B.C. is given for these books.

B. PURPOSE OF 1 SAMUEL

First Samuel is given to record the great transition in the national life of Israel, as Israel left the theocracy and went into the monarchy. Samuel was the key individual during this time, and 1 Samuel provides the account of his ministry.

C. BASIC OUTLINE OF 1 SAMUEL

    I. Samuel: Judge and Prophet in Israel (chaps. 1-7)
    II. Saul: The First King of Israel (chaps. 8-12)
    III. The Decline of Saul and the Rise of David (chaps. 13-31)

1. J. Carl Laney, *First and Second Samuel* (Chicago: Moody, 1982), p. 8.

D. IMPORTANT DATA ABOUT 1 SAMUEL

1. Key Word: King
2. Key Chapter: 8—the first king in Israel
3. Key Verses: 2:30; 8:7; 15:22-23; 16:7
4. Key Characters: Samuel, Saul, and David
5. Meaning of "1 Samuel": The first of two books named for the key figure of the early chapters
6. Geography of 1 Samuel: The land of Israel

E. SPECIAL CONSIDERATIONS ON 1 SAMUEL

The book begins with the birth of Samuel, which was about 1100 B.C., and ends with the death of Saul (1011 B.C.). This foundational book covers about ninety years.

A SUMMARY OF 1 SAMUEL

I. Samuel: Judge and Prophet in Israel (chaps. 1-7)
   A. The Birth of Samuel (1:1–2:10)
The significant role of Samuel in the history of Israel is often overlooked. He was born at a time when spiritually Israel was still in her descending spiral downward (Judg. 2:19); when Israel was weak and vulnerable before her enemies (1 Sam. 4:1-11); and when the voice of God was rarely heard in the land (3:1). Samuel was the last of the judges (7:6, 15); was a priest of God (1:1; 16:5 with 1 Chron. 6:33-36); and was the first notable prophet of God since Moses (3:19-21). From the human perspective, it was Samuel who changed Israel from a weak, idolatrous people to a nation spiritually alive and strong for the Lord God.

Samuel was born into the home of a Levite named Elkanah. (Note that they lived in the tribal area of Ephraim and were therefore called Ephraimites, but they were of the tribe of Levi.) Elkanah the Levite had two wives, which may suggest a low moral condition in Israel at that time. One wife was named Hannah, and she had no children. There was bitter antagonism between the two wives, much of which came from the fact that Hannah was childless. Evidently it took Hannah many years before she humbled herself before the Lord and prayed earnestly for a child (1:7, 10,

15). God honored her and gave her a son whom she named Samuel (1:27). She fulfilled the vow she had made and gave Samuel to the Lord for unique service in the Tabernacle (1:11, 28).

B. The Childhood of Samuel (2:11–3:21)

Samuel's environment at the Tabernacle had both positive and negative aspects to it. It was positive in that he was intimately involved with the high priest, Eli, and had the opportunity of serving God from his childhood. But it was negative in that he was exposed to Eli's two godless and immoral sons (2:11-12).

In those years it became clear to all in Israel that Samuel was uniquely God's man (3:19–4:1). God revealed an important life principle to Samuel in those early days—"those who honor Me I will honor" (2:30). This statement undoubtedly echoed in Samuel's thoughts all his life and was reflected in the life he lived.

C. The Ministry of Samuel (4:1–7:17)

Samuel was the key man in holding Israel together during the final, discouraging days of the theocracy. But even though some tragic events occurred (such as the military defeats at the hands of the Philistines and the capture of the Ark of the Covenant, 4:1-11), Samuel led the nation back to the Lord and into times of military victory (7:3-14). The majority of Samuel's significant ministry is summarized in just a few words (7:15-17).

II. Saul: The First King of Israel (8:1–12:25)

A. Israel's Demand for a King (8:1-22)

On several occasions in the era of the theocracy, the people of Israel had seriously considered the idea of having an earthly king rule over them (Judg. 8:22; 9:6). But the idea blossomed into reality when Samuel became quite old. It appeared to the elders of Israel that it was time to make the move to a monarchy (8:1-5). The matter was displeasing to Samuel and offensive to the Lord (8:6-7).

It must be noted that the idea of a king was within the plan of God (cf. Deut. 17:14-20). But on this occasion, the demand for a king was wrong for two basic reasons. First, the demand was premature. When God was ready to give them a king He would do so (David? the Messiah?). Second, the demand for a king was wrong because their attitude was wrong.

> Samuel's opposition . . . was a condemnation of the peo-
> ple's spirit and motives for requesting a king: they wished to be
> "like all the nations" in having a king (8:5, 20). It was also a
> tacit statement of disbelief in the power and presence of God:
> they wanted a king to go before them and fight their battles
> (v.20).[2]

The Lord offered Samuel comfort by telling him that the nation
was not rejecting Samuel, but they were rejecting God Himself
(8:7). This rejection of God's rulership climaxed here, but it had
been going on throughout the period of the judges.

God granted Israel's request and gave them what they wanted
but also warned them of what lay ahead in this new form of
government.

> This change of government called for heavy taxation of the
> people. Under God's "best" form, there had been no need for
> taxes to support a civil government. There was no king or ex-
> pensive court, to civil programs or authorities; the people could
> live tax-free. But this was radically changed when they re-
> ceived the monarchy. In this connection, God's instruction to
> Samuel at the time of the people's request for a king is note-
> worthy. . . . God wanted the people to recognize the unique
> benefit they had been enjoying under His prescribed theocra-
> cy.[3]

B. Saul's Anointing and Recognition as King of Israel
(9:1–12:25)

Evidently God gave Israel the kind of king they wanted (9:1-2)
but did intend to use him in a significant way (9:16). Samuel first
anointed Saul as king privately (9:3–10:16) and later anointed him
in a public ceremony (10:17-24).

> The oil of anointing, when used in worship, was a symbol of
> the divine Spirit; but in regal consecration it marked God's gift
> of His Spirit to aid the king of Israel in administering His rule.
> . . . this title of "the anointed one" . . . was only used abso-

2. Walter C. Kaiser, *Toward an Old Testament Theology* (Grand Rapids: Zondervan, 1981), p. 145.
3. Leon Wood, *Distressing Days of the Judges* (Grand Rapids: Zondervan, 1975),
p. 26.

lutely of the king. Subsequently the word became the title for the great Davidite who was to come and to complete the expected kingdom of God. All together, the noun "anointed" occurs thirty-nine times in the OT. Twenty-three times it is the title for the reigning king of Israel.[4]

Although he was anointed as Israel's king, some doubted that he could really lead Israel (10:27). But Saul's credentials as king were firmly established when he led Israel to a great military victory at Jabesh-Gilead (11:1-15). After this great victory, which brought Saul general recognition as king, Samuel stepped down as the judge in Israel. He turned the civil authority over to Saul and exhorted Israel to fear and obey the Lord (12:1-25).

III. The Decline of Saul and the Rise of David (chaps. 13-31)

The remainder of 1 Samuel chronicles the willful disobedience of King Saul. His deliberate, disobedient choices were based on his ignorance of God and His Word as well as on the fact that he feared men more than he feared God.

The first step down in Saul's life was when he impatiently intruded into the priestly role and sacrificed animals. When confronted with his sin, he put the blame elsewhere. Like Moses', Saul's one act of public disobedience cost him a great deal. In Saul's case, he would lose his kingship (13:8-14). The second step down in Saul's decline occurred when he refused to completely obey God's clear command. God had a score to settle with the Amalekites, a score that dated back to the time of the Exodus (15:2 with Ex. 17:8-16 and Deut. 25:17-19). Saul was to completely destroy all the Amalekites and all of their livestock. His obedience was incomplete (15:8-9, 20-26). Saul tried to argue his case (15:20-21) but was met with a scathing denunciation from Samuel (15:22-23, 28). As far as God was concerned Saul was through as king, and the Spirit left Saul (16:14). A new king, David, was chosen by God and was anointed in private by Samuel (16:1, 13). The emphasis of 1 Samuel now shifts away from Saul and toward David.

David's name became well-known in Israel after his amazing victory over the Philistine giant Goliath (17:1-52). More military

4. Kaiser, *Old Testament Theology,* pp. 148-49.

successes came to David after that event. David received the praise of the people ("Saul has slain his thousands and David his ten thousands," 18:7) but also the resentment and violence of Saul (18:8-11). Although Saul soon came to understand that David was God's choice as Israel's next king, he repeatedly tried to kill David. This willful refusal to submit to God's will was the third step down in the unhappy decline of Saul.

The final step in Saul's decline was his involvement with the witch of Endor (28:1-21). After the death of Samuel (25:1), it became clear to Saul that God had ceased all communication with him (28:6). When faced with another invasion by the Philistines, Saul was frightened and sought the Lord. When God failed to answer him, Saul entered the realm of the occult (cf. Deut. 18:9-11). A man with so much potential and with such a notable start ended up so poorly. The very next day Saul died on the battlefield. It was an unnecessary and tragic end, but the inevitable end of one who does not know and reverence God.

PERIOD OF THE KINGDOMS

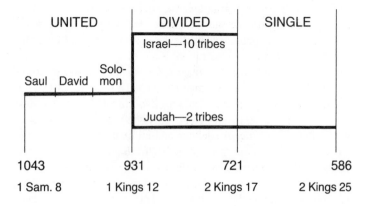

9

2 SAMUEL

Introduction to 2 Samuel

A. Authorship and Date of 2 Samuel

See the introduction to 1 Samuel for the discussion of authorship and date of this book.

B. Purpose of 2 Samuel

The purpose of 2 Samuel is to continue the account of the development of the monarchy in Israel. Second Samuel is the record of the reign of David, Israel's greatest king. The book also sets forth the elements of the Davidic Covenant.

C. Basic Outline of 2 Samuel

   I. David's Rule over Judah (chaps. 1-4)
  II. David's Rule over All Israel (chaps. 5-24)

D. Important Data About 2 Samuel

1. Key Word: David
2. Key Chapter: 7—The great Davidic Covenant
3. Key Verses: 7:8-16; 12:7-14
4. Key Characters: David, Nathan, Abner, Joab, and Absalom
5. Meaning of "2 Samuel": The second of two books named for the key figure of the early chapters of the first book
6. Geography of 2 Samuel: The land of Judah and Israel

E. SPECIAL CONSIDERATIONS ON 2 SAMUEL

The book of 2 Samuel records the years when David actually sat on the throne as king. His reign lasted for forty years (1011-971 B.C.).

A SUMMARY OF 2 SAMUEL

I. David's Rule over Judah (chaps. 1-4)

A. The Lamentation of David (1)

The book of 1 Samuel concludes with Saul's committing suicide on the battlefield after being wounded by the Philistines. The book of 2 Samuel begins with David's being informed about the deaths of Saul and his sons by an Amalekite, who was probably a mercenary soldier in Saul's army. The man claimed he had killed the nearly dead Saul, at Saul's request. Since the Scriptures indicate that Saul had indeed died by his own hand (1 Sam. 31:4-6), we know the man lied. No doubt he was hoping to be rewarded for eliminating David's enemy and removing the last obstacle to the throne. But David, who had himself repeatedly refused to kill Saul ("the Lord's anointed"), looked with anger on the Amalekite and had him executed, condemned by his own testimony (1:16).

Instead of rejoicing over the death of Saul and his sons, David grieved (1:17-27). His sorrow was particularly great for his close friend Jonathan.

B. The Crowning of David and the Years of Civil War (2-4)

David had the right to the throne at Saul's death, since he had been chosen and anointed by Samuel, God's prophet-priest. But only the tribe of Judah was willing to anoint David and recognize him as king (2:4). Most likely tribal jealousies, which emerged from time to time in Israel's history, kept the other tribes from immediately joining in. Instead Ishbosheth, a son of Saul, was made king over the northern area. He was supported by a mighty man by the name of Abner. This two-kingdom situation lasted for seven years. During that time wars were fought between the two nations. As time went on, however, it became clear that the kingdom of David was prospering and Ishbosheth's kingdom was declining (3:1). When the mighty Abner was murdered (3:30) and King Ishbosheth was assassinated (4:5-6), the northern tribes realized that they needed to unite under David.

II. David's Rule over All Israel (chaps. 5-24)

A. David's Early Reign in Power and Prosperity (5-10)

The leaders of the north recognized that it was not wise to be a divided people. They knew that David had been anointed to be king over all of Israel. They knew that David had played an important part in the recent military history of the north as well as the south. These truths plus the realization that they all had a common heritage brought the two groups together (5:1-3). Tens of thousands gathered in a great celebration at Hebron and made David king over all Israel (cf. 1 Chron. 12:23-40).

Several significant steps were taken immediately by David. First, he defeated Jerusalem and made it the political capital of the nation (5:6-10). David had been ruling from Hebron, located in the south. This move made Israel's capital more centrally located and more defensible. Second, he brought the Tabernacle to Jerusalem, thus making Jerusalem the religious capital of Israel also (6:12-19).

David was a capable military man who also sensed his need to depend on the Lord God. As a result, David won battle after battle, destroying enemy after enemy. In so doing, David expanded and secured the borders of Israel (5:17-25; 8:1-18; 10:1-19). David aggressively pushed the borders of Israel toward the boundaries granted under the Palestinian Covenant. Militarily David and Saul stand in sharp contrast. Saul's battles were primarily defensive, reacting to the hostile actions of some nation. David also responded to hostile nations, but David's battles were far more offensive in nature.

During a time of rest from war, David observed how beautiful his own house was in comparison to the Tabernacle, God's house. David's house was constructed out of expensive cedar wood, whereas God's house was a tent made out of cloth (7:1). To his friend and counselor Nathan the prophet, David expressed his desire to build a beautiful, permanent temple for the Lord. Nathan approved of the project but later that night was informed by God that since David was a man of war and bloodshed, he was not to build the Temple (7:5; 1 Chron. 22:8). But God responded to the heart desire of His servant David by entering into an eternal, unconditional covenant with him. The Davidic Covenant is a subdivision of the Abrahamic Covenant and develops further the promise of a nation and a king. Second Samuel 7 is the central passage on the Davidic Covenant, but many other Scriptures speak of it, including 1 Chronicles 17:11-27; Psalm 89; Jeremiah 33:14-22; Ezekiel 37:24-25; 2 Samuel 23:1-7; and Luke 1:32-33.

DAVIDIC COVENANT

1. DAVID'S NAME WILL BE GREAT

   This was fulfilled in David's own lifetime, as well as throughout history.

2. DAVID WOULD HAVE REST

   Rest from his enemies was one of the realities of David's life.

3. DAVID WOULD HAVE A *HOUSE*

   This does not refer to a physical structure but rather a ruling dynasty. His line would never be cut off.

4. DAVID WOULD HAVE A *THRONE*

   The right to rule Israel would always belong to David's line.

5. DAVID WOULD HAVE A *KINGDOM*

   This included an actual land area to rule over, as well as the other aspects of a kingdom.

(NOTE: Numbers 3, 4, and 5 await ultimate fulfillment in Jesus Christ.)

Since the Davidic Covenant looks ahead to David's greater Son, Jesus Christ, there are some clear prophetic implications to this covenant. They are: (1) Israel must be preserved as a nation and eventually returned to the land of Palestine; (2) David's Son, Jesus the Messiah, must return to rule over the covenanted kingdom; (3) a literal, earthly kingdom for the nation of Israel must be instituted, over which Christ will reign.[1]

1. J. Carl Laney, *First and Second Samuel* (Chicago: Moody, 1982), p. 99.

B. David's Later Reign of Sin and Trouble (11-24)

Often in times of great success and victory, when all seems well, defeat is experienced. So it was in the case of the great and victorious King David, when he committed adultery with Bath-sheba (11:1-4). The sequence of sin was common—he saw, he in-quired, and then he participated. His taking of another man's wife was bad enough, but the situation got worse because sin was not confessed. When David learned that Bathsheba was pregnant (11:5), he initiated a series of cover-ups, which finally ended in the death (actually murder) of Uriah, the unsuspecting husband of Bathshe-ba. David, therefore, was guilty of both murder and adultery. Both of these sins were capital crimes in Israel, and there was no sacrifice available to cover them. David the king faced death, but though burdened by terrible guilt (cf. Ps. 32:3-4), he would not confess. It took a story and declaration by his friend Nathan to bring David to the point of genuine confession (cf. Ps. 51). God extended mercy toward David. His sin was forgiven, but Nathan informed David that there would be two results of his sin: (1) the baby born to Bathsheba from their union would die, and (2) David would see and experience sin and rebellion in his own house for the rest of his life. And so it happened: one son raped one of his daughters; one son murdered another son; and one ran away from home only to foment a national rebellion when he returned (13:1–18:33). David's sins of murder and adultery had been forgiven, but even forgiven sin has its consequences. This spiritual and moral failure of King David has been recorded as a warning to all.

David did fail on a number of occasions, but he was still a "man after God's own heart." He dealt with his sin and drew upon the power and grace of God to live with the consequences of sin.

10

1 KINGS

Introduction to 1 Kings

A. AUTHORSHIP AND DATE OF 1 KINGS

The two books of 1 and 2 Kings were originally one book, and the author is unknown. It is generally agreed by commentators that the content of 1 and 2 Kings was compiled before the captivity of Judah, with the final editing taking place in the captivity period. Some believe that the author was a Jewish captive living in Babylon, whereas others point to the prophet Jeremiah as the most likely candidate. In either case, the date of writing would be about 600-575 B.C.

B. PURPOSE OF 1 KINGS

First Kings was written to continue the story of the united monarchy under David's son Solomon. It was also written to record the division of the kingdom into North and South. The book is not just a view of historical events but a commentary on the great spiritual issues that brought about those events.

C. BASIC OUTLINE OF 1 KINGS

    I. The Reign of Solomon over the United Kingdom (chaps. 1-11)

    II. The Early Days of the Divided Kingdom (chaps. 12-22)

D. IMPORTANT DATA ABOUT 1 KINGS

1. Key Word: Division
2. Key Chapter: 12—The dividing of the kingdom
3. Key Verses: 8:22-26; 12:16
4. Key Characters: Solomon, Rehoboam, Jeroboam, Ahab, Jezebel, Elijah, Asa, and Jehoshaphat
5. Meaning of "1 Kings": The first of two books named after the kings of Israel and Judah from Solomon to the Babylonian captivity whose histories they record
6. Geography of 1 Kings: The land of Judah and Israel

E. SPECIAL CONSIDERATIONS ON 1 KINGS

The book begins with Solomon's coming to the throne and ruling all of Israel, and it ends with Jehoshaphat's reigning in Judah and Ahaziah's ruling in Israel. This would, therefore, cover a period of about 125 years.

A SUMMARY OF 1 KINGS

I. The Reign of Solomon over the United Kingdom (chaps. 1-11)
   A. Solomon's Accession to the Thone (1:1-2:11)

As David neared the age of seventy (2 Sam. 5:4) and was weak and infirm, it became clear to all in Israel that a new king would be coming to the throne. David had evidently made a fundamental error by not clearly and publicly declaring which son would be his successor. Privately, David had promised Bathsheba that her son Solomon would be the next king (1:16-17). But in the absence of a clear, public statement, David's fourth son Adonijah (probably David's oldest living son) attempted to take the throne for himself (1:5, 18-19). This attempt was thwarted when David ordered Nathan the prophet, Zadok the priest, and other key individuals to publicly anoint and proclaim Solomon as king (1:32-40). Considering the potential for chaos and unrest, the transition of the throne to Solomon went fairly smoothly. After giving the new king some good advice, Israel's greatest king, David, died (2:1-11).

B. Solomon's Establishment of the Kingdom (2:12–5:18)

After removing several of his adversaries (2:12-46), Solomon put together a highly organized empire. He made numerous political alliances, engaged in many building projects, fortified the defenses of Israel, and developed a complex bureaucracy.

Solomon's wisdom (given him by God, 3:4-12) became well-known throughout the region (4:29-34). David's military victories, Solomon's wisdom, and God's obvious favor made it possible for all Israel to live in peace and prosperity (4:25).

C. Solomon's Building Program (6:1–10:29)

David had desired to build a house for God, but it was his son Solomon who actually built the Temple in Jerusalem. It took about seven years to build this multimillion-dollar structure. With its abundance of gold, silver, marble, and fine woods, the Temple was one of the wonders of the world.

The high point in Israel's history in the Old Testament was perhaps the dedication of this Temple. Never again do we find the nation, as a whole, living in such peace and prosperity and apparently so completely devoted to the Lord. Both king and people were united in obedience to the law of God. Solomon's marvelous prayer on that great day of dedication gives a fitting illustration of those prosperous days in Israel (cf. 8:1, 22-25, 54-56).

D. Solomon's Spiritual Failure and End as Israel's King (11:1-43)

Two Scriptures mentioned previously have great import in the following events. In 1 Samuel 8, God had warned Israel that heavy taxation would accompany the monarchy. In order to maintain his huge government, luxurious life-style, and numerous building projects, Solomon turned more and more to the taxation of his people. This tax burden caused deep unrest and became terribly oppressive (as the cries of the people later on indicate, 12:4). In Deuteronomy 17, God had warned kings not to multiply horses, silver, and wives. The horse was the basis of military might, but God wanted Israel to trust *Him*. Silver, and all other forms of wealth, would breed independence from God. Many wives (often part of treaties made with foreign kings) would bring their idols with them and in the process turn the king's devotion away from the Lord. Solomon flagrantly violated all three of these prohibitions (cf. 1 Kings 10:26; 2 Chron. 9:25; 1 Kings 10:14, 27; 11:1-5).

In his glory years Solomon did not act wisely, failing to remember that even kings are subject to the "constitution." He antagonized his subjects and offended the Holy One of Israel. His devotion to the many idols of his wives brought a word of judgment from God (11:11-13). As a result of his sin, the kingdom would be divided. Solomon's son would be king over but two tribes. Only the existence of the Davidic Covenant kept Solomon's line from being cut off.

The rest of Solomon's life is passed over quickly in the text of Scripture. The author of 1 Kings now introduces Jeroboam, who will become a central figure in the monarchy period. Jeroboam, a servant of Solomon, will become the first king of the Northern Kingdom (11:26-31).

II. The Early Days of the Divided Kingdom (chaps. 12-22)
    A. The Division of the Kingdom (12:1-20)

Solomon did not make David's error of failing to unmistakably set apart his successor. His son Rehoboam was made king. After Solomon's death, Rehoboam went to Shechem in north central Israel to be formally crowned as the fourth king of the united kingdom. However, it was at that time that the people demanded relief from the heavy taxation of Solomon as a prerequisite for their uniting under the kingship of Rehoboam (12:1-4). Rehoboam foolishly refused this legitimate request with the result that the northern tribes refused to acknowledge Rehoboam as king (12:13-16). Instead they made Jeroboam of Ephraim their king (12:20).

Although Rehoboam's lack of wisdom brought about the division of kingdom, it was not the cause of it. There were several reasons for the breakup of the kingdom of Israel. First and foremost was the spiritual defection of Solomon.

> Solomon's sin struck at the heart of the theocracy; to follow other gods in any sense was to deny the covenant with Yahweh and make the new temple a farce.[1]

This by itself would have brought about God's judgment. But a second reason for division can be found in a long-standing tribal jealousy that was promoted by Judah's being the preeminent kingly tribe. Solomon deepened this jealousy by taxing all the tribes but Judah, by concentrating his building projects in Judah, and by emphasizing the defense of Judah. His harsh treatment of certain northerners, by offering to give away their cities to another king (9:10-13), added to the already existing rivalry and antagonism.[2] And a third reason for the division can be found in Solomon's exploitation of the people.

> Solomon's personal pride and selfishness certainly contributed to the problem. . . . His vast building operations, though improving his power and prestige, did little to help his own people. . . . The people soon realized that they were being sacrificed for personal enrichment rather than for national welfare. . . . Unrest continued to increase.[3]

In light of these powerful forces already at work, the blame for the division belongs to Solomon and not Rehoboam. But division came and would continue for the next 210 years.

The year of the division was 931 B.C. The histories of the two kingdoms are interwoven in the Scripture text until the captivity of the Northern Kingdom in 721 B.C. (2 Kings 17). During those years the two kingdoms were often friendly and cooperative with one another, but at other times they were at war.

B. Rehoboam of Judah and Jeroboam of Israel (12:21–14:31)

Although political division had taken place, the two nations were still united religiously. Jerusalem, in the south, was still the center of Israel's worship and religious activity. Jeroboam rea-

---

1. Wayne Brindle, "The Causes of the Division of Israel's Kingdom," *Bibliotheca Sacra* 141 (July-September 1984): 231.
2. Ibid., pp. 224-27.
3. Ibid., p. 229.

APPROXIMATE BOUNDARIES OF THE TWO KINGDOMS IN THE DAYS OF THE DIVIDED MONARCHY

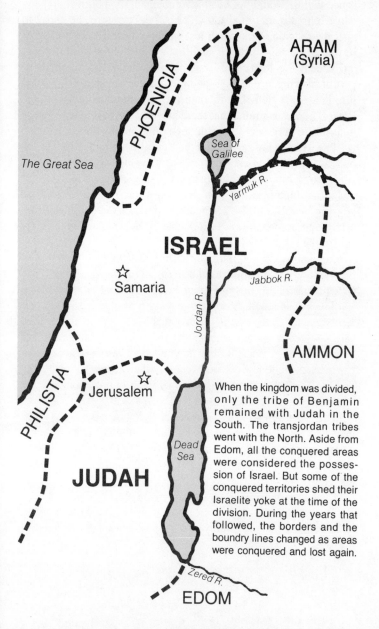

ARAM (Syria)

PHOENICIA

Sea of Galilee

The Great Sea

Yarmuk R.

ISRAEL

Samaria ☆

Jabbok R.

Jordan R.

AMMON

PHILISTIA

Jerusalem ☆

Dead Sea

JUDAH

When the kingdom was divided, only the tribe of Benjamin remained with Judah in the South. The transjordan tribes went with the North. Aside from Edom, all the conquered areas were considered the possession of Israel. But some of the conquered territories shed their Israelite yoke at the time of the division. During the years that followed, the borders and the boundry lines changed as areas were conquered and lost again.

Zered R.

EDOM

soned that he would not be able to maintain the political division while religious unity existed (12:26-27). Therefore, he chose to alter the religion of the north just enough to deprive Jerusalem of its role as the only center of a unified worship of the Lord. Jeroboam made two golden calves (bulls) and placed one in the northern part of his kingdom at Dan, and the other in the southern part of his kingdom at Bethel. Jeroboam was not introducing new gods. Rather, he was claiming that these calves were visible representations of the Lord who "brought them up from the land of Egypt" (12:28). He was not saying that the Lord was the calf. The calf, or bull, was revered in ancient times as a symbol of great strength. And, too, Jeroboam had history on his side. He could point to Israel's first high priest, Aaron, who once made a calf of gold for worship. Jeroboam also changed the religious calendar and the priesthood. Jeroboam was introducing his own version of the worship of the Lord.

Jeroboam's polluted religious system was the push that started the Northern Kingdom downhill to corruption and captivity. Gross forms of paganism entered easily once true worship of the Lord was abandoned. More than twenty times the Scriptures call Jeroboam the man "who made Israel sin." When the golden calves were set up and accepted by the Northern Kingdom, that kingdom took a notable step downward. The condition of the Northern Kingdom worsened rapidly when many godly people fled the North and went to live in the South in order to avoid the rampant idolatry (cf. 2 Chron. 11:14-17).

In the Southern Kingdom, however, Rehoboam proved to be an inept and evil king. The glory of Solomon's day faded quickly during Rehoboam's seventeen-year reign (15:21-31). And life was made worse by the war with Jeroboam that continued throughout his reign.

    C. Kings of Judah in 1 Kings (15:1-24; 22:41-50)

        1. Abijam

He reigned for just three years. He was not totally devoted to the Lord.

2. Asa

He was a godly king who ruled for forty-one years. He destroyed the places of idolatry in the Southern Kingdom.

3. Jehoshaphat

He was a good king who obeyed the Lord. He reigned for twenty-five years and made peace with the North.

D. Kings of Israel in 1 Kings (15:25–22:40, 51-53)

1. Nadab

He was evil like his father, Jeroboam. He was on the throne for just two years.

2. Baasha

He was a sinful king who ruled twenty-four years after completely destroying everyone in the family of Nadab.

3. Elah

He continued the sins and the policies of Baasha, his father, during his two years on the throne.

4. Zimri

He was a powerful general in the army who assassinated Elah and all of his family. He ruled for only seven days.

5. Omri

He was another leader in the army who came to power after killing Zimri. He was forced to rule alongside another claimant to the throne, Tibni. For three years these two ruled as kings in the North, until Omri finally won out. Omri made some effective long-range plans for Israel, such as moving Israel's capital to Samaria and strengthening Israel through alliances. One such alliance brought the evil Jezebel to Israel.

6. Ahab

Ruling for twenty-two years, along with his wife Jezebel, he brought Israel to its lowest spiritual level. Baalism became the religion of the Northern Kingdom, and the Scriptures declare that Ahab and Jezebel were the most wicked rulers in the entire history of the North (16:30-31; 21:25). In order to deal with this extreme crisis, God raised up the fiery prophet Elijah. Elijah was used to counter the evils of Baalism and call some in Israel back to Lord.

7. Ahaziah

This son of Ahab and Jezebel was wicked like his parents. Fortunately, he ruled for only two years.

A COMPARISON OF THE TWO KINGDOMS

	NORTH:	SOUTH:
NAME	Israel	Judah
FIRST KING: TRIBES: DURATION:	Jeroboam 10 209 years	Rehoboam 2 345 years
DYNASTIES: KINGS: CAPITAL:	9 20 Samaria	1 20 Jerusalem
CONQUERED BY: CONQUERED IN: LAST KING:	Assyria 721 B.C. Hoshea	Babylon 605 B.C. Zedekiah

11

2 KINGS

INTRODUCTION TO 2 KINGS

A. AUTHORSHIP AND DATE OF 2 KINGS

Please see the discussion on the authorship and date of 1 Kings.

B. PURPOSE OF 2 KINGS

Second Kings was written to continue the story of the divided kingdom period and to record the taking captive of both the Northern and the Southern Kingdoms. The book was written to show that God is faithful to His word in judging His people for their disobedience and idolatry.

C. BASIC OUTLINE OF 2 KINGS

    I. The History of Israel: The Northern Kingdom (chaps. 1-10)

    II. The History of Israel and Judah: The Divided Kingdom (chaps. 11-17)

    III. The History of Judah: The Single Kingdom (chaps. 18-25)

D. IMPORTANT DATA ABOUT 2 KINGS

    1. Key Word: Captivity

    2. Key Chapters: 17—The captivity of the Northern Kingdom; 25—The captivity of the Southern Kingdom

3. Key Verses: 17:7-18; 23:26-27; 25:8-12
4. Key Characters: Elisha, Jehu, Jeroboam II, Hezekiah, Josiah, and Manasseh
5. Meaning of "2 Kings": The second of two books named after the kings of Israel and Judah whose histories they record
6. Geography of 2 Kings: The land of Israel and Judah

E. SPECIAL CONSIDERATIONS ON 2 KINGS

The book of 2 Kings begins with the reign of King Ahaziah of Israel and concludes with King Zedekiah, the last king of Judah. The years covered by this book are approximately 250.

A SUMMARY OF 2 KINGS

I. The History of Israel: The Northern Kingdom (chaps. 1-10)

A. The Ministry of Elijah (1:1–2:11)

Most of Elijah's colorful ministry is recorded in 1 Kings in connection with the reign of the evil King Ahab (17:1–19:21). This section in 2 Kings continues the story of his miraculous ministry, recording the fire called down from heaven (1:9-12), crossing the Jordan River on dry ground (2:8), and his departure to heaven in a whirlwind (2:11).

B. The Ministry of Elisha (2:12–8:29)

Elijah's ministry was passed on to Elisha, who had to face the difficult times of spiritual and moral decay in Israel. Elisha's ministry, which lasted about half a century, greatly affected the people of his day. His influence was significant among the "sons of the prophets"—a group of young men trained at Bethel and Gilgal to serve the Lord in the Northern Kingdom. He influenced people through the miracles he worked—twice as many as Elijah performed. His influence extended beyond the border of Israel, and as he was known and respected in Syria. He was a great prophet raised up in difficult times.

C. The Role of Jehu (9:1–10:36)

The last recorded act of Elisha was to send one of the "sons of the prophets" to anoint Jehu, a captain in the northern army, to be the next king of Israel (9:1-3). Jehu was instructed to destroy all the family of Ahab and avenge the slain prophets of the Lord. With undisguised zeal, Jehu annihilated the house of Ahab and eradicated Baalism out of Israel (9:7-10; 10:10-28). Because of his obedience, the Lord prospered the dynasty of Jehu, causing it to be the longest in the Northern Kingdom. But since Jehu did not also rid Israel of the golden calves, the blessing was limited (10:29-31).

II. The History of Israel and Judah: The Divided Kingdom (chaps. 11-17)

A. Israel: The Northern Kingdom

All of the last nine kings who ruled Israel before the captivity of the North were worshipers of the golden calf. All of them were evil. None of them pleased the Lord. (See chart "Rulers in the Era of the Monarchy," p. 120.)

Of the last nine kings, one does stand out. Jeroboam II was the fourth king in the line of Jehu. He ruled for forty-one years and brought a degree of prosperity and victory to Israel. He extended the borders of Israel, reclaiming much territory that had been lost for many years. Israel also enjoyed material prosperity during his reign. But the man himself was wicked and worshiped the golden calves (14:23-24). His reign is particularly important because it is the setting for three of God's prophets—Amos, Hosea, and Jonah.

The years of prosperity went by quickly and the inevitable came. In 721 B.C., in the reign of Hoshea, the Lord brought the Assyrians down on Israel. For two centuries God had tolerated their wicked and idolatrous living. When they did not respond to the prophets who were sent to them, they were judged. The Northern Kingdom was destroyed, with many being killed and many being taken captive to Assyria. Though the Lord was amazingly patient with Israel, judgment eventually had to come (17:5-12).

B. Judah: The Southern Kingdom

During the last years of the Northern Kingdom, the Southern Kingdom experienced the wrath of a wicked ruler, Queen Athaliah, and the blessings of a righteous ruler, Jotham (11:1-3; 15:33-34). In contrast to the North, which had no righteous kings, the South did have some who sought to obey the Lord. This accounts for the longer duration of the Southern Kingdom. When the As-syrians swept down and crushed Israel, God preserved Judah.

III. The History of Judah: The Single Kingdom (chaps. 18-25)
    A. The Godly King Hezekiah (18:1–20:21)

It was God's own testimony that of all the kings of the South, Hezekiah was the most righteous (18:5). He removed idolatry out of his nation, even destroying the bronze serpent of Moses, which had become an object of worship. Hezekiah obeyed God, trusted God, and served God, and God honored him for it. Hezekiah's great test came when the arrogant but powerful Assyrian army be-sieged Jerusalem, demanding its surrender. Hezekiah pled with the Lord for deliverance. Through the prophet Isaiah deliverance was promised (19:5-7), and it came in a remarkable way when God destroyed a large number of the Assyrian army (19:35).

    B. The Wicked King Manasseh (21:1-16)

It is impossible to explain the enigma of Manasseh and Hezeki-ah. How could the godliest king of Judah be the father of the most wicked king in all of the monarchy period? But Manasseh was just that (21:10-12, 16). So great and pervasive was his sinful influ-ence that God pronounced irreversible judgment on Judah. The nation was now doomed for captivity. The evil done by Manasseh became so deeply rooted in Judah that the harvest of wickedness was sure—and captivity was sure.

    C. The Godly King Josiah (22:1-3)

Josiah was the last godly king to rule. He brought a revival to Judah, but it was basically external. Josiah himself was a truly godly man, but the hearts of the people were far from the Lord, and judgment remained on the horizon (23:26; 24:3).

    D. The Last Kings of Judah (22:31–25:30)

None of the last four kings of Judah were genuinely righteous men. In less than a quarter of a century after Josiah's death, the Southern Kingdom would disappear from the land.

On the world scene, the mighty Assyrian Empire had weakened and was falling steadily before the new Babylonian Empire. In the year 605 B.C., at the battle of Carchemish, Babylon defeated the combined forces of Assyria and Egypt and emerged as the world power. Nebuchadnezzar and his Babylonian army then came down and subjugated Judah. In the course of the next years, Nebuchadnezzar would come a total of three times to Judah.

1. 605 B.C.

Jehoiakim was king of Judah. Judah became a subject nation to Babylon, paying annual taxes. Judah was allowed to have her own king. Some captives and treasure were taken back to Babylon (Dan. 1:2).

2. 597 B.C.

When Jehoiakim refused to pay the tax, Nebuchadnezzar returned. A new king on the throne, Jehoiachin, submitted to him. The king, the rest of the Temple treasure, and some 10,000 captives were taken back to Babylon.

3. 586 B.C.

With Zedekiah on the throne of Judah, once again Judah withheld paying taxes. Nebuchadnezzar returned, destroying the city of Jerusalem and removing the last king of Judah.

With this third coming of Nebuchadnezzar the Southern Kingdom went into captivity, and the era of the monarchy ended.

RULERS IN THE ERA OF THE MONARCHY

★ SAUL (32)		
*★# DAVID (40)		UNITED
*★ SOLOMON (40)		KINGDOM

SOUTHERN KINGS	NORTHERN KINGS	
★ REHOBOAM (17)	★# JEROBOAM I (22)	
ABIJAM (3)	NADAB(2)	
* ASA (41)	# BAASHA (24)	
* JEHOSHAPHAT (25)	ELAH (2)	
	# ZIMRI (7 days)	
JEHORAM (8)	★# OMRI (11)	
AHAZIAH (1)	TIBNI (3)	
	★ AHAB (22)	DIVIDED
	AHAZIAH (2)	KINGDOM
	JEHORAM (12)	
★ ATHALIAH (7)	★# JEHU (28)	
* JOASH (40)	JEHOAHAZ (17)	
	JEHOASH (16)	
AMAZIAH (29)	JEROBOAM 11 (41)	
* UZZIAH (52)	ZECHARIAH (6 mos.)	
* JOTHAM (16)	# SHALLUM (1 mo.)	
AHAZ (16)	# MENAHEM 10)	
	PEKAHIAH (2)	
* HEZEKIAH (29)	# PEKAH (20)	
	# HOSHEA (10)	

HEZEKIAH	
★ MANASSEH (55)	
AMON (2)	
* JOSIAH (31)	SINGLE
JEHOAHAZ (3 mos.)	KINGDOM
JEHOIAKIM (11)	
JEHOIACHIN (3 mos.)	
★ ZEDEKIAH (11)	

( ) = years of the king's reign
  * = good kings—basically righteous
  ★ = kings who particularly influenced history
  # = founders of a dynasty

12

1 AND 2 CHRONICLES

A. AUTHORSHIP AND DATE OF 1 AND 2 CHRONICLES

The author of the Chronicles compiled these books from as many as ten different sources (1 Chron. 9:1; 2 Chron. 12:15). Tradition says that Ezra the scribe wrote these books, and he was certainly qualified to do so (Ezra 7:10-11). It has been suggested by many that the book of Ezra and the Chronicles were actually one consecutive history when they were first written (cf. Ezra 1:1-3 with 2 Chron. 36:22-23). If Ezra was the author, then a date after the captivity of about 450 B.C. is likely.

B. PURPOSE OF 1 AND 2 CHRONICLES

These books are complementary to 1 and 2 Samuel and 1 and 2 Kings. They were intended to strengthen the remnant of the nation who had made it through the period of the Babylonian Captivity. They needed to be reminded that the Lord was still with them and that they still had a glorious future because God was faithful to His covenants. The nation's apostasy had brought it down, but the nation would rise again.

> This historian's purpose is to show that the true glory of the Hebrew nation was found in its covenant relationship to God, as safeguarded by the prescribed forms of worship in the temple and administered by the divinely ordained priesthood under the protection of the divinely authorized dynasty of David. Al-

> ways the emphasis is upon that which is sound and valid in Israel's past as furnishing a reliable basis for the task of reconstruction which lay ahead. Great stress is placed upon the rich heritage of Israel and its unbroken connection with the patriarchal beginnings (hence the prominence accorded to genealogical lists).[1]

Chronicles, written after the Babylonian captivity, was both an encouragement and a warning. It was given to encourage Israel with the truth that God was not through with them. It was a warning that future apostasy or idolatry would again be dealt with severely.

C. BASIC OUTLINES OF 1 AND 2 CHRONICLES

1. Outline of 1 Chronicles
    I. The Genealogies (chaps. 1-9)
    II. The Reign of King Saul (chap. 10)
    III. The Reign of King David (chaps. 11-29)
2. Outline of 2 Chronicles
    I. The United Kingdom Under King Solomon (chaps. 1-9)
    II. The Southern Kingdom Under Judean Kings (chaps. 10-36)

D. IMPORTANT DATA ABOUT 1 AND 2 CHRONICLES

1. Key Word: Temple
2. Key Chapter: 12—David made King of Israel
3. Key Verse: 2 Chron. 7:14
4. Key Characters: David, Solomon, Asa, Jehoshaphat, and Hezekiah
5. Meaning of "Chronicles": Suggests that what is recorded are the official annals of the important affairs in the lives of Israel's kings
6. Geography of Chronicles: The land of Israel

1. Gleason L. Archer, *A Survey of Old Testament Introduction* (Chicago: Moody, 1964), p. 389.

E.   SPECIAL CONSIDERATIONS ON 1 AND 2 CHRONICLES

1. The Relationships of Chronicles

Because the contents of these books is repetitious of material in other neighboring books, it is helpful to see the relationship of Chronicles to other Old Testament materials. This can be quickly seen by consulting the following charts.

RELATIONSHIP

1 CHRONICLES		2 CHRONICLES	
1 SAMUEL	2 SAMUEL	1 KINGS	2 KINGS

COMPARISON

SAMUEL-KINGS	CHRONICLES
1. Viewed both North and South	1. Viewed only the South
2. Emphasis on the throne	2. Emphasis on the Temple
3. Civil/political history	3. Sacred history
4. Emphasis on the prophet	4. Emphasis on the priest
5. Wars prominent	5. Wars less prominent
6. Indictment of the two nations	6. Encouragement of the remnant

2. The Babylonian Captivity

The captivity of Judah officially lasted from 605-536 B.C., a period of seventy years. The prophet Jeremiah had not only warned the people of a coming captivity but also specified the length (Jer. 25:11; 29:10). The reason that the captivity lasted seventy years (and not fifty or one hundred years) is given in 2 Chronicles 36:21. Seventy times the nation had violated God's command to let the land rest every seventh (sabbath) year (cf. Lev. 25:1-7; 26:34, 43). Israel was not to plant or harvest during that year. But since the nation would not let the land rest voluntarily, God removed them from the land.

The years of the Babylonian captivity were painful but profitable ones for Judah. The pain of being in captivity to a pagan nation, of seeing Jerusalem burned and sacked, of witnessing the end of the monarchy, and of having no place to sacrifice and worship was terrible. But these years also brought great benefit to the people. They learned that serving idols was foolish, and, for the most part, they were cured of their idolatry. They also developed a new love and loyalty to the Scriptures. They had no temple and no functioning priesthood, but they did have God's Word. It is commonly believed that the synagogue, a local gathering place for the reading and teaching of Scripture, originated during the Babylonian captivity.

THE PERIOD OF CAPTIVITY IN BABYLON

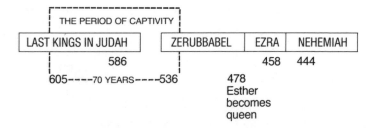

(a) The Jews in Babylon

Little is known of this period of history, since no "foundational book" covers it. What can be known about the Jews in Babylon is gleaned from Ezekiel, Daniel, and Ezra. The initial years in Babylon were discouraging ones (Ps. 137). Evidently, the Jews generally were not assimilated into Babylonian life but remained separate in detention camps (Ezek. 1:1; 3:15). Some, like Daniel and his three friends, were part of the court of the king. But even these never lost their Jewish identity (Dan. 5:13). Although as the years went by greater assimilation into Babylonian life probably took place, many were ready to "go home" when the opportunity came along.

(b) The Jews Left in Palestine

A great deal of information is available about those days immediately after the destruction of Jerusalem in 586 B.C. The prophet Jeremiah was allowed by Nebuchadnezzar to stay in Palestine. It is Jeremiah who records the situation of the Jews who remained in the land (Jer. 40-44).

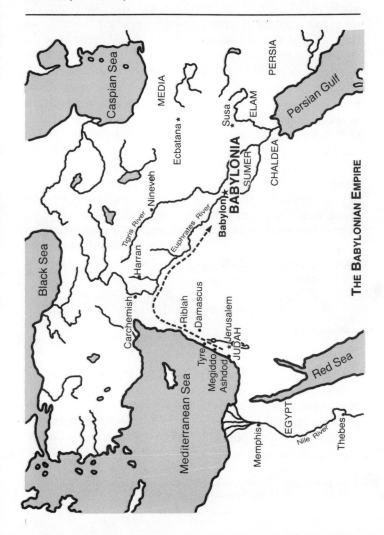

When Jerusalem was destroyed, the town of Mizpah became the political center of Judah and the new provincial capital. A Jew by the name of Gedaliah was selected by Nebuchadnezzar as the first governor of the area. Nebuchadnezzar probably thought it best to allow the Jews to have a Jew ruling over them, as long as he was not a king. With the population now greatly reduced there would be little chance that any large-scale rebellion could take place; thus very few Babylonian soldiers were left behind to aid Gedaliah at Mizpah. The number of people ruled over by Gedaliah was probably less than 50,000.[2] Gedaliah's rule was quite short, perhaps lasting two or three months. He was assassinated in office by Ishmael, who was part of the irreconcilable resistance party, which was based in Ammon. Jeremiah and the inhabitants were taken captive but were rescued by Johanan and a group loyal to Gedaliah. But fearing retaliation by the Babylonians (for the murder of the governor, Gedaliah), the group headed by Johanan retreated to a spot near Bethlehem and pondered their next move. Jeremiah was asked to inquire of the Lord as to what they should do. Ten days later Jeremiah returned with a word from God. The people were told to stay in the land and not to go down to Egypt, as they were now contemplating. But they would not listen to Jeremiah. Instead they fled to Egypt, forcing Jeremiah to go with them. With the departure of this group, there were almost no Jews left in the land.

A SUMMARY OF 1 AND 2 CHRONICLES

1 CHRONICLES

I. The Genealogies (chaps. 1-9)

These lists trace the lineage of Israel, beginning with Adam and ending with those of the Babylonian captivity. They reveal the hand of God at work during those many years as He selected certain ones to fulfill His purposes. This genealogy is important in tracing the line of the Messiah. These genealogies are not exhaustive, but are carefully selected. It is plain that the author is most

2. W. F. Albright, "The Biblical Period," in *The Jews: Their History,* ed. Louis Finkelstein (New York: Schocken, 1970), p. 49.

interested in the line of David, the tribe of Levi, and the tribes of Judah and Benjamin.[3]

II. The Reign of King Saul (chap. 10)

Even though Saul reigned for thirty-two years, little is given about his rule. His unfaithfulness and disobedience receive a brief treatment in order to contrast him with God's choice of a godly king, David.

III. The Reign of David (chaps. 11-29)

David is the standard used in Scripture for a righteous king. He is seen bringing the nation of Israel together and making it into a powerful force for the Lord. Emphasis is placed on David's desire to make Jerusalem the religious capital of the land and on his desire to build a temple for the Lord.

2 CHRONICLES

I. The United Kingdom Under King Solomon (chaps. 1-9)

In 2 Chronicles the history of Solomon's reign centers on two visions he received: one at Gibeon (1:1-13) and the other at Jerusalem (7:12-22). Because of his first vision, Solomon is given unusual wisdom from God, thus enabling him to build the Temple and lead Israel in God's paths of righteousness. The second vision took place in the Temple itself. God promised blessing and prosperity for obedience, but discipline for disobedience.

II. The Southern Kingdom Under Judean Kings (chaps. 10-36)

The emphasis in this section is on the godly kings of Judah who ruled after Solomon in the Southern Kingdom during both the divided and single kingdom periods. The focus is on Asa (14:1–16:14), Jehoshaphat (17:1–20:37), Hezekiah (29:1–32:33), and Josiah (34:1–35:27). Evil kings are given little space by the author. The final chapter describes the fall and deportation of Judah.

3. Irving L. Jensen, *Jensen's Survey of the Old Testament* (Chicago: Moody, 1978), p. 211.

13

EZRA AND ESTHER

EZRA

INTRODUCTION TO EZRA

A. AUTHORSHIP AND DATE OF EZRA

Tradition says that Ezra himself wrote this book. It is clear that he was certainly capable of doing so, as he is called "a man of letters" (7:11). With Ezra as the author, the date of writing would be about 450 B.C.

B. PURPOSE OF EZRA

The purpose of the book of Ezra is to record the faithfulness of God in the reestablishing of the Jews in their land.

C. BASIC OUTLINE OF EZRA

    I. The Return Under Zerubbabel (chaps. 1-6)
    II. The Return Under Ezra (chaps. 7-10)

D. IMPORTANT DATA ABOUT EZRA

    1. Key Words: Spiritual Restoration
    2. Key Chapter: 6—The rebuilding of the Temple
    3. Key Verses: 1:1-4; 6:14-15
    4. Key Characters: Zerubbabel, Joshua the high priest, and Ezra
    5. Meaning of "Ezra": Named after its principal character
    6. Geography of Ezra: Babylon and Palestine

E. SPECIAL CONSIDERATIONS ON EZRA

1. Years Covered by Ezra

The entire book of Ezra covers a period of about eighty years. There is a large gap between chapters 6 and 7, where there is no recorded history.

2. Background Points on Ezra

In order to understand the events surrounding the restoration of the people of Judah to their land, several facts need to be grasped, including the chronology of the period and the Persian kings who ruled during this time.

(a) The Chronology of the Restoration

THE CHRONOLOGY OF THE RESTORATION

PERSIAN KING	DATES	BIBLICAL CHAR- ACTERS	SCRIP- TURE	EVENT
Cyrus	539-530	Zerubbabel, Joshua, Haggai, Zechariah	Ezra 1-4	First return Temple begun then stopped
Cambyses	530-521	---	---	No work on Temple
Darius I	521-486	Haggai, Zechariah	Ezra 4-6	Temple work completed
Xerxes (Ahasuerus)	486-465	Esther, Mordecai	Esther 1-10	Story of Jews' preservation
Artaxerxes	465-423	Ezra, Nehemiah, Malachi	Ezra 7-10 Nehemiah	Second return under Ezra Third return Nehemiah Ministry of Malachi

END OF OLD TESTAMENT HISTORY

(b)   The People of the Restoration

It was the Southern Kingdom of Judah that was taken captive to Babylon, and it was the Southern Kingdom that returned to the land of Palestine. But it must be kept in mind that there were elements of the northern tribes present also. Sometimes the northern tribes are called the "ten lost tribes." They were not lost in the sense of disappearing. The Northern Kingdom ceased to exist as a separate kingdom, but there were significant numbers from the northern tribes living in the South.

There were several emigrations from the North to the South. At the time of the division of the kingdom many elected to remain under the Davidic king (1 Kings 12:23; 2 Chron. 11:14-16). And again in King Asa's day many came from the north (2 Chron. 15:9). Even after the fall of the Northern Kingdom in 721 B.C., northerners with a heart for the Lord (and still living in the northern area) joined with Hezekiah (2 Chron. 30:11) and later with Josiah (2 Chron. 34:9).

During the captivity, the prophet Ezekiel ministered to the "House of Israel" (3:1-5), which would indicate that even in captivity there was a mingling of the two kingdoms.

At the time of the restoration, the tribes of Judah and Benjamin were definitely the leaders (Ezra 1:5). Yet, the northern cities of Bethel and Ai are included among those in the return (2:28).

> Ezra 7:7 records that "there went up some of the children of Israel." At the dedication of the temple, a sin offering was made for all of the twelve tribes (Ezra 6:17). Later another burnt offering was made by those who had come out of the captivity for all the twelve tribes of Israel (Ezra 8:35). These returned exiles certainly seemed to consider themselves as representatives of the whole nation. Furthermore, Zechariah . . . addressed his messages to Judah and Israel (Zech. 1:19; 8:13; 10:6).[1]

It can be said with certainty that all of Israel "came home" in the era of restoration. Certainly in New Testament times all the

1. Paul N. Benware, *Ambassadors of Armstrongism* (Fort Washington, Pa.: Christian Literature Crusade, 1984), p. 90.

tribes were in evidence (Luke 2:36; Matt. 10:6; Acts 26:6-7; James 1:1). And all twelve tribes will be part of the final, great restoration of Israel (Ezek. 36:22-32; 37:11-22).

(c) Notable Dates in Ezra

538: The edict of Cyrus, which permitted the Jews to return to their homeland

537: The return of some 50,000 Jews under the leadership of Zerubbabel

536: The altar for sacrificing rebuilt

535: Work on the Temple begun then stopped

535-520: No further work on the Temple

520: Decree of Cyrus confirmed by Darius I; he aids in the construction of the Temple; the prophet Haggai begins his ministry

516: The completion and dedication of the Temple

458: Second return to Judah, led by Ezra

A SUMMARY OF EZRA

I. The Return Under Zerubbabel (chaps. 1-6)

A. The Decree of Cyrus (1)

The Persian Empire had defeated and taken over the empire of Babylon in 539 B.C. The Persian government had established itself but still desired the loyalty of its new subjects. Most likely with the help of Daniel, Cyrus issued a decree allowing the Jews to return to their homeland and rebuild their Temple.

B. The Return to Palestine (2)

Those who were willing to leave Babylon and return to the desolate land of Palestine were carefully listed. Zerubbabel would lead a group of almost 50,000 (2:64-65).

C. Rebuilding the Temple (3)

Upon arriving in the land, the first order of business was to rebuild the sacrificial altar (3:2). Then preliminary work was done on the Temple, clearing away debris and laying the foundation (3:10).

D. The Opposition to Rebuilding (4)

Not everyone was glad to see the Jews back in their land. Some made it their business to oppose the Temple project by threatening the Jews and also by hiring lawyers to thwart them in the law courts (4:1-5). The enemies of the Jews succeeded in stopping the work for fifteen years.

E. The Return to Rebuilding (5)

Challenged and motivated by the prophets Haggai and Zechariah, the people realized the need to get back to Temple building. They came to understand that they had been disobedient and unbelieving. And even though the circumstances had not changed, they went back to work and saw God work on their behalf.

F. The Temple Completed (6)

After four years of hard work the construction was finished and the Temple was dedicated (6:14-18).

II. The Return Under Ezra (chaps. 7-10)

A. The Decree of Artaxerxes (7)

About eighty years after the first return, under Zerubbabel, Ezra the scribe returned with 1,500 people. Ezra undoubtedly had not been born when the first return took place. His purpose in going to the land was to bring a substantial offering to help the people there and to teach the law of God.

B. The Return to Palestine (8)

The people of the land were glad for the financial relief brought by Ezra, and Ezra was delighted to finally see Jerusalem.

C. Reformation under Ezra (9)

Unfortunately, the people of Israel were once again beginning to compromise God's laws, especially in the matter of marrying pagans. Ezra knew the law, and he knew recent history. He knew that if the situation was not dealt with, more disciplinary action from God would be forthcoming. It was a brokenhearted man who cried to the Lord and mourned greatly (9:1-3). Many observed Ezra and came to realize the sinfulness of their sin. Ezra was the catalyst that made them do the right thing. One godly man, who knows and obeys the Word of God, can impact large numbers of people. Revival (which is a new beginning of obedience) came to the people of the nation of Israel.

ESTHER

This book complements Ezra. It describes a fascinating story of God's providence that transpired back in Persia while many of God's people were resettling Palestine.

INTRODUCTION TO ESTHER

A. AUTHORSHIP AND DATE OF ESTHER

Once again the author is not identified. But it is likely that the author was a Jew who lived through the events described in this book. His knowledge of Persian words and customs and his detailed descriptions of the palace of Susa (1:6-8; 7:8) strongly suggest one who was an eyewitness. Based on Esther 9:20, many believe that Mordecai the Jew penned this book. Others do not think that the words of praise in chapter 10 would have been written by Mordecai of himself. But if the book was written during the days of Ahasuerus (Xerxes), then the date would be about 475 B.C.

B. PURPOSE OF ESTHER

The book was written to show God's providential care for His people even while they were in captivity and in a poor spiritual condition. Because of the Abrahamic Covenant, God would never allow these descendants of Abraham to be exterminated. He still blesses those who bless Israel and, as in this case, curses those who curse Israel.

C. BASIC OUTLINE OF ESTHER

    I. Royal Crisis for God's People (chaps. 1-5)
        A. Queen Vashti Deposed (1)
        B. Esther Becomes Queen (2)
        C. Haman's Murderous Plot (3)
        D. Mordecai's Intercession (4)
        E. Esther Receives Favor (5)

II. Divine Protection for God's People (chaps. 6-10)
   A. Mordecai Receives Honor (6)
   B. Haman's Execution (7)
   C. The Jews Avenged (8)
   D. Purim Instituted (9)
   E. Mordecai Becomes Premier (10)

D. IMPORTANT DATA ABOUT ESTHER

   1. Key Word: Providence of God
   2. Key Chapter: 6—The hand of God changes the situation
   3. Key Verses: 4:13-14; 6:13; 8:17; 9:26-28
   4. Key Characters: Mordecai, Esther, Haman, and Ahasuerus
   5. Meaning of "Esther": The book is named after the key character in the story
   6. Geography of Esther: The land of Persia

E. SPECIAL CONSIDERATIONS ON ESTHER

Esther's story took place in the time period of the book of Ezra. These events occurred between the first and second returns, and therefore come between Ezra 6 and 7. (See the chart "The Chronology of the Restoration," p. 129.)

A SUMMARY OF ESTHER

I. Royal Crisis for God's People (chaps. 1-5)
   A. Queen Vashti Deposed (1)

The first chapter sets the stage for the story by informing the reader of the removal of the Persian queen Vashti. Her husband, King Ahasuerus, demanded that she appear before him and the leaders of the nation. Perhaps in a state of drunkenness (1:10), the king was actually demanding a lewd display on the part of the queen. At any rate, she refused. In his anger and humiliation, the king removed her from her position as queen (1:12, 19).

   B. Esther Becomes Queen (2)

In order to fill the vacancy of queen, a nationwide beauty contest was held (2:3). Young women would join the king's harem, and then the king would decide which would be queen. Esther the Jewess became part of this situation (2:5-8). Esther had lost her parents and was raised by Mordecai, her cousin. He instructed her not to reveal that she was Jewish. (These two do not seem to be sterling examples of spirituality, as were Daniel and Joseph.) Esther was winner of the contest, and she became the queen.

    C. Haman's Murderous Plot (3)

The king elevated Haman to a position of great authority in the kingdom of Persia. But Haman became offended by the Jew Mordecai. In his anger, Haman decided to get rid of all the Jews.

    D. Mordecai's Intercession (4)

When Mordecai came to understand that the Jews were scheduled for destruction because of his actions, he persuaded Esther the queen to intervene on behalf of the Jews.

    E. Esther Receives Favor (5)

At the risk of her own life, Esther approached the king. She asked him to come to a banquet, and it was at the banquet that she would make her appeal. Haman was to come also.

II. Divine Protection for God's People (chaps. 4-10)

    A. Mordecai Receives Honor (6)

Through a set of divinely arranged circumstances Haman was forced to publicly praise Mordecai the Jew, the man he hated. To Haman's wife and friends this indicated that Haman was doomed (6:13). Their viewpoint suggests that the unseen hand of God had often moved on behalf of His people.

    B. Haman's Execution (7)

At the banquet Esther pleaded for her own life and pointed to Haman as the villain in the matter. The king, who did not have the slightest idea of what was going on, was enraged and ordered the execution of Haman.

    C. The Jews Avenged (8)

The law that allowed the Jews to be killed could not be changed. In Persian society the law was greater than any person, even the king. And once a law had been set in place it could not be annulled. But another law could be instituted that could counteract the previous law. This was done, and the Jews were allowed to defend themselves with no penalty for doing so.

D. Purim Instituted (9)

The annual Jewish feast of Purim came out of these events in Persia and celebrates the Jews' deliverance from their enemies.

E. Mordecai Becomes Premier (10)

The king elevated Mordecai to a position of great prominence in his kingdom. In that position, Mordecai was used to help the Jews of the Persian Empire.

14

NEHEMIAH

Introduction to Nehemiah

A. AUTHORSHIP AND DATE OF NEHEMIAH

Nehemiah himself was probably the author of this book (1:1). The date of writing would be about 425 B.C., in the reign of Artaxerxes, king of Persia (see chart "The Chronology of the Restoration," p. 129.)

B. PURPOSE OF NEHEMIAH

The book was written to show the work of God through a godly leader, Nehemiah. The book records the building, fortifying, and reestablishing of the city of Jerusalem. The book also reveals the beautiful balance in the life of Nehemiah between zealous human effort and planning, and divine empowering.

C. BASIC OUTLINE OF NEHEMIAH

   I. Rebuilding the Walls (chaps. 1-7)
  II. Revival and Reform (chaps. 8-13)

D. IMPORTANT DATA ABOUT NEHEMIAH

  1. Key Words: Political restoration
  2. Key Chapter: 6—The rebuilding of Jerusalem's walls
  3. Key Verses: 1:4-11; 2:17; 5:14; 6:15
  4. Key Characters: Nehemiah, Artaxerxes, and Ezra

> 5. Meaning of ''Nehemiah'': Named after the central person in the narrative
> 6. Geography of Nehemiah: Persia and Palestine

E. SPECIAL CONSIDERATIONS ON NEHEMIAH

> 1. Years Covered by Nehemiah

The book of Nehemiah covers a period of twelve years from 444-432 B.C. This is based on the two time notations in 1:1 and 13:6, the twentieth and the thirty-second years of Artaxerxes' reign.

> 2. Background Points on Nehemiah
>> (a) The Historical Setting

When Nehemiah, living in Persia in 445 B.C., received news that Jerusalem's walls were broken down and its gates were burned, his response was that of intense sorrow (1:3-4). It is highly unlikely that Nehemiah's sudden grief was due to Nebuchadnezzar's destruction of Jerusalem over a century earlier (in 586 B.C.). Ezra 4:6-23, which provides some background information for the book of Nehemiah, furnishes a plausible answer. This passage records the opposition of the Jews' enemies in Palestine from the days of Cyrus to the days of Artaxerxes (4:5, 7). In the days of Artaxerxes, some Jews were evidently beginning to rebuild the walls of Jerusalem (4:12). This probably refers to some kind of activity connected with the coming of Ezra in 458 B.C. When informed of the building and of the Jews' past rebellion, King Artaxerxes ordered a halt to the building (4:21). He did not order the walls and gates destroyed, but the enemies of Israel took it upon themselves to do so. Hearing about this terrible setback, a frustrated and depressed Nehemiah agonized over Israel's future.

>> (b) The Contemporaries of Nehemiah

When Nehemiah arrived at Jerusalem in 444 B.C., Ezra the scribe-priest had been there for more than a decade. The Scriptures are clear that these two men of God ministered and worked together (Neh. 8:1-18; 12:26). After staying in Jerusalem for twelve years, Nehemiah returned to Persia in 432 B.C.(the thirty-second year of Artaxerxes, 13:6). After an undetermined length of time, he returned to Jerusalem (13:6). He found that certain sins (such as withholding the tithe, intermarriage with pagans, etc.) were quite visible among the people. The prophet Malachi dealt with the same sins, which strongly suggests that either Malachi ministered while Nehemiah was in Jerusalem the second time, or he prophesied during those days when Nehemiah was absent from Jerusalem.

A SUMMARY OF NEHEMIAH

I. Rebuilding the Walls (chaps. 1-7)

A. Nehemiah's Prayer for the Remnant at Jerusalem (1:1-11)

When informed by his brother Hanani of the desolation of Jerusalem, Nehemiah spent about four months in prayer. He confessed the sin of Israel and prayed for the favor of King Artaxerxes. At this time, Nehemiah was the cupbearer to the king. The position of cupbearer was important in the kingdom of Persia. Nehemiah would have been a man highly trusted by the king.

B. Nehemiah's Request and Return to Jerusalem (2:1-16)

Since no one was to appear sad or depressed before the king, Nehemiah was afraid when the king noted his sadness (2:1-2). But it provided the opportunity for Nehemiah to request a leave of absence from the king's service in order to go to Jerusalem and rebuild the walls. Nehemiah was given permission to go to Jerusalem, and he was given access to building materials for the project. Upon arriving in Jerusalem, Nehemiah quietly surveyed the damage and then presented his plan to the people.

C. Nehemiah's Exhortations to Rebuild the Walls (2:17–3:32)

Nehemiah identifed himself with the people and the problem as he addressed them and shared his vision (2:17-18). The project was well organized and involved everyone.

D. Nehemiah's Response to Opposition (4:1–6:19)

Even when a person is doing the will of God there can be problems and stiff opposition. Nehemiah faced a series of people and situations that could have brought the rebuilding project to a halt (4:1-4, 11; 5:1; 6:1). Opposition came from the enemies on the outside and from the Jews themselves on the inside. But Nehemiah,

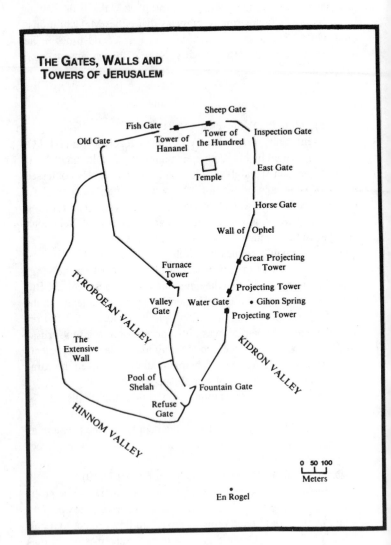

THE GATES, WALLS AND
TOWERS OF JERUSALEM

Sheep Gate

Fish Gate

Inspection Gate

Old Gate

Tower of
Hananel

Tower of
the Hundred

Temple

East Gate

Horse Gate

Wall of Ophel

Great Projecting
Tower

TYROPOEAN VALLEY

Furnace
Tower

Projecting Tower

Valley
Gate

Water Gate

Gihon Spring

Projecting Tower

The
Extensive
Wall

KIDRON VALLEY

Pool of
Shelah

Fountain Gate

Refuse
Gate

HINNOM VALLEY

0 50 100
Meters

En Rogel

a man of prayer and wisdom, brought the people through the difficult times. In just fifty-two days of work the walls of Jerusalem
were finished (6:15)

    E. Nehemiah's Registration of the People (7:1-73)

Once the walls were completed, thus affording some protection, Nehemiah asked one-tenth of the people to come and live
within the city. He also organized a militia to defend the city. It
should be noted that although the walls were essentially finished,
much more work needed to be done both in strengthening the
walls and rebuilding the city itself.

II. Revival and Reform (chaps. 8-13)

    A. The Great Bible Reading Led by Ezra (8:1-18)

It is a mistake to think that Nehemiah was concerned only about
the physical restoration of the nation. Nehemiah was deeply committed to teaching the nation to live according to its "constitution" (the Mosaic law code). Ezra read from the law and explained its meaning to the thousands who gathered (8:1-8).

    B. Revival and its Results (9:1–10:39)

Any genuine revival is based squarely on the Word of God.
(Revival is a new beginning of obedience to God and His Word.)
Any genuine revival will bring about changed behavior. These
chapters record not only the confession of sin (9:2-3) but also a
change in living (10:30-39).

    C. The People in the Land (11:1–12:26)

It was necessary to populate the city of Jerusalem, once the
walls were completed (11:1). Nehemiah was concerned that the
city be repopulated by those of pure Jewish descent. Nehemiah
handled this and other issues of organization in a forthright man-
ner.

    D. Reform and Results (13:1-31)

When Nehemiah left Jerusalem, much of his influence left also.
During his absence certain sins were once again tolerated in national life. But when Nehemiah returned he zealously dealt with
the offenders (13:7-11, 23-25). Nehemiah knew that to tolerate
clear violations of the law would inevitably bring discipline from
God.

With the reforms of Nehemiah the Old Testament closes. There is no inspired record for the next four hundred years of Israel's history. The silence of God was finally broken when the angel Gabriel appeared in the holy place of the Temple announcing the coming birth of John the Baptist, the one who would prepare the way for Jesus the Messiah (Luke 1:11-18).

Part 3

The Poetic Books

15

HEBREW POETRY

Poetry is found everywhere in the Old Testament Scriptures, but six entire books of poetry were written during the era of the monarchy. The time of the united monarchy would be considered Israel's "golden age of literature." These days of peace, in the reigns of David and Solomon (found in the foundational books of 2 Samuel and 1 Kings), were the most productive in the writing of the songs and poems that became such an important part of life in Israel. These books of poetry spoke not only to ancient Israel but have had a continuing impact on God's people.

> Reflected in this literature are the problems, experiences, beliefs, philosophies, and attitudes of the Israelites. Such a wide variety of interests are expressed that these writings well-nigh have a universal appeal. The frequent use by the common people throughout the world and the voluminous literature written since Old Testament times indicate that the poetical books deal with problems and truths familiar to all mankind.[1]

THE BOOKS OF HEBREW POETRY

The poetical books do indeed speak to the issues and needs experienced by believers then and now. (1) *Job* wrestles with the

---

1. Samuel J. Schultz, *The Old Testament Speaks* (New York: Harper & Row, 1970), p. 279.

problem of suffering that righteous people endure in this life. (2) The *Psalms* basically are songs of praise, though they express the full range of human emotions. (3) The book of *Proverbs* provides valuable insights into all realms of life and gives needed instruction on living wisely. (4) *Ecclesiastes* approaches the matter of wise living from a unique point of view, but makes clear that apart from a right relationship with God life is empty. (5) *Song of Solomon* is a dramatic poem that expresses the joys and dangers of human love. (6) *Lamentations* is an expression of deep human grief coupled with trust in a covenant-keeping God.

TYPES OF HEBREW POETRY

There are different ways of catagorizing Hebrew poetry, but the following five types are the main kinds.[2] (1) *Lyric* poems are so named because they were originally designed to be accompanied by music. Most of the psalms fall into this category. (2) *Didactic* poetry intended to teach people to observe and evaluate life. The mind, rather than the emotions, was appealed to. Proverbs and Ecclesiastes would be considered didactic. (3) *Prophetic* poems are not found in these six books of poetry, but rather in Isaiah and some other places. (4) *Elegaic* poetry records human grief and sorrow. The Lamentations of Jeremiah fit into this category. (5) *Dramatic* poems, such as Job and the Song of Solomon, convey ideas and truth through dialogue and monologue, much like modern plays.

PARALLELISM IN HEBREW POETRY

Unlike poems and verse that we are most familiar with, Hebrew poetry is not achieved by rhyme. The basic structure of Hebrew poetry is parallelism.

> We do not find any emphasis at all on rhyme and very little on metre compared to that of other languages. The principal

2. Eugene Merrill, *An Historical Survey of the Old Testament* (Grand Rapids: Baker, 1980), p. 232.

feature is that of parallelism, the idea that the second or following lines of a strophe somehow parallel the thought of the first.[3]

In the structure of Hebrew poetry, a statement is made in the
first line and then the second line repeats or expands or contrasts
that thought. It is the "thought" or "sense" rhyme in Hebrew poetry that makes it much easier to translate these great truths from
Hebrew into other languages.

Numerous kinds of parallelism could be mentioned. Five will
be defined here, though the first three are usually considered to be
the main types:[4] (1) *synonymous*: the second line repeats the same
thought as the first line in very similar or identical terms (e.g. Ps.
24:1; 19:2); (2) *antithetic*: the second line contrasts the idea of the
first line (e.g. Ps. 1:6; 37:9); (3) *synthetic*: the second (and perhaps later) line(s) completes or enlarges upon the thought of the
first line (Ps. 2:6; 19:7); (4) *climactic*: a word is built upon until a
climax in thought is reached (e.g. Ps. 29:1; 103:1); (5) *emblema-
tic*: a metaphor or simile in one line is used to illustrate the truth of
another line (Ps. 42:1; Prov. 25:25).

Hebrew poetry possesses many other features such as beautiful
word pictures and figures of speech, acrostic arrangement, si-
miles, metaphors, and personification of ideas or objects. But the
value of this portion of the Old Testament is not necessarily found
in the variety of literary devices, but in the beautiful balance that
exists between the inspiring work of the Holy Spirit and the deep-
est and widest of human emotion and expression. The believer
can not only identify with these writers but is also assured that the
truth received is an authoritative, unchanging message from God.

3. Ibid., p. 232.
4. John Walton, *Chronological Charts of the Old Testament* (Grand Rapids: Zondervan, 1981), p. 75.

16

JOB

INTRODUCTION TO JOB

A. AUTHORSHIP AND DATE OF JOB

Since the author is not identified in the book, it is not possible to determine authorship and the date of composition. Many men, including Moses and Job himself, have been suggested as authors.[1] Generally speaking, conservative scholars believe that the book was written in the days of King Solomon, though the man Job lived in patriarchal times.[2]

Job was a historical character (cf. Ezek. 14:14, 20; James 5:11). Several facts indicate that he lived in those days after the Flood of Noah and before the time of Moses. First, the length of Job's life points to that time shortly after the Flood in which men had long lifespans. Job lived 140 years *after* he had fathered ten children who were adults in the drama and after he had experienced the traumatic events of this story (42:16). Second, Job is seen functioning as a priest for his family, a typical role in the patriarchal days (1:5). And third, the Mosaic law and the important revelations of the prophets are never referred to in all the theological discussions of Job and his friends. It is highly unlikely that they would speak of God and His ways and never refer to the authoritative Scriptures, if they existed at that time. The setting of the book of Job is, therefore, in the days of the patriarchs. The writing of the book, however, may have been much later.

1. Roy B. Zuck, *Job* (Chicago: Moody, 1978), pp. 8-9.
2. Merrill F. Unger, *Introductory Guide to the Old Testament* (Grand Rapids, Zondervan, 1950), p. 379.

DATING THE WRITING OF JOB

GENESIS	EXODUS	NUMBERS	JOSHUA	JUDGES	SAMUEL	KINGS

The life of Job in patriarchal times

The writing of the book of Job in the
time of King Solomon

B. PURPOSE OF JOB

The book of Job addresses the issue of the suffering of people who are righteous. Whereas the suffering and distress of the wicked has not been as great a problem to most people, the suffering of people who love and serve the Lord God is another matter. If God is sovereign and loving, then why does He permit His own to experience terrible (and apparently needless) suffering? Although the book of Job might suggest some answers to this issue, an intellectual solution is not really given. A spiritual solution is given; namely, the absolute sovereignty of God. When Job met God, he did not demand answers but humbly submitted himself to his sovereign God, recognizing in a fresh way the Creator-creature relationship.

C. BASIC OUTLINE OF JOB

    I. The Prologue (1:1–2:13)
    II. Human Wisdom and Suffering (3:1–37:24)
    III. Divine Wisdom and Suffering (38:1–42:6)
    IV. The Epilogue (42:7-17)

D. IMPORTANT DATA ABOUT JOB

    1. Key Word: Suffering, sovereignty
    2. Key Chapter: 1—Setting the stage for the drama of Job
    3. Key Verses: 1:20-22; 8:3-7; 40:1-2
    4. Key Characters: Job, Eliphaz, Bildad, Zophar, and Elihu
    5. Meaning of "Job": Named after the main character in the story
    6. Geography of Job: Palestine

E. SPECIAL CONSIDERATIONS ON JOB

Job is the longest poem in the Old Testament. It is a combination of prose and poetry and utilizes both dialogue and monologue. The prose sections are simply interpreted normally as one would interpret any historical writing. The poetry section is also approached with normal interpretation, but recognizing the special features of poetic literature—the parallelisms, the vivid word pictures, and expressive figures of speech. It must also be remembered that the speakers in the book of Job did not have the direct revelations of Moses and the prophets to rely on. Therefore, they were limited in their knowledge of numerous subjects. In the progress of God's revelation in the centuries that would follow, a much clearer understanding of God and His purposes would be possible.

A SUMMARY OF JOB

The dramatic poem of Job begins with a prologue that sets the stage for the main dialogue of the book. The prologue is the testimony of God that Job was a genuinely righteous man (1:1, 8). He was also a man of great wealth (1:3). After these essential facts about Job are related, the scene shifts to heaven, where Satan and other angelic beings are seen appearing before God.

God pointed out the true righteousness of Job to Satan. But Satan declared that Job only served God because it was profitable for him to do so (1:9-10). God then allowed Satan to attack Job, in order to reveal Satan's faulty thinking. In a series of four catastrophic attacks, Job lost all of his great wealth and experienced the loss of all ten of his children (1:13-19). In spite of these terrible events, the brokenhearted Job still worshiped the Lord. Satan then took away the good health of Job, inflicting him with a horrible disease (2:4-8; 7:5). In all this, Job remained true to the Lord.

Three of Job's friends heard of these events and came to see Job. The majority of the book is taken up with their discussions about Job's sufferings (2:11–31:40). In three rounds of speeches, the three friends (Eliphaz, Bildad, and Zophar) discussed and often debated with Job the reason for Job's condition. Though much was said by these three men, their basic argument can be simply stated. They saw these events in Job's life as out of the realm of the ordinary. This was the hand of God. They reasoned that truly righteous people are not punished by God, whereas wicked men are punished by Him. Therefore, since God was clearly punishing Job, he must not be truly righteous but guilty of secret sin. Assuming Job's guilt, they encouraged him to confess his sinfulness and be restored by God. Job responded to these three friends by protesting his innocence and rebuking his friends for not giving him answers or comfort.

After the three rounds of speeches concluded, a younger man named Elihu appeared and discussed his observations of Job's situation and the reasonings of the three friends (32:1–37:24). Elihu came closer to the truth than the others. He rebuked Job for justifying himself before God, and he rebuked Job's friends for talking a great deal but exhibiting no wisdom. Elihu pointed out that suffering can be for instruction rather than for punishment.

God then broke the silence of heaven and revealed Himself to Job (38:1–42:6). In two magnificent addresses Job quickly learned how great God is and how insignificant he was. Job's response was one of submission and surrender. God did not explain to Job why he suffered. God simply wanted Job to trust Him and bow before Him.

In the conclusion of the drama, God severely rebuked the three friends of Job because they misrepresented Him (something we must be careful not to do). The story ends with Job's being restored to health, receiving twice the wealth he had originally, and once again being blessed with ten children (42:7-17).

17

PSALMS

A. AUTHORSHIP AND DATE OF PSALMS

Approximately two-thirds of the psalms have known authors, and the remaining one-third are anonymous. Of the one hundred psalms that have identifiable authors, David is the most prolific, writing seventy-three of them (he may have written many of the anonymous psalms also). Asaph, one of David's court musicians, wrote twelve; ten were written by the sons of Korah; two by Solomon; and one each by Moses, Heman, and Ethan.

In identifying the authors, it is clear that the great majority of the psalms were written during the era of the united monarchy (the foundational books of 2 Samuel and 1 Kings). Technically, the psalms cover a thousand years of history from Moses (1500 B.C.) to the post-exile times (500 B.C.). But the vast majority were written in the hundred-year period from 1030-930 B.C.

There is an ongoing discussion on how the psalms were collected. But we can be sure that the Holy Spirit inspired men to write poems of praise and worship. Sometimes these poems were composed in the crucible of difficult personal experiences. Others were penned specifically with public worship in mind. As thousands of poems and songs were written, undoubtedly they were put in various collections (e.g. the psalms of David, Ps. 72:20). The Holy Spirit, using men and natural processes, preserved those that were to be included in the canon of Scripture. Many scholars believe that the 150 psalms found in our Bible reflect the work of one final editor, who is usually identified as Ezra the scribe.[1]

B. PURPOSE OF PSALMS

The various psalms cover a wide range of subjects. But the single element found in just about every psalm is that of praise. The Psalms constituted the hymnal of Israel, and a key to worship is praise.

God undoubtedly inspired and preserved the psalms because they accurately reflect the full range of human emotions. They help God's people find their way through the varying experiences of life. They serve as expressions of human feeling in joy or sorrow, in depression or jubilation, in darkness or light. This book not only constituted the hymnal of ancient Israel but also has served as the basis for many Christian hymns down to the present day.

C. BASIC OUTLINE OF PSALMS

There is really no way to outline Psalms except by the organization of the book as found in our Bibles. The Psalms are divided into "five books."

Book   I: Psalms 1-41
Book   II: Psalms 42-72
Book III: Psalms 73-89
Book IV: Psalms 90-106
Book   V: Psalms 107-150

D. IMPORTANT DATA ABOUT PSALMS

1. Key Word: Praise
2. Key Chapter: 23—The favorite psalm that reflects the general tone of many other psalms
3. Key Verses: 1:1-6; 23:1-6; 34:1-22; 51:1-13; 119:129-52
4. Key Characters: David and Asaph

1. Samuel J. Schultz, *The Old Testament Speaks* (New York: Harper & Row, 1970), p. 286.

5. Meaning of "Psalms": "Praise" (the element that is found in almost all psalms)
6. Geography of Psalms: The land of Israel

E. SPECIAL CONSIDERATIONS ON PSALMS

Since the Psalms are poetry (and often were to be sung), they cannot be approached as one would interpret prose. The figures of speech, the graphic imagery, the parallelisms, and the various literary devices must be kept in view when interpreting the Psalms.

Interpretation of some psalms is greatly aided by certain titles and terms that were placed by the authors at the beginning of those psalms. Sometimes there is an explanatory note at the beginning of the psalm that reveals the historical setting of the psalm (e.g. Pss. 7, 34, 51, 54, 56, 57, 59, 60). Sometimes a notation indicates the occasion on which the psalm was to be used (e.g. Pss. 92, 100, 120) or why the psalm was written (e.g. Pss. 81, 84, 85). Other times a musical notation is given that suggests the tune to be used or the way it was to be sung (e.g. Pss. 6, 7, 9). All of these explanatory notes help give a better feel for the psalm.

Again it must be remembered that most of the Psalms were written before the revelations of the prophets, and all of them were written before the New Testament. Therefore, in interpreting the Psalms care must be taken not to incorrectly read later revelation into the statements made by the psalmists.

A SUMMARY OF PSALMS

There are numerous types of psalms, and scholars will construct differing lists and categories. It is best not to attempt to come up with a rigid list. The categories given below should not be seen as fixed categories, since often a single psalm will have elements of several psalm types in it. But the following will give a basic idea of the differences that exist in the Psalms.

I. Messianic Psalms
These are psalms that prophetically speak of the Person and the work of the Messiah. Some of these psalms refer only to the Lord

Jesus Christ. Others refer to the king on the throne at the time the psalm was composed, but await the final fulfillment in the Lord Jesus Christ (e.g. Pss. 2, 8, 22, 69, 110).

II. Lament Psalms

In these psalms there is a cry to God for help because of some trouble that the psalmist finds himself (or his nation) in. God is petitioned to act on behalf of the psalmist (or Israel). Within this type of psalm there will be found a confession of trust in God (e.g. Pss. 7, 26, 60).

III. Testimonial Psalms

The essential feature of this psalm is the declaration by the writer that he will tell others what God has done for him (''I will praise . . . ''). The psalm looks back to some moment of need in his life and records how God met that need. It is a testimony (e.g. Pss. 30, 34).

IV. Pilgrim Psalms

Also known as ''songs of ascent,'' these psalms have to do with pilgrimages to the holy city of Jerusalem. These songs were evidently sung as the Israelites ascended to Jerusalem for the great annual feasts (e.g. Pss. 120-134).

V. Imprecatory Psalms

These are psalms that ask for judgment on wicked men who are enemies of the writer. These wicked men have not just offended the author but also God who is holy (e.g. Pss. 58, 109).

VI. Penitential Psalms

Mostly written by David, these psalms reveal the heart of the penitent individual, sorrowing over his sin (e.g. Pss. 32, 51).

VII. Wisdom Psalms

These psalms give guidelines to godly people living in this ungodly world. A philosophy of life is offered to the righteous man to help him view life more from God's perspective (e.g. Pss. 37, 73).

VIII. Historical Psalms

In the historical psalms, the writer looks back on God's dealings with the nation of Israel. The power and faithfulness of God are spoken of. These psalms often provide a "divine commentary" on some past event in Israel's history, giving added insight to that event (e.g. Pss. 78, 105, 106).

IX. Nature Psalms

The handiwork of God in His creative work is the emphasis of these psalms. The greatness, goodness, and power of God inspired the psalmist to write (e.g. Pss. 8, 19).

The various types of psalms reflect the common experiences of God's people. They help us express ourselves to the Lord in times of great joy, sorrow, frustration, or fear. There is probably no situation of life that some psalm does not directly address.

18

PROVERBS

A. AUTHORSHIP AND DATE OF PROVERBS

It is generally agreed that King Solomon wrote a major share of the book of Proverbs. The book itself testifies to his authorship (1:1; 10:1; 25:1), and 1 Kings 4:29-32 records both the great wisdom and the prolific writing of Solomon. Since most of the proverbs were written by Solomon (chaps. 1-29), a date of about 950 B.C. is given for the book.

The final two chapters of the book were written by Agur and King Lemuel. We know nothing of certainty about either of these two men.

B. PURPOSE OF PROVERBS

Proverbs gives wisdom on all areas of human experience. Wisdom is not simply a matter of the intellect—it is viewing life and self from God's perspective, which is the only true and valid perspective. A wise person is able to deal with life's issues and problems with the advantage of God's viewpoint.

A proverb is a brief saying that is used to communicate much truth. In a concise, striking way, truth is expressed so as to be caught by the mind and retained by the memory. The root of the word *proverb* carries the idea of "to govern" or "rule." Therefore, proverbs are wise, concise sayings that are to be used in governing our lives.

C. BASIC OUTLINE OF PROVERBS

    I. Solomon's Proverbs (chaps. 1-29)
      A. On Wisdom's Value (1-9)
      B. On Righteous Living (10-29)
   II. Agur's Proverbs: On Diverse Subjects (chap. 30)
 III. Lemuel's Proverbs: On Diverse Subjects (chap. 31)

D. IMPORTANT DATA ABOUT PROVERBS

1. Key Word: Wisdom
2. Key Chapter: 1 and 2—The importance and attaining of wisdom
3. Key Verses: 1:2-7; 1:20–2:7
4. Key Characters: Solomon
5. Meaning of "Proverbs": Refers to short sayings that are designed to govern life and conduct
6. Geography of Proverbs: Israel

E. SPECIAL CONSIDERATIONS ON PROVERBS

Since Proverbs is a book of poetry, parallelism is the key interpretive element. Synonymous parallelism is often identified in Proverbs by the use of "than," "so," or "as"; antithetic parallelism is recognized by the word "but"; and synthetic parallelism is often identified by the word "and."

The words "wise" and "wisdom" are repeated many times, along with "knowledge" and "understanding." The key phrase "the fear of the Lord" is found more than a dozen times in the book.

A SUMMARY OF PROVERBS

The book of Proverbs was written to bring us to wisdom and into a disciplined life (1:2-7). Solomon is convinced that wisdom begins with a right relationship with God (1:7; 9:10). Until a man "fears the Lord" (meaning he has the proper view of God, which results in a right relationship with God) he has no real hope of living an abundant kind of life. Until a man sees God rightly, he cannot rightly view life (cf. 1 Cor. 1:18-31).

Wisdom continues as the theme in chapters 1 through 9, and it is personified in several places as a woman (1:20-33; 8:1–9:18). She is seen walking in the streets of the city inviting people to come and to receive true understanding from her.

A person's response to wisdom places him into one of four groups: *The wise* is one who heeds and receives the truth and thus becomes discerning; *the naive* is one who does not listen to wisdom and is easily deceived in life, believing what he wants to believe; *the scoffer* is cynical and sarcastic in regard to the wisdom of God and spiritual things, making it impossible to live correctly; *the fool* has rejected God's wisdom and as a result is dull and wicked both morally and spiritually. The effect on one's life of either receiving or rejecting wisdom is great (1:24-33).

All wisdom comes from the Lord, but man has a responsibility to search and seek after wisdom (2:1-12). So although the "fear of the Lord" is the beginning of wisdom, man needs to study and to learn God's truth and increase in wisdom (cf. 2 Tim. 2:15). Having true wisdom will keep one from making some terrible errors in judgment (e.g. 7:6-23) and will bring a person into an abundant kind of life (8:35).

After the section on the value of wisdom (1:1–9:18), Proverbs becomes a collection of individual proverbs dealing with a wide range of subjects. In chapters 10-29 there is a general theme of righteous living but no particular order or grouping of these proverbs. Some of the major subjects dealt with in this section are the use and abuse of the tongue, the benefits and blessings of work and diligence, good friends, child training, the positive and negative aspects of sex, wealth, God's guidance, and the blessings of being wise.

Because Proverbs touches on every area of life, it is a favorite book of believers. It is not only relevant to life but shows that God is interested in every area of life.

19

ECCLESIASTES

A. AUTHORSHIP AND DATE OF ECCLESIASTES

The authorship of Ecclesiastes is greatly debated. Many hold to Solomonic authorship, whereas others adamantly oppose that position. Some statements in the book make Solomonic authorship difficult. Nevertheless, the best position is still that King Solomon wrote this book. The author does say that he was the "son of David, king in Jerusalem" (1:1, 12). Solomon certainly fits that statement. Furthermore, the wisdom, wealth, and great building projects spoken of in Ecclesiastes (1:13-16; 2:4-10) are obviously true of the life of Solomon (1 Kings 3:12; 4:29-32; 10:14-29). And Solomon certainly had the time and the money to do all the things discussed in Ecclesiastes.[1]

Seven times the author identifies himself as "Koheleth," or the "Preacher." In many ways Ecclesiastes is a sermon in which "Koheleth" sets forth certain conclusions based on his observations and on certain Old Testament passages.

It is probably best to assume that Solomon wrote this book toward the end of his life, after he had experienced so very much. Solomon had begun his reign walking with the Lord and ruling with great wisdom. But Solomon sinned by turning from the Lord to serve idols, and so experienced life apart from the true God.

---

1. Walter Kaiser Jr., *Ecclesiastes: Total Life* (Chicago: Moody, 1979), pp. 24-29. Ardel B. Caneday, "Qoheleth: Enigmatic Pessimist or Godly Sage?" *Grace Theological Journal* 7, no. 1 (Spring 1986), pp. 21-56.

After he repented and turned back to the Lord, Solomon could reflect insightfully on his failure and his foolishness. He understood experientially the emptiness of living away from the Lord. Since Solomon died in 931 B.C., a date shortly before that would be assigned to this book.

B. PURPOSE OF ECCLESIASTES

Ecclesiastes records man's struggle to find meaning and fulfillment in life. The basic theme is that life is empty and meaningless apart from a right relationship with God. Unless a man comes to know the Creator, nothing in the creation can bring him peace and satisfaction. Everything will be "vain" (1:2; 12:8). All of man's pursuits will eventually leave him discontent and empty.

C. BASIC OUTLINE OF ECCLESIASTES

    I. Prologue: Introductory Thoughts on Human Futility (chap. 1:1-3)
    II. Some Demonstrations on Human Futility (chaps. 1:4–3:22)
    III. Some Developments on Human Futility (chaps. 4:1–12:8)
    IV. Epilogue: Concluding Thoughts on Human Futility (chaps. 12:9-14)

D. IMPORTANT DATA ABOUT ECCLESIASTES

    1. Key Word: Vanity
    2. Key Chapter: 12—The conclusion of the issue
    3. Key Verses: 1:2-11; 12:8-14
    4. Key Character: Solomon
    5. Meaning of "Ecclesiastes": Comes from the Greek word for "preacher" (Ecclesiastes is a sermon.)
    6. Geography of Ecclesiastes: Israel

E. SPECIAL CONSIDERATIONS ON ECCLESIASTES

Solomon wrote Ecclesiastes from a concealed premise. He did not come right out and say that people need to have a right relationship with God in order to be happy and contented in life. Instead he took a seemingly secular approach, intending to meet the unsaved man on his own level and way of thinking. He wished to show man that knowledge, pleasure, wealth, material possessions, and even hard work cannot bring lasting contentment. Solomon's writing is really an apologetic for living according to God's standards (12:13).

In approaching the subject as he did, Solomon used several words and phrases repeatedly. The word "vanity" (used thirty-seven times) refers to that which "vanishes away" like a mirage. So much of man's pursuits fall into this category. "Vanity of vanities" (1:2) is not a verdict on life in general, but on life lived apart from God.

The phrase "under the sun" (used twenty-seven times) speaks of the reasonings of the secular man, as he views life on the purely natural plane. It is at this point that many have had difficulty with some statements found in Ecclesiastes (e.g. "For the fate of the sons of men and the fate of beasts is the same," 3:19). But it must be remembered that much of this book is written from the perspective of secular human reasoning. These are the thoughts of the man who lives "under the sun."

Solomon also spoke of man's pursuits in life as "striving after wind." This phrase emphasizes that apart from God, man spends his life engaged in matters that cannot bring contentment, but rather bring emptiness and dissatisfaction.

When interpreting this book, Solomon's "secular" approach must be kept in mind. The book is, of course, fully inspired by God. Solomon wrote down accurately the reasonings of the unsaved man (much like Satan's statements in the book of Job were accurately recorded).

A SUMMARY OF ECCLESIASTES

Solomon began by noting that man's life, like nature, is an endless cycle (1:3-11). Everything "under the sun" is empty and meaningless. He then recalled those things to which he had given his life: knowledge, pleasure, wealth, material possessions, and hard work. But these things did not bring contentment and peace. All of them turned out to be "vain."

Interwoven in the pessimism of the book is the positive idea that a true relationship with God does bring joy and satisfaction (e.g. 2:24-26; 3:12-15; 5:7, 18; 8:12). Solomon concluded the book by exhorting young people to seek God early in life, thus avoiding the emptiness of life without Him (12:1-7). He encouraged men to fear God; that is, to reverence and commit themselves to Him. They were also told to obey His commandments (12:13). Adherence to these truths brings joy and contentment (cf. John 15:10-11). A man can enjoy the creation if he knows the Creator.

20

SONG OF SOLOMON

INTRODUCTION TO SONG OF SOLOMON

A. AUTHORSHIP AND DATE OF SONG OF SOLOMON

The book was written by King Solomon, perhaps about 960 B.C. (early in his reign). Although Solomonic authorship has been questioned, it has been the traditional viewpoint of the Jewish rabbis and conservative Christian scholars that the entire book was written by Solomon.[1] The book itself states that Solomon wrote it (1:1), and his name is mentioned several times in the text (1:5; 3:7, 9, 11; 8:11-12).

B. PURPOSE OF SONG OF SOLOMON

This lengthy poem elevates human, sexual love to the place that God intended. Although the Bible often warns of the negative consequences of immorality, it also extols the blessings that come from moral behavior. This book records the reminiscences of a bridegroom and his bride. In so doing, this Scripture shows the joys of physical love within the boundaries of marital commitment.

---

1. Paige Patterson, *Song of Solomon* (Chicago: Moody, 1986), pp. 14-17. Weston Fields, "Early Jewish and Medieval Interpretation of the Song of Songs," *Grace Theological Journal* 1, no. 2 (Fall 1980), pp. 221-31.

C. BASIC OUTLINE OF SONG OF SOLOMON

  I. Courtship: Preparation for Marriage (chaps. 1:1–3:5)
 II. Consummation: Fulfillment Within Marriage (chaps. 3:6–5:1)
III. Commitment: Realities of Marriage (chaps. 5:2–8:14)

D. IMPORTANT DATA ABOUT SONG OF SOLOMON

1. Key Word: Love
2. Key Chapter: 4—The joy of wedded love
3. Key Verses: 3:6-11; 5:1
4. Key Characters: Solomon and his bride
5. Meaning of "Song of Solomon": Emphasizes the author of this love poem
6. Geography of Song of Solomon: Jerusalem; the hill country of Ephraim

E. SPECIAL CONSIDERATIONS ON SONG OF SOLOMON

There have been a number of divergent interpretations of this book, but two are prominent: the allegorical and the literal.[2] The book has been a problem to many Bible students because of the explicit discussion of physical love. A widely held attitude is that God would not include such an explicit love poem in the sacred Scriptures. As a result, they view the Song as an allegory of God's love for Israel or Christ's love for the church. Although it is true that both Israel and the church are seen in the motif of a wife or bride of God, the motif is not found in this book. It is far better to interpret this book normally as a poem of human love.[3]

> Even if the Song of Solomon is merely a collection of songs describing the bliss of lovers in wedlock, it is not thereby rendered unworthy of a place in the Bible, unless marriage is to be regarded as a fall from a state of innocency . . . The entire range

2. Patterson, *Song of Solomon*, pp. 17-27.
3. S. Craig Glickman, *A Song for Lovers* (Downers Grove, Ill.: InterVarsity, 1978), pp. 173-87.

of man's legitimate joys finds sympathetic and appreciative description in the Bible.[4]

It should be remembered that the Bible speaks clearly and forcefully on human sexuality in other places as well as this one. Sex rightly used is a joy and blessing (e.g. Prov. 5:15-19; Heb. 13:4), whereas sex wrongly used brings pain and grief (Prov. 7:21-23; 1 Thess. 4:5-7). Should the story of Lot's committing incest with his daughters in a cave belong in the Bible, and Solomon's love for his new bride be excluded? The Song of Solomon should be interpreted literally as a personal love poem, giving additional wisdom from God on human sexuality.

A SUMMARY OF SONG OF SOLOMON

This poem consists mainly of the reminiscences of Solomon and his bride (the Shulammite girl) as they think back over their meeting, courtship, and marriage. The girl was from a poor family in Ephraim. One day she met a young shepherd (who was really King Solomon in disguise). It was love at first sight for both of them. The shepherd had to leave her but promised to return. After an extended absence he did return, but in the grandeur as king of Israel. It was only then that she realized that her shepherd lover was none other than Israel's king. Solomon took her back to his palace in Jerusalem as his bride. The poem records their joy and pleasure, as well as some of the difficulties they faced. Their love relationship reveals that genuine love in the context of marital commitment is beautiful, uplifting, and satisfying. It carries with it pleasant memories without any guilt or self-reproach.

4. John Sampey, "Song of Songs," in *International Standard Bible Encyclopedia* (Grand Rapids: Eerdmans, 1949) 5:2833.

21

LAMENTATIONS

INTRODUCTION TO LAMENTATIONS

A. AUTHORSHIP AND DATE OF LAMENTATIONS

The evidence points to the prophet Jeremiah as the author of Lamentations.

> Such evidence includes the following: (1) the Septuagint and Vulgate introductions to the book, which read in part: "Jeremiah sat weeping and lamented with the lamentation over Jerusalem, and said . . . ," (2) Hebrew and Gentile tradition, (3) similarities between Lamentations and poetical portions of Jeremiah . . . , (4) the writer was an eyewitness of Jerusalem's destruction, with a sensitivity of soul (cf. Jer. 9:1; 14:17-22) and an ability to write.[1]

In light of the sequence of events found in 2 Kings 25 and Jeremiah 40-44, it is likely that Jeremiah penned the book at Mizpah in 586 B.C.[2] He was at Mizpah when Jerusalem was burned and reduced to rubble. The deep sorrow expressed in Lamentations suggests a time of writing shortly after the destruction of Jerusalem.

1. Irving L. Jensen, *Jeremiah and Lamentations* (Chicago: Moody, 1966), p. 121.
2. C.F. Keil, *Biblical Commentary on the Old Testament: The Prophecies of Jeremiah,* trans. James Kennedy (Edinburgh: T. and T. Clark, 1874), 1: 16.

B. PURPOSE OF LAMENTATIONS

The book is a lament over the destruction of Jerusalem at the hands of the Babylonian armies, following months of a devastating siege of the city. It displays enormous emotional and physical pain. This poem is a sequel to the book of Jeremiah.

C. BASIC OUTLINE OF LAMENTATIONS

    I. The First Lamentation: Jerusalem's Grief (chap. 1)
    II. The Second Lamentation: God's Wrath (chap. 2)
    III. The Third Lamentation: Continuing Hope (chap. 3)
    IV. The Fourth Lamentation: Sin's Consequences (chap. 4)
    V. The Fifth Lamentation: Prayerful Confession (chap. 5)

D. IMPORTANT DATA ABOUT LAMENTATIONS

1. Key Word: Lament
2. Key Chapter: 3—Hope in the midst of affliction
3. Key Verses: 1:1-12; 3:22-23
4. Key Characters: Jeremiah and Jerusalem (personified)
5. Meaning of "Lamentations": Reflects the dirge-like quality of the poem
6. Geography of Lamentations: Jerusalem

E. SPECIAL CONSIDERATIONS ON LAMENTATIONS

The unique feature about the poetry of Lamentations is its acrostic arrangement.

> In arrangement the first four chapters are alphabetic acrostics. Each chapter has 22 verses or a multiple thereof. The 22 letters of the Hebrew alphabet are used successfully to begin each verse in 1 and 2. Chapters 3 and 4 allot three and two verses respectively to each Hebrew letter. Although 5 has 22 verses it does not represent an alphabetic acrostic.[3]

It may well be that Jeremiah employed this literary device as a memory aid for his countrymen, who would read this poem.

3. Samuel J. Schultz, *The Old Testament Speaks* (New York: Harper & Row, 1970), p. 341.

A Summary of Lamentations

Lamentations expresses the reaction of one who was an eyewitness and deeply involved in a terrible event. Even though Jeremiah had warned Judah for some forty years that such judgment would come, the event itself was overwhelming.

Great grief is expressed over the wrath of God poured out on Judah (e.g. 3:49). As the covenant people witnessed the removal of their king, the burning of their Temple, and the destruction of their land, they could find no comfort anywhere (e.g. 1:2, 12; 2:7). False prophets were partly to blame for their condition (2:14). The people had not listened to men like Jeremiah, and the nightmare of the long siege came upon them. Starvation and cannibalism became part of life in the city (2:11-12; 4:5-10). In all of this, Jeremiah acknowledged that God was holy, righteous, and faithful (3:21-33). And as the poem ended, he pleaded for mercy, confessing the sin of his people (5:1-22).

Part 4

The Prophetic Books

22

GOD'S PROPHETIC MESSENGERS

For a thousand years of Israel's history there appeared men (and a few women) who received messages from God and delivered those messages to Israel. These prophets had a profound impact on the national life of Israel. Although they did not appear in unbroken order (cf. 1 Sam. 3:1), they did come on the scene in every era of Israel's history.

The prophet Amos makes clear that prophets were a gift from God (Amos 2:11). The divine origin of the prophetic office is affirmed by Jeremiah, who also reveals that it began with Moses (Jer. 7:25). (Note that God spoke directly to men like Abraham, before Moses, but the prophetic office with its various functions began with Moses.)

A primary passage in understanding the prophetic office is Deuteronomy 18:9-22. In this passage, Moses declared that God would raise up the prophetic institution and that someday a great Prophet would arise. This message was given as Israel prepared to enter the land of Canaan. The first thing Moses told the Israelites was that when they entered the land they were not to involve themselves in the Canaanite practices of witchcraft, spells, omens, spiritism, or similar observances. These wicked, superstitious rituals were not to be used to obtain direction or information. Instead, God would raise up a prophet (Deut. 18:18). At first, Moses seemed to be speaking about just one prophet. But the context of Deuteronomy, as well as the continuing need for the prophetic office over the years does not permit us to understand that only one person is in view.[1] Jesus Christ, of course, would be the great Prophet who would give final and complete fulfillment to this passage.

THE NAMES FOR THE PROPHETS

A. THE PROPHET

The primary term for the prophet in the Old Testament is *nabhi*. The origin of this Hebrew word is uncertain even though numerous ideas for the root of the word have been suggested.[2] But the precise meaning of the word can still be understood even though there is uncertainty about its origin. This is possible because of the way the term is used in the Old Testament. In Exodus 7:1-2 an excellent picture of the function of the prophet is given: "Then the Lord said to Moses, 'See, I make you as God to Pharaoh, and your brother Aaron shall be your prophet. You shall speak all that I command you, and your brother Aaron shall speak to Pharaoh.'"

When Moses stood before Pharoah, Aaron did the speaking— though the words were Moses' words. Aaron would also speak on Moses' behalf to the people of Israel (Ex. 4:16). The prophet is to God what Aaron was to Moses. The prophet spoke God's words on God's behalf.

Other Scriptures develop the concept further. When Jeremiah was called by God to be a prophet, he was told, "All that I command you, you shall speak" (Jer. 1:7). The prophet not only would speak God's words, but he was seen as "God's mouth"— the place where God speaks (e.g. Jer. 15:19; Isa. 1:20; 1 Kings 8:15).

Therefore, the prophet (*nabhi*) spoke a message on behalf of his superior, God. The prophet did not originate the message, but simply proclaimed it.

---

1. Edward J. Young, *My Servants the Prophets* (Grand Rapids: Eerdmans, 1968), pp. 20-37.
2. Ibid., pp. 56-57.

B. THE SEER

A less frequently used word for the prophet was "seer" (Hebrew word *ro'eh*, and sometimes *hozeh*). From its usage in the Old Testament it was a common name used by the people for the prophet of God (e.g. 1 Sam. 9:9-11). But there is no difference in the function of the prophet and the seer. An individual could be called by either designation. There is perhaps a difference in emphasis.

> The word has primary reference to the prophet's relation to God. Herein lies the difference. The word nabhi stresses the active work of the prophet, in speaking forth the message from God. The word ro'eh, on the other hand, brings to the fore the experience by means of which the prophet was made to "see" that message.[3]

Therefore, the emphasis of the word "seer" is on the reception of the message from God. He got his information through "seeing"—by dreams, visions, or perhaps supernatural illumination.

C. MAN OF GOD

This phrase emphasized the holy calling, moral character, and God-given ministry of the prophet.[4] This term is found in numerous passages (e.g. 2 Kings 1:9, 11; 1 Sam. 9:10).

D. SERVANT OF THE LORD

The Scriptures frequently refer to the prophets as "My servants" (Dan. 9:6; Ezek. 38:17; 2 Kings 9:7; 17:13), emphasizing "the close and holy relationship between God and His faithful messengers."[5]

3. Ibid., p. 65
4. Hobart Freeman, *An Introduction to the Old Testament Prophets* (Chicago: Moody, 1968), p. 41.
5. Ibid.

THE ROLE OF THE PROPHETS

In Israel there were two kinds of mediators. First was the priest, who represented the people before God in their worship and sacrifice. Second was the prophet, who spoke for God to the people. There were three basic aspects to the mediatorial role of the prophets: they were preachers, predictors, and watchmen.[6]

First, the prophets were preachers of the already revealed law. Not everything the prophets spoke was new truth. In fact, their ministries were clearly based on God's truth that had been revealed through Moses (and others). The Israelites, in every generation, needed to be instructed in the "constitution" (law) of Israel and to be reminded of their obligation, as Israelites, to adhere to that constitution. The prophets (perhaps assisting the priests) expounded forcefully truth that was neglected, misunderstood, or unknown (Mal. 4:4; Dan. 9:4-13; Jer. 11:1-5).

Second, the prophets predicted coming persons and events. Based on the needs of their time, they foretold coming judgment or blessing.

> Although the prophets spoke primarily to people of their own day, their divinely inspired messages often springing out of the historical situation in which they lived, there was, nevertheless, a predictive element pervading their messages . . . Predictive prophecy was concerned with judgment, salvation, the Messiah and His kingdom.[7]

Third, the prophets functioned as watchmen over the leaders and the people of Israel. The prophets were the guardians of Israel's constitution. They were the preservers and defenders of the principles on which the theocracy had been built. They did not just preach the law, but called on Israel to obey the law, warning them of certain judgment if they refused. This is probably the primary function of the prophet.

6. J. Carl Laney, "The Role of the Prophets in God's Case Against Israel," *Bibliotheca Sacra* 138 (October-December, 1981): 315.
7. Freeman, *Introduction to the Old Testament Prophets*, p. 49.

The major role of the biblical prophets was that of royal dip-
lomats who functioned as prosecuting attorneys on behalf of
Yahweh. They indicted the people of Israel for their violations
of the Mosaic covenant, called for repentance, and warned of
coming judgment for continued disobedience.[8]

In his ministry, the prophet not only spoke to the people of Israel but was often seen associating with the rulers and kings of Israel. The reason for this is important to understand.

It would be a grave mistake, however, to assume that, because of the great interest of the prophets in the monarchy, they
were themselves primarily politicians. Their political activity is
always subservient to a religious end. They did serve as the
counsellors, but they did so in order that the theocratic kingdom might prosper.[9]

It was through the king (or ruler) that the prophet could often
best influence the nation for the truth of God (e.g. Elijah and
Ahab; Isaiah and Hezekiah; Haggai and Zerubbabel; Jeremiah and
Zedekiah).

THE LAND OF THE PROPHETS

The prophets frequently referred to the land of Israel in their
messages (see Joel, Amos, Micah, Isaiah, Jeremiah, Ezekiel,
Haggai, Zechariah, and Malachi). The condition of the land was a
visible indicator of Israel's spiritual condition. Obedience to the
law of God (Israel's "constitution") brought prosperity from
God's hand, while disobedience brought discipline on the land in
the form of drought, famine, and plagues. The prophets drew
heavily on Leviticus 26, and Deuteronomy 11 and 28. Because
the land was an integral part of God's covenant relationship with
Israel, the prophets regularly pointed to this visible reality.

8. Laney, "The Role of the Prophets," p. 323.
9. Young, *My Servants*, p. 82.

CONCLUSION

Two final observations must be made at this point in our study. First, there are sixteen prophetic books, which are the written messages of some of God's prophets. But it should be remembered that God sent hundreds of prophets to His people over the centuries. Our focus is naturally on those whose messages were written down and preserved. Second, our approach to the prophets is chronological. We will study them in the order that they appeared in history. The usual designations of "major" and "minor" prophet will not be followed. These terms do not indicate the importance of a prophet (unlike someone's being a major league or minor league baseball player). The term "major" prophet simply means the prophet's message is of greater length and there is a greater variety of subject matter to be found in his writings.

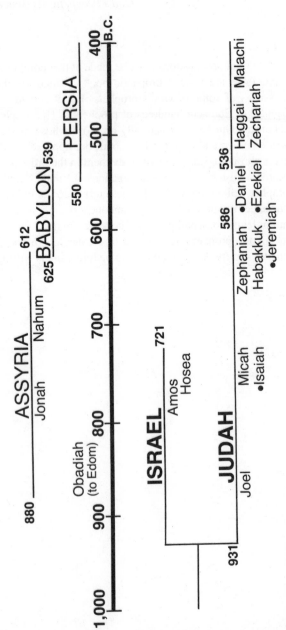

CHRONOLOGY OF THE PROPHETS
of ISRAEL AND JUDAH

B.C.

PERSIA

BABYLON 539

ASSYRIA

400 — 500 — 550 600 — 700 — 800 — 900 — 1,000

Malachi
Haggai
536 Zechariah

•Daniel
586 •Ezekiel
Zephaniah
Habakkuk
•Jeremiah

612
Nahum
625

880
Obadiah
(to Edom)

Amos
721 Hosea

ISRAEL

Micah
•Isaiah

JUDAH

Joel

931

• - Major Prophet

The Prophetic Books
Group 1:

Prophecies During the
Divided Kingdom

PROPHET	DATE	MESSAGE TO	RULERS
OBADIAH	845	JUDAH	JORAM, JEHORAM
JONAH	780	NINEVEH	JEROBOAM II
AMOS	760	ISRAEL	JEROBOAM II
HOSEA	750	ISRAEL	JEROBOAM II–HOSHEA
ISAIAH	740	JUDAH	UZZIAH–HEZEKIAH
MICAH	735	JUDAH	JOTHAM–HEZEKIAH

23

OBADIAH

INTRODUCTION TO OBADIAH

A. AUTHORSHIP AND DATE OF OBADIAH

This shortest of all Old Testament books was written by an unknown prophet named Obadiah (the name means "servant of the Lord"). The author gives no other information about himself, his background, or the time in which he lived. His name is a common one in the Old Testament; about a dozen individuals are so named. All attempts to identify this author with one of the dozen Obadiahs found in the text of the Old Testament have failed.

A date of 845 B.C. is given for this book, making it the earliest of all the prophets. The key to establishing the date of Obadiah is found in verses 10-14 of the book. These verses reveal that an attack was made on the city of Jerusalem, an attack in which the Edomites participated or at least encouraged the attackers. The Old Testament records seven times when Jerusalem was attacked. The second of these attacks (2 Kings 8:20-22; 2 Chron. 21:8-17) in the days of King Jehoram best fits the event described in Obadiah. At that time, the Philistines and the Arabians attacked Jerusalem. Instead of helping "brother Jacob," the Edomites assisted the enemies of Judah.[1] This event took place about 845 B.C.

Evidence for this early date for Obadiah is found in the writings of Jeremiah, Amos, and Joel. These three prophets show an acquaintance with Obadiah's message, indicating that Obadiah antedates these other prophets (e.g. Jer. 49:7-22; Joel 3:19).

---

1. Gleason Archer, *A Survey of Old Testament Introduction* (Chicago: Moody, 1964), p. 288.

B. PURPOSE OF OBADIAH

The message of Obadiah was directed to Israel's southern neighbors, the Edomites. The Edomites were the descendants of Esau and had a history of hostility toward Israel. God held them accountable for what they did to Israel. (For a further discussion of the Edomites, see Note E, "Israel and the Nations," p. 252.)

C. BASIC OUTLINE OF OBADIAH

    I. The Overthrow of Edom (vv. 1-9)
   II. The Offenses of Edom (vv. 10-14)
  III. The Outlook for Edom (vv. 15-21)

D. IMPORTANT DATA ABOUT OBADIAH

  1. Key Word: God's retributive justice
  2. Key Chapter: No chapter divisions
  3. Key Verses: 10-14—Edom's sins
  4. Key Characters: Edomites
  5. Meaning of "Obadiah": The name of the prophet who is writing
  6. Geography of Obadiah: Edom

E. SPECIAL CONSIDERATIONS ON OBADIAH

Based on the date given above, the ministry of Obadiah took place in the reign of Judah's king Jehoram. Jehoram was an unusually evil king (cf. 2 Chron. 21:1-7). It was because of his wickedness that God allowed Edom to revolt (21:8). But nevertheless, God held Edom accountable for the evil that they did to Judah a little later.

A SUMMARY OF OBADIAH

The subject matter of this prophet is that of coming judgment on Edom. Because of Edom's two sins of pride (1:3) and injury done to Judah (1:10), they would be thoroughly judged. Because of the natural fortification Edom enjoyed (in the canyons and cliffs of their capital city of Petra), they were confident that they would never be destroyed. But God, through Obadiah, vividly describes the completeness of the destruction coming on them (1:5-6). Edom would discover, when trouble came, that her allies would not come to her support (1:7). It was bad enough for a nation to attack the people of God, but for a blood relative to do so was far worse (1:10-14), bringing God's judgment on themselves.

Looking ahead to the great period of the Tribulation, Obadiah declared Edom and the other nations would be severely judged (1:15-16), but God would preserve Israel, giving them the whole land promised to Abraham, which included land occupied by the Edomites (1:15-21).

24

JOEL

A. AUTHORSHIP AND DATE OF JOEL

The author identifies himself as "Joel, the son of Pethuel" (1:1). Other than this brief statement, almost nothing is known about the man himself. (His name means "Jehovah is God.") He probably was not a priest, since he addresses the priests as a class to which he did not belong (2:17).

A date of 830 B.C. is given for this prophecy. Since Joel does not date his ministry by the reign of any king, exact dating is somewhat difficult. But a general date can be established by comparing Joel with Amos. Evidently Joel's prophecy was given and widely received by the time Amos came along. Amos's prophecy can be dated with some exactness (cf. Amos 1:1, 760 B.C.). By comparing Joel and Amos, it becomes apparent that Amos took the keynote of his prophecy from the closing words of Joel's prophecy. The whole force of Amos's thought depends on Joel's words being recognized by his hearers (cf. Amos 1:2 and Joel 3:16; also Amos 9:13 and Joel 3:18). As a result of this comparison, Joel is dated somewhere around 830 B.C., thus making him one of the earliest of the prophets.

B. PURPOSE OF JOEL

Joel's message is aimed at the Southern Kingdom of Judah. There is little doubt that he was living in the center of the public worship of God (Jerusalem). He speaks to the priests as though they were present (e.g. 2:17). On several occasions he refers to

Zion, Jerusalem, and Judah (e.g. 2:1, 15). When he does mention "Israel" on three occasions it is a reference to the people of God generally and not to the Northern Kingdom.

C. BASIC OUTLINE OF JOEL

    I. The Historical Visitation (chap. 1)
    II. The Prophetic Revelation (chaps. 2-3)

D. IMPORTANT DATA ABOUT JOEL

    1. Key Word: Day of the Lord
    2. Key Chapter: 2—Events of the Day of the Lord
    3. Key Verses: 2:1-2; 2:28–3:2
    4. Key Characters: The Israelites
    5. Meaning of "Joel": The name of the prophet who is writing
    6. Geography of Joel: Judah

E. SPECIAL CONSIDERATIONS ON JOEL

Based on the date of 830 B.C., Joel ministered in the days of Joash of Judah. This king was a godly king who was supported and given direction by Jehoiada the priest, a great man of God (cf. 2 Chron. 23:1–24:14). Judah had survived the reign of the wicked queen Athaliah. But after her death at the hands of Jehoiada, the nation of Judah prospered spiritually. However, when the godly priest Jehoiada died, Joash and Judah lost their intensity for the things of the Lord. It was perhaps after the death of Jehoiada that God sent Joel to Judah with His warnings (cf. 2 Chron. 24:15-22).

A SUMMARY OF JOEL

The theme of Joel's message is "the day of the Lord" (see the discussion below). As with many of the prophets who spoke of coming judgment, Joel's message had application to the nation of his day as well as that great future day of judgment, the Tribulation. Joel warned Judah that if they did not repent, judgment was certain.

Joel built his message on two recent events in nature: a great plague of locusts (1:2-4) and a time of drought (1:15-20). The people of Israel should have remembered that anything that hurt the land was to be interpreted as disciplinary action of God (cf. Deut. 11:10-17; 28:15, 23-24, 38; Lev. 26:14-21). Joel told the drunken nation to sober up and to lament and mourn because of these events (1:5-12). Joel warned them of the coming "day of the Lord." The "day of the Lord" (the Tribulation) would have its foreshadowing during the Assyrian and Babylonian invasions (2:1-11).

Judah, however, still had time to repent, so an invitation to repent was given (2:18-32). Joel 2:28-32 are significant verses because Peter made reference to them in his sermon on the Day of Pentecost (Acts 2). The outpouring of the Holy Spirit on the Day of Pentecost was a foreshadowing of His coming in the last days. The church, in this present dispensation, has received the Spirit of God as never before, but even this is just a partial fulfillment of Joel 2 and the events of the "day of the Lord." What is mentioned briefly in Joel 2:30-31 is expanded and detailed in the judgments of Revelation 6, 8, 9, and 16. Joel 3 speaks of the day when God will judge the nations at Armageddon ("the valley of Jehoshaphat").

Joel, then, using the vivid desolation caused by a locust plague and a drought looks into the future and sees two times of great desolation—one in the near future with Babylon and the other in the distant future in the Tribulation. Mixed in with the judgment there is blessing and mercy.

THE DAY OF THE LORD

This phrase is used by a number of the prophets. It is used in Obadiah 1:15; Joel 1:15; 2:1, 11, 31; 3:14; Amos 5:18, and in a dozen other places. In addition to these, the phrase "that day" or "the great day" or "the day" can be found more than seventy-five times in the Old Testament. It is used to refer to a time of intense judgment (the Tribulation), a time of great blessing (the Millennium), and the time when the Messiah will come to His own people (the Second Coming). The context determines which aspect of "the day" is in view.

25

JONAH

INTRODUCTION TO JONAH

A. AUTHORSHIP AND DATE OF JONAH

This is the message of Jonah the son of Amittai (1:1), who was a prophet of God in the Northern Kingdom of Israel (2 Kings 14:25). Since Jonah ministered for the Lord during the reign of Israel's king Jeroboam II, his message is dated 780 B.C.

B. PURPOSE OF JONAH

The book reveals that God desired the salvation of Gentiles and extended His grace toward them. Although God had established a covenant relationship with Israel alone, He did not abandon the rest of mankind. Jonah's message was directed to the powerful nation of Assyria, with its capital city at Nineveh. (For a further discussion of the Assyrians, see Note E, "Israel and the Nations," p. 252.)

C. BASIC OUTLINE OF JONAH

    I. The Request to Jonah (chap. 1:1-2)
    II. The Reluctance of Jonah (chap. 1:3-17)
    III. The Repentance of Jonah (chap. 2:1-10)
    IV. The Recommissioning of Jonah (chap. 3:1-4)
    V. The Reception of Jonah (chap. 3:5-10)
    VI. The Reproof of Jonah (chap. 4:1-11)

D. IMPORTANT DATA ABOUT JONAH

1. Key Word: The grace of God
2. Key Chapter: 4—Revelation of God's character
3. Key Verses: 1:2; 3:4-10; 4:2
4. Key Character: Jonah
5. Meaning of "Jonah": The name of the prophet who is writing
6. Geography of Jonah: Israel and Nineveh

E. SPECIAL CONSIDERATIONS ON JONAH

Jonah prophesied in the Northern Kingdom during the prosperous reign of Jeroboam II (cf. 2 Kings 14:23). God called him to go with His word of judgment on Nineveh. The brutal Assyrians, with their great war machine, were hated and feared by many nations, including Israel. Jonah, being a patriotic Israelite, also hated this Gentile power. This hatred combined with his fear that God just might be merciful to the Assyrians caused Jonah to resist God's command to go.

Nineveh was a large city (cf. Jonah 4:11) that was highly fortified. The walls and the series of moats made this city almost impregnable. Their army was known for its might, discipline, and ferocity. Why then would they repent when an Israelite prophet wandered into their city? It may be that the people of Nineveh were beginning to seek the true God in light of several plagues that had hit the city and a total eclipse of the sun.[1] These events may well have been thought of as signs of coming judgment. If this assumption is correct, then Nineveh was prepared when Jonah arrived at the gates of the city.

A SUMMARY OF JONAH

This account out of the life of Jonah was written to offset the narrow nationalism of the Israelites. Even though God was in a covenant relationship with Israel, He was still interested in the Gentiles and wanted them saved. And furthermore, the nation of

1. John Walton, *Jonah* (Grand Rapids: Zondervan, 1982), pp. 40-48.

Israel had a responsibility to be a light to the Gentiles. The book of Jonah is a study in the power and the grace of God. It is a book filled with miraculous events, but more important, it is further evidence that God is rich in mercy and grace.

When Jonah received God's command to go to the Assyrians, he refused because he knew his God was indeed longsuffering and full of mercy (4:2). Fortunately for Jonah that was true, because God showed great mercy to Jonah, even though he was disobedient, angry, and stubborn. When Jonah finally arrived at Nineveh (after his short stay in the great fish, 2:1-10), he preached his message of judgment (3:4). When all Nineveh repented, God withdrew His planned judgment (cf. Jer. 18:7-8). Jonah was very displeased with this revival (4:1-3). The book ends with an instructive contrast between God's great compassion and Jonah's lack of it (4:5-11).

26

AMOS

Introduction to Amos

A. AUTHORSHIP AND DATE OF AMOS

Evidently Amos was a humble individual who had spent most of his life caring for someone else's sheep and cultivating the fruit of the sycamore tree. He was not trained in one of the schools of the prophets, which had been started by Samuel (Amos 1:1; 7:14-15). He was from the southern town of Tekoa, which was located some twelve miles south of Jerusalem and was a defense city to protect Jerusalem (Amos 1:1; 2 Chron. 11:6).

Amos dates his ministry by the reign of King Uzziah of Judah and Jeroboam II of Israel. Uzziah ruled from 787-735 B.C., and Jeroboam II reigned from 790-749 B.C. Therefore, a date of 760 B.C. is given for Amos.

B. PURPOSE OF AMOS

In the days of Amos, the Northern Kingdom of Israel was still deeply involved in their worship of the golden calves. Although Amos was from a town in the Southern Kingdom of Judah, God chose him to go to the Northern Kingdom to deliver His message of coming judgment. Some of that message was delivered in the corrupt city of Bethel, which was one of the centers of calf worship (7:10-17).

C. BASIC OUTLINE OF AMOS

    I. The Visitation of Judgment (chaps. 1:1–2:10)
    II. The Declaration of Charges (chaps. 3:1–6:15)
    III. The Warning of Judgment (chaps. 7:1–9:10)
    IV. The Restoration of Israel (chap. 9:11-15)

D. IMPORTANT DATA ABOUT AMOS

    1. Key Word: Prepare to meet God
    2. Key Chapter: 4—Climax of the message
    3. Key Verses: 3:1-3; 4:6-12
    4. Key Characters: Amos and Amaziah
    5. Meaning of "Amos": The name of the man whose prophecy is recorded
    6. Geography of Amos: Israel

E. SPECIAL CONSIDERATIONS ON AMOS

The Northern Kingdom of Israel under Jeroboam II had become wealthy and prosperous. Because of the temporary balance of power in the world, they had been relatively free of war and had therefore enjoyed a peaceful situation. The nation had become brazen in its idolatry and moral corruption, as calf worship and Canaanite idolatry were firmly established in the Northern Kingdom. Material prosperity only made matters worse. The people were characterized by wealth, moral laxity, and religious indifference. It was the task of Amos (and later Hosea) to try to stop wicked Israel from its plunge to ruin and to turn the nation back to the Lord. Amos preached a potent message of reproof and judgment.

A SUMMARY OF AMOS

Amos began his message by pronouncing judgment on six nations that surrounded Israel. God condemned these nations for their many sins ("for three transgressions and for four") against God's people (1:3–2:3). Amos probably gave these messages as a reminder to Israel that God was well aware of Israel's oppressors and that He was both sovereign and powerful. But although Israel may have enjoyed this part of Amos's message, they hated the rest. After a brief word against Judah for sinning in the light of knowledge (2:4-5), Amos targeted Israel. Israel was guilty of many terrible violations of God's laws (2:6-16). Amos reminded Israel that God had been disciplining them now for many years, but so far they had not responded to any of His disciplinary action (3:1–4:11 with Lev. 26:14-33). Since they had not responded and repented, Israel was told to "prepare to meet your God" (4:12). Amos then gave some descriptions of the devastating judgments to come (e.g. 5:3). But the message ended with Amos's looking into the future and seeing the time when God will again restore Israel (9:11-15). The marvelous restoration will take place when Messiah comes and establishes His kingdom.

27

HOSEA

INTRODUCTION TO HOSEA

A. AUTHORSHIP AND DATE OF HOSEA

Except for what can be gleaned from the text itself, nothing is known about Hosea. He was probably from the Northern Kingdom, as there are numerous geographic notations in the message (e.g. 4:15; 5:1; 6:8).

His ministry is clearly dated by the reigns of four Southern kings (Uzziah, Jotham, Ahaz, and Hezekiah) and Jeroboam II of the North (1:1). 750 B.C. would be a reasonable date for this prophecy.

B. PURPOSE OF HOSEA

This prophecy was God's last voice to the Northern Kingdom of Israel before its destruction. It was a gracious attempt to rescue individuals out of the doomed nation. This message of judgment was fulfilled within a few years.

C. BASIC OUTLINE OF HOSEA

    I. The Unfaithful Wife (chaps. 1-3)
    II. The Unfaithful People (chaps. 4-14)

D. IMPORTANT DATA ABOUT HOSEA

    1. Key Word: God's love for Israel
    2. Key Chapter: 2—A description of love

3. Key Verses: 1:2-9; 2:5-8; 3:1-5
4. Key Characters: Hosea and Gomer
5. Meaning of ''Hosea'': Name derives from God's faithful prophet
6. Geography of Hosea: Israel

E. SPECIAL CONSIDERATIONS ON HOSEA

Hosea calls the Northern Kingdom by several names: Israel, Ephraim, and Samaria (e.g. 4:16-17; 5:9-13; 7:1; 10:6-7). Israel, of course, is the usual designation; Samaria was the capital city of the Northern Kingdom and its name symbolized the entire nation; Ephraim is used because the tribe by that name was the most powerful of the tribes in the Northern Kingdom.

Hosea did not minister in pleasant times. Israel was in as bad a spiritual and moral situation as she had ever been. And it was just as bad politically. After the death of Jeroboam II, murder and intrigue were common in Israeli politics. Out of the last six kings on the throne, only one died a natural death in office (cf. 2 Kings 15:10-30). Morally and spiritually the people were almost completely defiled.

> Blood was shed like water until one stream met another and overspread the land with one defiling deluge. Adultery was consecrated as an act of religion. Those who were first in rank were first in excess. People and king lived in debauchery, and the sottish king joined and encouraged the freethinkers and blasphemers of his court. The idolatrous priests loved and shared in the sins of the people . . . Corruption had spread throughout the whole land; even those places once sacred through God's revelations or other mercies to their forefathers, Bethel, Gilgal, Gilead, Mizpah, Shechem, were especially scenes of corruption or of sin.[1]

The nation had degenerated morally and spiritually so that they were much like the nations Joshua had driven out of the land many centuries before. Hosea was sent, as God's last prophet, into this decaying situation.

1. E. B. Pusey, *The Minor Prophets* (Grand Rapids: Baker, 1965), 1:12.

For a short period of time Hosea probably ministered as a contemporary of Amos in the North and Isaiah and Micah in the South.

A SUMMARY OF HOSEA

Extreme times often call for extreme methods. Israel had not listened to the prophets. Their preaching had fallen on insensitive people. So God chose to use His prophet (and his family) as an object lesson to Israel. Hosea's family, or more specifically Hosea's relationship with his wife, would become an illustration of God's love for Israel. Hosea would love his wife even though she would be unfaithful to him; and God loved Israel even though she had been totally unfaithful to Him.

The first word that came to Hosea from God was a strange one. God commanded him to marry a woman who would prove to be unfaithful in their marriage relationship. The term "wife of harlotry" (1:2) strongly suggests that Gomer (Hosea's wife) was guilty of sexual immorality before the marriage, perhaps as a temple prostitute. The picture of prostitution ("harlotry") is used by Hosea throughout his message (2:2-5; 3:3; 4:10-19; 5:3-4; 6:10; 9:1). It was a motif entirely appropriate for the nation of Israel in their relationship with God. Hosea married Gomer, and three children were born and were given names that would say something about God's relationship with Israel (1:4, 6, 9). The firstborn was named *Jezreel* (a name symbolizing judgment); the second was *Lo-ruhamah* (meaning "no pity"); and the third was called *Lo-ammi* ("not my people").

Evidently Gomer tired of the marriage and left Hosea and went back to her life of immorality (2:2, 5). For a while she lived the "good life" of material pleasure and prosperity but eventually ended up on the auction block as a slave. God then instructed Hosea to go and buy back his wife and reinstate her as his wife (3:1-3). So Gomer was purchased and restored as the wife of the prophet. This experience in the life of Hosea, showing what real love was like, would be a vivid object lesson to the people of Israel. And it would serve as a basis for Hosea's preaching ministry.

The nation of Israel was "married" by covenant to the Lord but had forsaken her "husband" and gone after other gods—spiritual adultery. Her forsaking of the Lord had bred a multitude of sins which were enumerated by Hosea—unfaithfulness, swearing, deception, murder, stealing, adultery, rebellion, idolatry, disobedience, pride, stubbornness, and involvement in spiritism (4:1-2, 10-14, 16; 5:5; 6:8-10). The leaders were just as sinful as the people (4:9, 18; 5:1; 7:5; 9:15). Sin had so hardened Israel that she would not repent (5:4). Judgment was sure. But Hosea was just as sure that God would restore Israel in the future (14:4-9).

28

ISAIAH

INTRODUCTION TO ISAIAH

A. AUTHORSHIP AND DATE OF ISAIAH

The prophet Isaiah lived and ministered in Jerusalem, where he was the court preacher. Tradition says that he was the cousin of King Uzziah. Isaiah, whose name means "the Lord saves," was married and had at least two sons (cf. 8:18). According to rabbinic tradition, he was sawed in two by order of the wicked king Manasseh. Isaiah lived when the nation of Assyria was the great power in the Middle East, and he was ministering when Assyria invaded Palestine and took the Northern Kingdom of Israel captive.

Some critics of the Bible have denied that Isaiah wrote all sixty-six chapters of this book. It is claimed that another man (referred to as "Deutero-Isaiah") wrote chapters 40-66. But conservative scholars have answered this theory clearly and convincingly. There is just one human author of this great prophecy.[1]

Isaiah had a long ministry, which began in the year that King Uzziah died (740 B.C.) and continued into the reign of Manasseh (696-642 B.C.). Isaiah probably ministered for about fifty years, and a date of 740 B.C. is given for this book (1:1).[2]

1. Merrill F. Unger, *Introductory Guide to the Old Testament* (Grand Rapids; Zondervan, 1956), pp. 315-22.
2. Edwin R. Thiele, *A Chronology of the Hebrew Kings* (Grand Rapids: Zondervan, 1977), pp. 27-32, 67.

B. PURPOSE OF ISAIAH

Isaiah was raised up by God to speak of coming judgment on Judah because of her many sins and to reveal the coming of "the servant of the Lord." Isaiah was one of the last prophets who offered the nation (as a nation) the opportunity to repent and avoid a national calamity. He also was among the greatest revealers of truth about the person, work, and kingdom of the coming Messiah.

C. BASIC OUTLINE OF ISAIAH

I. Prophecies of Punishment (chaps. 1-35)
II. Parenthesis for History (chaps. 36-39)
III. Prophecies of Peace (chaps. 40-66)

D. IMPORTANT DATA ABOUT ISAIAH

1. Key Word: Servant of the Lord
2. Key Chapter: 1—An overview of the book
3. Key Verses: 1:2-18
4. Key Characters: Isaiah and Hezekiah
5. Meaning of "Isaiah": Name of the man often called "the evangelical prophet"
6. Geography of Isaiah: Judah

E. SPECIAL CONSIDERATIONS ON ISAIAH

The primary thrust of Isaiah's message and ministry was toward the Southern Kingdom of Judah (1:1). Some elements of his message applied to Israel before 721 B.C. (the time of Israel's captivity). Also, there is a large section devoted to the foreign nations (13:1–27:13).

Isaiah began his ministry while there were still two kingdoms. During his ministry the Northern Kingdom was taken captive by the Assyrians. Isaiah was a contemporary of Micah in the South and Hosea in the North (and possibly Amos). He was a great help and support to the godly king Hezekiah.

A SUMMARY OF ISAIAH

A. PROPHECIES OF PUNISHMENT

Like the other prophets, Isaiah fearlessly pointed out the sins of God's people. In so many ways they had broken the covenant that they had made with God. Isaiah pointed out their rebelliousness and thanklessness, their religious formalism and hypocrisy (e.g., 1:2-15, 24-26). Judah at this time was not involved in the gross idolatry of Israel, but she was in grave spiritual danger because she was living by the externals of the law but with no real heart for God. Throughout the book, Judah is warned of coming judgment if she fails to turn back to the Lord (e.g., 1:24-25). At this point in history Judah could still repent and avoid coming judgment (1:16, 18-20). But God was clear that time was running out. He had worked with them, and they were still a fruitless nation (see the graphic illustration of the vineyard, 5:1-30).

One of Isaiah's greatest and unique contributions is his discussion of the coming Messiah and His kingdom. The Messiah would be born of a virgin[3] (7:14), would be God (9:6-7), would be of the line of David (11:1), would be Spirit-filled (11:2), would rule the nations (11:10-12), but would die as a sacrifice for the sins of all men (53:1-12). The Messiah's kingdom would be characterized by righteousness (11:4-5), peace (2:4), knowledge (2:3), the lifting of the curse (Gen. 3:17) from both plants and animals (11:6-8; 35:1-2), the removal of physical infirmities (35:5-6), and great joy (35:10). No doubt Isaiah and his contemporaries did not understand all about these matters as he spoke of "the sufferings of Christ, and the glories to follow" (1 Pet. 1:11).

B. PARENTHESIS FOR HISTORY

The book of Isaiah contains a historical parenthesis that discusses several events in the life of godly king Hezekiah (36:1–39:8). Chronologically, chapters 38 and 39 precede chapters 36 and 37. Isaiah evidently changed the historical order because of the structure of his book. In chapters 1-35 he speaks of the As-

---

3. Hobart Freeman, *An Introduction to the Old Testament Prophets* (Chicago: Moody, 1968), pp. 203-9.

syrians invading and being used by God as instruments of His judgment. So in chapters 36 and 37 he continues his train of thought, recording an Assyrian invasion and the reaction of King Hezekiah to that invasion. In chapters 40-66, Isaiah will sometimes refer to the Babylonians. Since chapters 38 and 39 speak of the emissaries from Babylon who came to visit Hezekiah when he was ill, these chapters are grouped together.

C. PROPHECIES OF PEACE

In chapters 40-66, Isaiah emphasizes several key matters. First, he gives great comfort to God's people by reminding them of some significant truths about their relationship to God or about the character of God. For example, God is a great and awesome God (40:12-26); He has a marvelous future for Israel (40:9-11); He claims Israel as His own (43:1); and He will redeem them (44:21-24). These great truths, along with others, were designed to encourage Israel even though there were pronouncements of judgment to come.

A second important emphasis in this section of Isaiah is his discussion of the ''servant of the Lord'' (41:8-10; 42:1-7; 42:19-35; 43:10; 44:1-2, 21; 48:20-22; 49:1-13; 50:4-11; 52:13–53:12). The identification of the ''servant of the Lord'' is crucial in Bible interpretation.[4] The term *servant* is used in three ways by Isaiah: first, in reference to all Israel (e.g. 41:8); second, in reference to a remnant within Israel (e.g. 43:10); and third, in reference to the coming Messiah (e.g. 52:13–53:12). The climax, of course, is the application to the Lord Jesus Christ, the greatest servant of the Lord. The word ''servant'' emphasizes the idea of work, and the greatest work of the ''servant of the Lord'' is the work of redemption (53:1-12 with Mark 10:45).

Isaiah rebuked the people for their sinfulness and warned them of coming judgment if there was no repentance. But he also revealed that there were marvelous days ahead for Israel, as the Messiah would redeem them and establish His kingdom on this earth.

4. Alfred Martin, *Isaiah: The Salvation of Jehovah* (Chicago: Moody, 1956), pp. 71-73, 84-100.

29

MICAH

INTRODUCTION TO MICAH

A. AUTHORSHIP AND DATE OF MICAH

Micah was from the village of Moresheth, which was located twenty miles southwest of Jerusalem. His name means "who is like Jehovah."

Micah dated his ministry by the reigns of three Southern kings —Jotham, Ahaz, and Hezekiah. A date of 735 B.C. is assigned to this book.

B. PURPOSE OF MICAH

Micah was sent by God to call Judah back to practical righteousness. He particularly denounced the leaders of Judah for oppressing the poor and for using their positions for their own personal gain. He brought a message of coming judgment on Judah. This foreboding message was coupled with a message of hope centered on the coming Messiah.

C. BASIC OUTLINE OF MICAH

    I. A Message of Punishment (chaps. 1-2)
   II. A Message of Promise (chaps. 3-5)
  III. A Message of Pardon (chaps. 6-7)

D. IMPORTANT DATA ABOUT MICAH

1. Key Word: Personal righteousness
2. Key Chapter: 3—An attack on Judah's leadership
3. Key Verses: 3:9-12; 5:1-2; 7:18-20
4. Key Characters: Micah and Judah's leaders
5. Meaning of "Micah": Named after the humble prophet whose message is written here
6. Geography of Micah: Judah

E. SPECIAL CONSIDERATIONS ON MICAH

Micah had a word for both the Northern and the Southern kingdoms (1:1), but it is clear from the content of the book itself that Micah's ministry centered almost exclusively in the south, in the city of Jerusalem.

The ministry of Micah was contemporary with at least two other writing prophets. In the Northern Kingdom, Hosea was illustrating and preaching the love of the Lord, while in the Southern Kingdom, Isaiah was preaching in the court. There is no doubt, therefore, that Micah played an important role in influencing Hezekiah for the Lord.

A SUMMARY OF MICAH

Speaking in the same situation as Isaiah did, Micah had much the same message. The messages of the two prophets are clearly similar (e.g., Micah 4:1-3 and 5:2-4 with Isa. 2:2-4 and 9:6-7). Some have suggested that whereas Isaiah ministered in the court, Micah focused his ministry on the common people.

Micah began his message on the subject of judgment. He noted that the city of Samaria would become nothing more than a pile of rocks because of their idolatrous practices (1:5-7). Judah would escape the judgment that would fall on the North (the Assyrian invasion). But Micah was grief-stricken because what was going to happen to Samaria would eventually happen to Judah (1:8-16). In 2:1-13 the reasons for Judah's judgment are given, which include numerous crimes against their fellow Israelites. Micah then foretold the coming judgment on the rulers (3:1-4), on the false prophets who led the nation away from God (3:5-8), and on the city and Temple (3:9-12). This last section was well-known a century later in the days of Jeremiah (cf. Jer. 26:16-19).

When the godly Jew heard all these messages of judgment, he might wonder about the covenant commitments of God. Micah, looking ahead to the latter days, declared that God would indeed fulfill His covenant promises (4:1-5) and bring the Messiah to them (5:2-15).

God then reminded the people of all the things that He had done for them. He had never failed them (6:1-5). What did God want from His people? He wanted obedience (6:6-8). Micah was deeply distressed by the absence of righteousness in Judah (7:1-6). He was assured, however, that this judgment would not wipe out Israel (7:7-20). The book concludes with yet another reminder of the true character of God (7:18-20 with Jonah 4:2 and Joel 2:13). God is not quick-tempered and hateful. He is loving and merciful. He does not delight in judging men.

The Prophetic Books
Group 2:

Prophecies During the
Single Kingdom

PROPHET	DATE	MESSAGE TO	RULERS
NAHUM	650	NINEVEH (Assyria)	MANASSEH
ZEPHANIAH	635	JUDAH	JOSIAH
JEREMIAH	626	JUDAH	JOSIAH–ZEDEKIAH
HABAKKUK	609	JUDAH	JEHOIAKIM

30

NAHUM

INTRODUCTION TO NAHUM

A. AUTHORSHIP AND DATE OF NAHUM

The author identifies himself as Nahum the Elkoshite. The name *Nahum* means "comforter." The designation *Elkoshite* has given rise to much speculation as to his origin. Some believe that Elkosh was a village in Assyria, others believe it was a town southwest of Jerusalem; still others hold that Capernaum ("the village of Nahum") in Galilee was his place of residence.

Although Nahum does not date his message by the reign of any king, the date of 650 B.C. is fairly certain. This is based on the content of the book. The message of Nahum declares judgment on Nineveh, which took place in 612 B.C. Therefore, the message had to be given before that date. Also, Nahum uses the illustration of the destruction of the Egyptian city of Thebes (or No-amon). The destruction of this city took place in 661 B.C. So the writing of this book took place somewhere between these two dates.

B. PURPOSE OF NAHUM

Nahum was called to deliver a message of judgment on a nation that previously had been given revelation of the true God. The Assyrians, with their capital at Nineveh, were the ones addressed in this message (1:1; 2:8; 3:18). They had heard about the true God through the ministry of Jonah. Since then they were sinning in spite of the light of revealed knowledge.

C. BASIC OUTLINE OF NAHUM

   I. The God of Judgment (chap. 1)
  II. The Execution of Judgment (chap. 2)
 III. The Vindication of Judgment (chap. 3)

D. IMPORTANT DATA ABOUT NAHUM

  1. Key Word: The vengeance of God
  2. Key Chapter: 2—The character of God
  3. Key Verses: 1:2-3, 7; 3:19
  4. Key Characters: The people of Nineveh
  5. Meaning of "Nahum": The name of the ministering prophet
  6. Geography of Nahum: Nineveh in Assyria

E. SPECIAL CONSIDERATIONS ON NAHUM

The prophet Jonah had given his message to Nineveh more than a century earlier (780 B.C.). Since that time, Assyria had brutally crushed the Northern Kingdom of Israel (721 B.C.). Nineveh was now ripe for judgment because of her sins—she was now sinning in the light of knowledge. Assyria (Nineveh) had destroyed Israel and caused Judah much grief. As part of the covenant with Abraham, God had sworn that He would "curse" those nations that "cursed" Israel (Gen. 12:3), and this prophecy illustrates the validity of that declaration.

A SUMMARY OF NAHUM

The theme of this prophecy is judgment on deserving Nineveh. Chapter 1 discusses the holy nature of the judge and also the deserving nature of the evildoers. (See below for a discussion of the character of God.) The Lord is good (1:7), and He is very patient with sinners (1:3), but the time comes when He will tolerate wickedness no longer. Chapter 2 describes the carrying out of the judgment on Nineveh—the preparation of the army, the siege, and finally the capture and destruction of the city. Chapter 3 gives the reasons judgment was deserved. Nineveh sowed brutality, immorality, and idolatry, and she reaped destruction. The message of irreversible judgment ends with the statement that Nineveh's "wound is incurable" (3:19). There is no hope for Assyria. Unlike Israel and Judah, who were in an unconditional covenant relationship with God, Nineveh had no future. The importance of the Abrahamic Covenant is illustrated here. The sins of Israel and Judah were essentially no different from the sins of Nineveh. But Israel and Judah were in a covenant relationship with the Lord. And though they experienced some terrible disciplines from the hand of God, the covenant (and their future) remained intact.

THE CHARACTER OF GOD

For many, the God of the Old Testament is angry, quick-tempered, and always judging or threatening judgment. Those people point out how unlike the Lord Jesus that God is. But such a view of God is absolutely false. The character of God, whether discovered in the Old or in the New Testament, is really the very opposite. God revealed much of His character to Moses, and the prophets built their preaching squarely on the Mosaic covenant.

Exodus 34:6-7 is a particularly important revelation of God's nature, and apparently the prophets were well aware of this declaration (e.g. Jonah 4:2; Joel 2:13; Mic. 7:18; Nah. 1:2). Up on the mountain of Sinai God revealed Himself as One who was "compassionate and gracious."

> "Compassion" . . . is related to the word for "womb," and aptly describes the "deep love" (usually of a "superior" for an "inferior") rooted in some "natural bond." . . . It can also imply that this compassion is being extended to one who does not deserve it. . . . "Gracious" . . . is a close synonym of "compassion."[1]

God also informed Moses that He was "slow to anger," which is the exact opposite of being quick-tempered. God was

1. John R. Kohlenberger, *Jonah and Nahum* (Chicago: Moody, 1984), p. 116.

very patient with sinful people. He still is, according to Romans 2:4. It is true that there are many words of coming judgment in the prophets, but it is essential to have the perspective of history. For example, God pronounced judgment on the totally corrupt world of Noah's day, but judgment did not come for 120 years. He told Abraham that the Canaanites were wicked and would be punished, but He waited four centuries to do so. Sinning in the light of full knowledge, Israel purposely entered into idolatry, but did not receive deserved punishment for 210 years; and likewise Judah, committing the sins of the Canaanites, did not experience the full discipline of God for well over a century. If God were not "slow to anger," no flesh would have survived the Old Testament era, and no man would be alive on the planet today.

God further told Moses that He was "abounding in lovingkindness and truth." The word *lovingkindness* is a marvelous word that

> combines the ideas of affection and absolute loyalty, thus is often rendered "loyal love" or "unfailing love." "Faithfulness" . . . by itself is often translated "truth" or "true" . . . These words appear as a pair more than a dozen times in Scripture (e.g. Gen. 32:10; Ps. 25:10; 26:3; 115:1; Isa. 16:5). Together they emphasize the dependability of God's love.[2]

As God continued to reveal Himself to Moses, He told Moses that He does remove the sins of men. But it was also true that those who did not repent of sin would be punished for that sin. And when He did punish sin, He would be perfectly just in doing so.

The Lord Jesus told His disciples that He revealed the true character of God (John 14:8-9). What is seen in the character of Christ is exactly the same as the character of the God of the Old Testament: One who is holy and righteous and yet is slow to anger and loyal in His love.

2. Ibid.

31

ZEPHANIAH

INTRODUCTION TO ZEPHANIAH

A. AUTHORSHIP AND DATE OF ZEPHANIAH

Zephaniah begins his book by tracing his lineage back to his great-grandfather, King Hezekiah. He was, therefore, of the royal line and a relative of the reigning king, Josiah.

He dates his prophecy during the days of King Josiah, which would place his time of ministry around 635 B.C.

B. PURPOSE OF ZEPHANIAH

Zephaniah was raised up by God to assist the godly King Josiah in his attempt to bring Judah back to God. The message of Zephaniah revealed, however, that it was too late for the nation of Judah. Judgment was coming, though some individuals could still be saved.

C. BASIC OUTLINE OF ZEPHANIAH

    I. Coming Judgment on National Judah (chaps. 1:1–2:3)
   II. Coming Judgment on Surrounding Nations (chap. 2:4-15)
  III. Coming Judgment on National Judah (chap. 3:1-8)
  IV. Coming Blessings on All Nations (chap. 3:9-20)

D. IMPORTANT DATA ABOUT ZEPHANIAH

   1. Key Word: The day of the Lord
   2. Key Chapter: 1—Judgment on Judah

3. Key Verses: 1:7-9; 2:3
4. Key Characters: The people of Judah
5. Meaning of "Zephaniah": Author's name applied as title to the prophecy
6. Geography of Zephaniah: Judah

E. SPECIAL CONSIDERATIONS ON ZEPHANIAH

In order to understand the ministry of Zephaniah and his two contemporaries, Habakkuk and Jeremiah, it is essential to understand the recent history of Judah. Zephaniah ministered in the days of a godly king. There was revival during the reign of Josiah. But far more important was the reign of an earlier king of Judah, Manasseh. Manasseh ruled longer than any other king of Israel (fifty-five years), and he was the most wicked king in all of Israel's history (cf. 2 Kings 21:1-18). Because of the incredible evil of Manasseh, God pronounced a coming irreversible judgment on Judah. Because of Manasseh, evil so thoroughly pervaded Judah that the nation would never turn back to God. Even the revival of Josiah was unable to reverse what Manasseh had done (cf. 2 Kings 21:10-12; 23:26-27; 24:3). The three prophets who spoke for God after the reign of Manasseh could not change the fate of the nation, but they could rescue people individually from the coming events.

King Josiah began his rule in 640 B.C., and his revival began ten years later in 630 B.C. Zephaniah may have played a part in this revival. It should be noted that the revival simply slowed Judah down as she rushed toward judgment.

A SUMMARY OF ZEPHANIAH

The theme of Zephaniah is the "Day of the Lord." This phrase occurs seven times in the book (a total of thirteen times if "that day" is included). Several things are said about the Day of the Lord—it is imminent, it will be a time of terror, it is coming as a judgment for sin, it will be accompanied by great convulsions in nature, it will fall upon all creation, and only a remnant will survive. These statements have both a near and a far view (the coming Babylonian invasion and the Tribulation period).

Idolatry and immorality are once again the causes given for this sure judgment of the Lord. If individuals would repent, they would be saved spiritually and perhaps spared the horrors of the judgment. Nationally it is too late. Judgment is also announced on the Gentiles.

As with the previous prophets, Zephaniah sounded a hopeful note as he spoke of the future restoration and blessing of Israel.

Godly King Josiah died in 609 B.C., and in just four years the Babylonians invaded and took Judah. Since Judah did not heed the warnings of the prophets of old, she now would experience the discipline of God.

32

JEREMIAH

INTRODUCTION TO JEREMIAH

A. AUTHORSHIP AND DATE OF JEREMIAH

Jeremiah was a priest, the son of Hilkiah. Jeremiah lived in the priestly city of Anathoth, which was located a few miles north of the city of Jerusalem.

Jeremiah's ministry lasted about fifty years and spanned the reigns of five kings. His ministry lasted for forty years in Judah (from 626 to 586 B.C.) and beyond that in Egypt, where he ministered to a rebellious remnant.

B. PURPOSE OF JEREMIAH

Jeremiah's messages were given to the kings, rulers, and the people of Judah. His message was heavy with irreversible judgment on Judah. This earned him the characterization of "weeping prophet." Most of the people despised and rejected his message.

C. BASIC OUTLINE OF JEREMIAH

    I. Introduction (chap.1)
   II. Prophecies Against Judah and Jerusalem (chaps. 2-45)
  III. Prophecies Against Various Gentile Nations (chaps. 46-51)
  IV. Supplement (chap. 52)

D. IMPORTANT DATA ABOUT JEREMIAH

1. Key Word: New Covenant
2. Key Chapter: 31—The revelation of the New Covenant
3. Key Verses: 1:4-10; 21:8-10; 31:31-34
4. Key Characters: Jeremiah and the contemporaneous kings of Judah
5. Meaning of "Jeremiah": The name of the stedfast prophet who wrote the book
6. Geography of Jeremiah: Judah and Egypt

E. SPECIAL CONSIDERATIONS ON JEREMIAH

The historical background to Jeremiah is found in 2 Kings 21-25. As with Zephaniah, Jeremiah's ministry was shaped by events that had taken place before he became a prophet of God. The total wickedness of Manasseh's reign had doomed the kingdom of Judah. Jeremiah did not have hopes of the nation's repenting. However, he did try to deliver some from judgment and to keep Jerusalem from suffering the horrible destruction that eventually took place.

Jeremiah prophesied during the time when there was a three-cornered struggle for world domination among Assyria, Egypt, and Babylon. Babylon emerged victorious and swept down on Jeremiah's land in 605 B.C.

A SUMMARY OF JEREMIAH

God informed Jeremiah that He had set him apart as a prophet even before his birth. Jeremiah felt he was too young to have such a ministry but was assured that the Lord was with him and would speak through him (1:4-19).

Over the forty years of his ministry to Judah, the message of Jeremiah was essentially the same. It was a call for individuals to repent and for the nation to submit to the Babylonians (and thus to God), avoiding needless destruction and agony (cf. Jer. 21:1-9; and 27:6-15 for a good summary of Jeremiah's ministry and message). He used a variety of illustrations and object lessons to get his point across: for example, the harlotry of Israel and Judah,

3:6–6:30; the marred belt and broken jars, 13:1-27; and the potter's house message, 18:1–20:18. He warned them not to trust in the presence of the Temple as some sort of lucky charm to keep away judgment (7:1-11). Evidently many Jews believed that God would never allow "His house" to be destroyed by Gentiles, so there was a feeling of security. Like the rest of the prophets, Jeremiah rebuked Judah for willful violations of their "constitution," thus breaking the covenant that they made with God at Mount Sinai (e.g. 11:1-10; 31:31-32).

Even though his message was true, and eventually verified by the events that took place, Jeremiah was rebuked, rejected, and persecuted for his message (e.g. 26:10-15; 32:1-5). He was viewed as a traitor because of his insistence that Judah submit to the Babylonians and was treated badly because he would not compromise his message of coming judgment.

One of Jeremiah's main contributions was his message on the New Covenant (31:31-34). The New Covenant is a sub-covenant of the Abrahamic Covenant (see chart "God's Covenants with Israel," p. 41). The New Covenant is largely occupied with the issue of salvation and is based on the cross. It was God's declared purpose to save His people Israel from their sins. The New Testament is clear that animal sacrifices could only cover ("atone") sin, but could not take away sin (e.g. Heb. 9:11-15, 24-28; 10:4-14). Only the blood of Christ can remove sin and make it possible for sinful men (Israelite or Gentile) to fellowship with a holy God. Jesus spoke of His death as the basis of the New Covenant (Luke 22:20). In Jeremiah 31, Israel and Judah are the subjects of God's salvation, whereas the New Covenant is applied to Gentiles in the church age (Heb. 8:8-13; 2 Cor. 3:1-18). Salvation, based on the New Covenant, has come to the Gentiles and in the future will come to the nation of Israel (cf. Rom. 11:25-27; Dan. 9:24).

The book of Jeremiah gives us most of our information about those days immediately after the destruction of Jerusalem in 586 B.C. (40:1–45:5). And it gives a valuable supplement to 2 Kings 25 in recording the events involved with the fall and destruction of Jerusalem at the hands of the Babylonians.

THE LAST DAYS OF THE KINGDOM OF JUDAH

JUDEAN KINGS		PROPHETS	BABYLONIAN INVASIONS
MANASSEH	- 697-642	NAHUM	
AMON	- 642-640		
JOSIAH	- 640-609	ZEPHANIAH JEREMIAH	
JEHOAHAZ	- 609-598	HABAKKUK JEREMIAH DANIEL	1st (605) captives taken, including Daniel
JEHOIACHIN	- 598-597	JEREMIAH EZEKIEL	2d (597) captives taken, including Ezekiel
ZEDEKIAH	- 597-586	JEREMIAH	3d (586) Jerusalem destroyed

33

HABAKKUK

INTRODUCTION TO HABAKKUK

A. AUTHORSHIP AND DATE OF HABAKKUK

The prophet does not identify himself either by family lineage or even place of residence. He does refer to himself as a prophet (1:1), and it seems that he was recognized as such since his message would bring a response (2:2). Also the two musical notations might suggest that he was a member of the Temple choir and thus a Levite (3:1, 19).

A date of 609 B.C. is assigned to the book. Although Habakkuk gives no specific king's reign, the reference to the Chaldeans (Babylonians) indicates that the time of his ministry was probably shortly before the Babylonian invasion of Palestine. It would place the prophecy in the reign of Jehoiakim, shortly after the death of godly King Josiah.[1]

B. PURPOSE OF HABAKKUK

Habakkuk's message weighs the important question how God's pateince with sin can be related to His holiness. The dialogue between the prophet and God gives insight into this matter for all time. The sinful, law-breaking people of Judah were a concern to Habakkuk. His distress is registered in his conversation with the Lord.

1. Cyril Barber, *Habakkuk and Zephaniah* (Chicago: Moody, 1985), p. 17.

C. BASIC OUTLINE OF HABAKKUK

    I. Habakkuk and God: The First Dialogue (chap. 1:1-11)
    II. Habakkuk and God: The Second Dialogue (chaps. 1:12–2:20)
    III. Habakkuk and God: Praise and Prayer (chap. 3:1-19)

D. IMPORTANT DATA ABOUT HABAKKUK

    1. Key Word: The holiness of God
    2. Key Chapter: 1—The revelation of the issue of sin and holiness
    3. Key Verses: 1:2, 12; 2:4; 3:2
    4. Key Character: Habakkuk
    5. Meaning of "Habakkuk": Named after the prophet whose prophecy is written
    6. Geography of Habakkuk: Judah

E. SPECIAL CONSIDERATIONS ON HABAKKUK

If the date of 609 B.C. is accurate, Judah was only four years away from the Babylonian invasion. The Babylonian empire was on the rise, having taken the Assyrian capital of Nineveh, thus fulfilling the prophecy of Nahum. In 605 B.C., the Babylonians would defeat the Egyptians and Assyrians at the battle of Carchemish. From there they would sweep down and take Jerusalem. Time was just about up for the Southern Kingdom of Judah. It needs to be recalled that the reign of the wicked Manasseh had started Judah down the road to captivity. (See also p. 207, "Special Considerations on Zephaniah.")

A SUMMARY OF HABAKKUK

Habakkuk was deeply concerned about the holiness of God. He complained that wickedness was everywhere, but God did nothing about it (1:2-4). How could God allow such lawlessness and violence? God responded by telling Habakkuk that He was aware of what was happening and was about to act. He was going to bring the Chaldeans (Babylonians) down on Israel, and they would be His rod of discipline for sinful Judah (1:5-11). (See the map, p. 216.)

Habakkuk could not believe that God would do such a thing. His point was that the Chaldeans were more wicked than Judah (1:12-17). God's second response explained to the prophet that He was aware of the sins of the Chaldeans, and they would be judged also (2:2-20).

The final part of the book records the prayer and the praise of Habakkuk. He was completely overwhelmed by this word of judgment, and prayed that God would "in wrath remember mercy" (3:2, 16). He also expressed his personal faith in the Lord and the works of the Lord (3:17-19). Habakkuk was one of the righteous who would live by his faith (2:4).

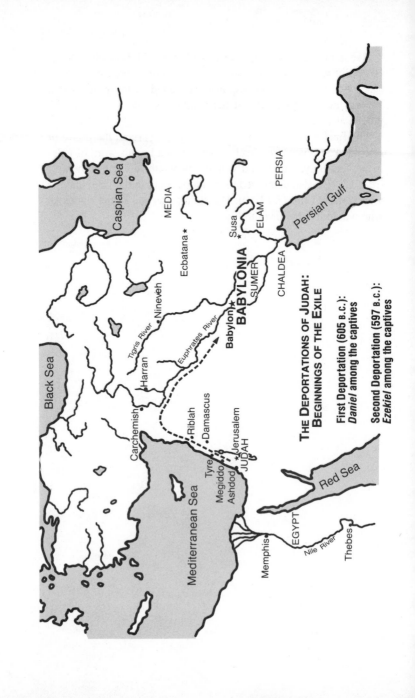

THE DEPORTATIONS OF JUDAH:
BEGINNINGS OF THE EXILE

First Deportation (605 B.C.):
Daniel among the captives

Second Deportation (597 B.C.):
Ezekiel among the captives

The Prophetic Books
Group 3:

Prophecies During the Exile

PROPHET	DATE	MESSAGE TO	RULERS
DANIEL	605	EXILES AND GENTILES IN BABYLON	NEBUCHADNEZZAR THROUGH CYRUS II
EZEKIEL	593	REMNANT IN JUDAH AND IN BABYLON	NEBUCHADNEZZAR

34

DANIEL

Introduction to Daniel

A. AUTHORSHIP AND DATE OF DANIEL

The book of Daniel was written by a Jewish captive, Daniel, who lived in Babylon from 605 to at least 536 B.C. This book probably was written toward the end of this time period.

Liberal critics have disputed the authorship and date of the book of Daniel, claiming that it was written by an anonymous author about 167 B.C. They have held to their position tenaciously because of a basic bias against miracles and prophecy, and their claim that the book has overwhelming linguistic and historical problems. But their contentions have been fully answered by conservative scholars.[1] Archaeological findings (especially those of the "Dead Sea Scrolls") support conservative scholars and point to a date much earlier than 167 B.C.[2] And the objections raised by liberal critics have been carefully analyzed.[3]

The book itself presents Daniel as the author (e.g. 7:2; 8:1; 9:2; 12:4). The very important testimony of the Lord Jesus Christ is that this book was written by "Daniel, the Prophet" (Matt. 24:15). The historicity of Daniel is found in his contemporary Ezekiel, who speaks of him several times (Ezek. 14:14, 20; 28:3).

1. John F. Walvoord, *Daniel: The Key to Prophetic Revelation* (Chicago: Moody, 1971), pp. 16-27.
2. Bruce Waltke, "The Date of the Book of Daniel," *Bibliotheca Sacra* 133 (October-December, 1976): 319-29.
3. K. A. Kitchen, *Notes on Some Problems in the Book of Daniel* (London: Tyndale, 1965), pp. 9-31.

The book claims to come out of the era of Babylon and Medo-Persia. Either these claims are true, or the whole book is fraudulent (1:1; 2:1; 7:1; 8:1; 9:1; 10:1).

B. PURPOSE OF DANIEL

Since Daniel lived and ministered in the city of Babylon, it must be assumed that his primary audience was the Jews of the captivity. But the contents of the book indicate that all of Israel needed to know and understand its prophecy. The book would have encouraged Israel by revealing that God was not through with them as a nation. God did have an order of events for the future, and Israel had a significant place in this program.

C. BASIC OUTLINE OF DANIEL

    I. The Personal History of the Prophet (chap. 1)
   II. The Prophetic History of the Gentiles (chaps. 2-7)
  III. The Prophetic History of Israel (chaps. 8-12)

D. IMPORTANT DATA ABOUT DANIEL

   1. Key Word: Times of the Gentiles
   2. Key Chapter: 2—Outline of the times of the Gentiles
   3. Key Verses: 1:8; 2:36-45; 9:24-27
   4. Key Characters: Daniel, Nebuchadnezzar, Belshazzar, and Darius
   5. Meaning of "Daniel": Named after the author-prophet who is also the central figure in the story line of the book
   6. Geography of Daniel: Judah and Babylon

E. SPECIAL CONSIDERATIONS ON DANIEL

Nebuchadnezzar and the armies of Babylon came to Jerusalem the first time in 605 B.C. Daniel, who was about fifteen years old at the time, was taken with a select group of captives to Babylon. He lived there for the rest of his life, perhaps until 530 B.C. For the first twenty years of his captivity Judah existed as a nation. Then Jerusalem was destroyed in 586 B.C., thus raising the question about Israel's future—a question answered in the book.

A SUMMARY OF DANIEL

The theme of Daniel is "the times of the Gentiles." This term speaks of the period of time from 605 B.C. to the second coming of Jesus Christ—that time when the nation of Israel is under the domination of the Gentile nations. Daniel gives the basic outline of that time—a period that continues right to the present.

Daniel gives Bible students a prophetic framework that is important in understanding Bible prophecy. But this book also is significant because it gives a great deal of information about Daniel himself, a man who honored God and was in turn "highly esteemed" by God (1 Sam. 2:30; Dan. 9:23; 10:11, 19). The quality of Daniel's life in his devotion to the Lord, to the Scriptures, and to serving the Lord gives a high standard for spiritual excellence.

The book begins with a brief account of Daniel's life, which explains how a young Jewish boy ended up in the court of the pagan Babylonians. This captivity of the treasures and young men of Judah by the Babylonians was a fulfillment of prophecy (cf. Isa. 39:5-7). Daniel had numerous natural attributes that made him special (1:3-4), but it was his devotion to his God that made him unique (e.g. 1:8).

Chapter 2 is the key to the book. It is the record of a dream that Nebuchadnezzar the king had one night. In this dream, which Daniel was able to interpret, God outlined the "times of the Gentiles." Four nations (Babylon, Medo-Persia, Greece, and Rome) would come upon the scene of world history before God would establish His great kingdom. The fourth kingdom (Rome) would have two phases to it, the second of which would be in the last days of human history. In the days of Rome, phase two (which will be the kingdom of the Antichrist in the Tribulation period), the Son of Man (Christ) will establish His kingdom. (See the chart below.) This basic outline of history is detailed in the chapters of Daniel that follow chapter 2. The other chapters focus on one or more of these four key empires, using a variety of imagery. Chapter 9 is also quite important because it records the "seventy weeks" prophecy. In this prophecy, God declares that He will accomplish a number of things in the life of the nation of Israel.

These matters include the redemption and the restoration of Israel. The basis for what God said He would do is the cross of Jesus Christ, but the actual fulfillment has yet to take place. The book of Daniel is clear that God is the covenant-keeping God.

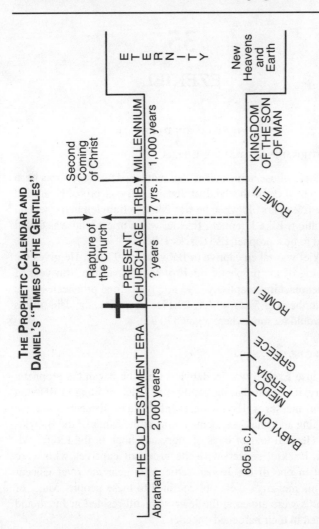

THE PROPHETIC CALENDAR AND DANIEL'S "TIMES OF THE GENTILES"

35

EZEKIEL

A. AUTHORSHIP AND DATE OF EZEKIEL

Ezekiel, whose name means "strengthened by God," was born about 622 B.C. in the land of Judah. He was probably around twenty-five years old when he was taken to Babylon in the second deportation. Like Jeremiah, Ezekiel was a priest who was called by God to be a prophet also (Ezek. 1:1-3).

Ezekiel was taken captive to Babylon in 597 B.C. He gives the beginning of his prophetic ministry as being in the fifth year of King Jehoiachim's captivity (593 B.C.). His final prophecies were given in the year 570 B.C. (cf. 29:17). Therefore, the date of this book would be somewhere about 570 B.C.

B. PURPOSE OF EZEKIEL

Because Ezekiel was in Babylon when he began his prophetic ministry, it is clear that the captives of Judah residing in Babylon heard his messages. His messages informed his listeners about the impending and final judgment coming at the hands of the Babylonians. He also told of days of glory and hope in the future. Although Ezekiel settled with the group of captives who were located in one of the Jewish settlements near the river Chebar (1:1), his messages were not confined to these people. Many of his words were aimed at the Jews who still resided in Judah and remained in their hardened unbelief.

C. BASIC OUTLINE OF EZEKIEL

I. Introduction: Ezekiel's Commission (chaps. 1-3)
II. Prophecies of Judgment on Judah (chaps. 4-24)
III. Prophecies of Judgment on Gentiles (chaps. 25-32)
IV. Prophecies of Restoration for Israel (chaps. 33-39)
V. Prophecies of Reestablishment for Israel (chaps. 40-48)

D. IMPORTANT DATA ABOUT EZEKIEL

1. Key Word: Coming judgment and restoration
2. Key Chapter: 36—Restoration after judgment
3. Key Verses: 2:1-7; 36:16-28
4. Key Characters: Judeans in Judah and Babylon
5. Meaning of "Ezekiel": Named after its chief person and author
6. Geography of Ezekiel: Judah and Babylon

E. SPECIAL CONSIDERATIONS ON EZEKIEL

Ezekiel lived in Babylon during those final days of the Southern Kingdom of Judah. It is important to note that chapters 1-24 of Ezekiel were given before the final overthrow and destruction of Jerusalem in 586 B.C. These chapters speak of the sin and unbelief of Judah and are very stern pronouncements. But after the fall of Jerusalem in 586 B.C., Ezekiel's messages change dramatically to prophecies of hope and consolation (chaps. 33-48). The ministry of Ezekiel pivots on that key historical event of the fall of Jerusalem.

A SUMMARY OF EZEKIEL

When God called Ezekiel to minister as His prophet (2:1–3:21), He told Ezekiel he was being sent to a stubborn, hardened, rebellious nation. His ministry would not be well received when he spoke of judgment. But Ezekiel was to view himself as a watchman. A watchman is obligated to do one basic thing, and that is to sound the alarm. He is not responsible for the response to the alarm.

One of the unique aspects to Ezekiel's ministry was the large number of visual aids he used in his preaching. This attracted the interest of people who had grown tired of listening to the prophets of God. But the message (with or without visual aids) was the same—judgment was coming on Judah because of her sin. The people in captivity knew full well that judgment had come. But the Jews living in Judah assumed that it was just the wicked Jews whom God had shipped to Babylon. They refused to acknowledge that they were sinful covenant breakers. (In fact, both Jeremiah and Ezekiel suggest that God preserved the righteous of Judah from the times of terrible judgment by taking them to Babylon. The wicked were left in Judah!)

Following his messages of judgment on Judah, and after his words of judgment on the Gentile nations, Ezekiel looks ahead to the glorious days of restoration. Israel has a great future. Ezekiel speaks of a twofold restoration of Israel. First, Israel will be restored politically and geographically. God Himself will bring scattered Israel back to the land of the covenant in the "latter days" (34:11-16, 25-30; 37:24-28; 38:8, 16; 39:25-29). Following this physical restoration, there will be a spiritual restoration of Israel (36:25-27; 37:14, 23-28; 39:22). The order of restoration is clear—first physical and then spiritual. As He did throughout their history, God will use Gentile nations to accomplish His purposes in the life of Israel (36:19-24; 38:1–39:22). When the events of the last days are over, God will have accomplished His purposes to save Israel and bring them under the New Covenant (cf. Dan. 9:24; Rom. 11:25-27; Jer. 31:31).

Ezekiel 40-48 contains information about the millennial Temple and life in the kingdom age. There is much detail here, but basically it is teaching that Messiah will be worshiped in the capital of the kingdom, Jerusalem. The few blood sacrifices that are mentioned (e.g. 40:38-44) are apparently memorial in nature. Only the blood of Christ can take away sin, and the Scriptures are clear that no more need for sacrifice exists now (cf. Heb. 10:10-14). These sacrifices are evidently a graphic reminder (in a near perfect age) of the terrible results of sin and of the great sacrifice of Christ on the cross.

Both prophets of the exile, Daniel and Ezekiel, give hope to downtrodden Israel that they have a glorious future ahead of them because of their covenant-keeping God.

The exile lasted for seventy years (Jer. 25:11-12; 29:10; 2 Chron. 36:20-21). They were difficult and discouraging years for God's people. Those years raised many questions about their future and about the covenant that had been made with the Lord. But those years of captivity were also valuable years for Israel. They learned that God is holy and that sin will eventually be punished. Particularly they were, for the most part, cured of the sin of idolatry. This, coupled with a new love for the Scriptures, brought God's people out of the exile period a stronger nation spiritually.

When the years of captivity were over, God allowed His people to return to the land of the covenant and begin life there again. The last three prophets in the Old Testament—Haggai, Zechariah, and Malachi—ministered in Judah after the exile.

The Prophetic Books
Group 4:

Prophecies After the Exile

PROPHET	DATE	MESSAGE TO	RULERS
HAGGAI	520	JEWS OF THE FIRST RETURN	GOVERNOR: ZERUBBABEL
ZECHARIAH	520	JEWS OF THE FIRST RETURN	GOVERNOR: ZERUBBABEL
MALACHI	430	JEWS IN THE LAND OF ISRAEL	GOVERNOR: NEHEMIAH

36

HAGGAI

A. AUTHORSHIP AND DATE OF HAGGAI

Haggai was the first post-exilic prophet to minister to the returned remnant of Israel. He evidently was part of the first group that returned to Judah from Babylon. He is identified as a prophet (1:1; Ezra 5:1; 6:14) and is linked closely to the prophet Zechariah.

There is no question as to the date of his messages, since he carefully dates them (1:1, 15; 2:1, 10, 18, 20). The year is 520 B.C., about fifteen years after they returned to Judah.

B. PURPOSE OF HAGGAI

Haggai was raised up by God to call the people of God back to divine priorities. Haggai spoke to the leaders and to the people who had returned from Babylon to begin a new life in Judah. The purposes of his ministry were to remind the people of their primary task of rebuilding the Temple and to warn them of the ongoing consequences of disobedience.

C. BASIC OUTLINE OF HAGGAI

    I. The Lord's Warning to His People (chap. 1:1-11)
   II. The People's Reaction to God's Warning (chap. 1:l2-15)
  III. The Lord's Response to His People (chap. 2:1-23)

D. IMPORTANT DATA ABOUT HAGGAI

1. Key Word: Consider your ways
2. Key Chapter: 1—The issue of wrong priorities
3. Key Verses: 1:2-8, 12; 2:4
4. Key Characters: Haggai, Zerubbabel, and Joshua the high priest
5. Meaning of "Haggai": Named after the author
6. Geography of Haggai: Judah

E. SPECIAL CONSIDERATIONS ON HAGGAI

The people of Israel had been given the opportunity by Cyrus, king of Persia, to return to their own land and to rebuild the Temple of the Lord in Jerusalem (Ezra 1:1-4). Some 50,000 people had responded to the invitation of Cyrus and had gone home. The rebuilding project was hampered by enemies of Israel and soon came to a complete halt. It was in this setting that Haggai preached to the people. Several key dates set the background for the ministries of both Haggai and Zechariah.

538 - Cyrus issued a decree allowing the people to return.

536 - Upon the people's return, an altar for sacrifice was built and the work of rebuilding the Temple begun.

535 - Threats and a legal suit caused the people to stop work on the Temple. Only the foundation had been laid.

520 - After fifteen years of inactivity on the Temple, the prophet Haggai preached a message of rebuke.

516 - Four years later the Temple has been rebuilt.

(See chart "The Chronology After the Exile," p. 230.)

A SUMMARY OF HAGGAI

For fifteen years the returned exiles had lived in the land without working on the Temple. The threats of their enemies and the legal injunctions against building seemed to make their inactivity legitimate. But God viewed their reasons as merely excuses. Their problem was that of misplaced priorities. Instead of doing the will of God, the people were trying to live the "good life" (1:4). But

THE CHRONOLOGY AFTER THE EXILE

PERSIAN KINGS	PROPHETS	THE RETURNS TO JUDAH	SCRIP- TURE
Cyrus 539-530	Haggai and Zechariah	First return under Zerubbabel	Ezra 1-6
Cambyses 530-521	—	—	—
Darius I 521-486	—	—	—
Xerxes 486-465 (Ahasuerus)	(Story of Esther)	—	Esther
Artaxerxes 465-423		Second return under Ezra	Ezra 7-10
Malachi		Third return under Nehemiah	Nehemiah 1-6

with all of their efforts to be happy and satisfied, they were discontent (1:6). God would not allow them to be content while living in the condition of disobedience (1:9-11). When Haggai confronted the leaders and the people with the reality of the situation, they immediately responded in fear and obedience (1:12). God then informed the people that He was no longer against them but was with them (cf. 1:13; 2:4, 19). They went back to work on the Temple, and God took care of the threats and the lawsuits (cf. Ezra 5, 6). God assured them that even though their Temple did not have the splendor of Solomon's Temple, He would still dwell with them. And He told them that Israel did indeed have a great future (2:20-23).

37

ZECHARIAH

INTRODUCTION TO ZECHARIAH

A. AUTHORSHIP AND DATE OF ZECHARIAH

Zechariah was careful to identify himself by his family line (1:1). He was the "son of Berechiah, the son of Iddo." This information is helpful since Nehemiah 12:4, 16 reveals that Iddo was one of the priests that returned from Babylon to Judah. So Zechariah was another priest who was called to the prophetic office.

Ezra 5:1 and 6:14 place Zechariah alongside Haggai with the first group of returned exiles. Zechariah also dated his ministry carefully (1:1; 7:1). This would put the messages of Zechariah in the time frame of 520-518 B.C.

B. PURPOSE OF ZECHARIAH

Zechariah's prophecies were given to the people who had returned from Babylon. These people had already responded to Haggai's message and had resumed the construction of the Temple. Now Zechariah ministered encouragment to them (cf. Ezra 5:2). The prophet told of God's abundant future blessings on the nation. This filled the people with courage and hope.

C. BASIC OUTLINE OF ZECHARIAH

    I. Introduction (chap. 1:1-6)
    II. The Night Visions of Zechariah (chaps. 1:7–6:8)
    III. The Four Messages of Zechariah (chaps. 7:1–8:23)
    IV. The Two Burdens of Zechariah (chaps. 9:1–14:21)

D. IMPORTANT DATA ABOUT ZECHARIAH

1. Key Word: The coming Messiah
2. Key Chapter: 14—Messiah's advent
3. Key Verses: 12:10; 14:1-4
4. Key Characters: Zechariah and the people of Israel
5. Meaning of "Zechariah": Named for the prophet
6. Geography of Zechariah: Judah

E. SPECIAL CONSIDERATIONS ON ZECHARIAH

Zechariah began his ministry about two months after Haggai spoke to the people about their neglect of the Temple.

A SUMMARY OF ZECHARIAH

Zechariah began his prophecy with a short history lesson. He reminded Israel that their forefathers had paid a high price for their sin. They had disobeyed the law, rejected the reproof of the prophets, and had suffered in exile as a result. If Israel wanted to experience the blessing of the Lord, she must turn from sin to the Lord (1:2-7).

The first major section of Zechariah's prophecy is his "night visions." He received all eight of these visions in one night, and they contain a great variety of information about Israel's future. The visions are highly symbolic. Zechariah needed help from an interpreting angel in order to come to some understanding of the visions. The subject matter of the visions is diverse. For example, in the first vision Israel's place of subjection under the Gentile nations is in view, but also communicated is the assurance that God will someday end Gentile domination (1:7-17). In the fourth vision Zechariah saw Joshua the high priest in filthy garments standing before the Lord (3:1-10). Joshua was representing the nation of Israel in its high priestly status. But Israel was filthy with her sin. How can God do anything for such a sinful, back-slidden people? The answer given in this vision is that someday God will step in and give His people clean robes (righteousness) and reestablish them as a priestly nation (the "turban" representing that role). In the final night vision, four war chariots are seen.

They seem to represent end time judgments (similar to Rev. 6:1-8). This section ends with the crowning of Joshua the high priest, symbolic of what will occur in the Millennium (6:10-15) when the Messiah will be crowned as the king.

The second section is messages that came out of questions or events in Zechariah's day. For example, in the first message (7:1-7), Zechariah was asked by fellow Jews if they should continue to fast in the fifth month. Jerusalem had fallen in the fifth month, and it had become customary to fast in remembrance of that event. The response of Zechariah was rather harsh. He attacked their self-righteousness and told them to mourn over the sin that caused the events and not the events themselves.

Zechariah's two burdens compose the next part of the book. Generally the first burden focuses on the first advent of the Messiah (e.g. 9:9), and the second burden emphasizes the second advent (e.g. 14:3-8).

The scope of subject matter makes Zechariah fit the pattern of the "major prophets." He speaks of the times of the Gentiles, the period of the great Tribulation, the coming of Israel's Messiah, and the glorious days of the kingdom. To a people recently returned from captivity, who were powerless, these messages were messages of hope. God was not finished with them. They still had a future.

38

MALACHI

A. AUTHORSHIP AND DATE OF MALACHI

The author simply calls himself Malachi, with no further information (1:1). The name Malachi means "my messenger," and this has caused some to believe that it is not a proper name, but simply a title for the prophecy. But most likely it is a proper name, as it would be most unusual for this book to be preserved without giving the name of the author. Malachi was the last of the prophets sent to the remnant at Jerusalem. Tradition has it that he was a member of the Great Synagogue organized by Nehemiah.

In contrast to Haggai and Zechariah, Malachi does not give the date of his prophecy. But certain internal evidence helps us arrive at a date of about 430 B.C. Malachi probably ministered at the same time as Nehemiah. They addressed similar issues. For example, the Temple was completed but being misused (Mal. 1:7-10 with Neh. 3:10); there was corruption in the priesthood (Mal. 1:7–2:9 with Neh. 13:1-9); there was some intermarriage with the heathen (Mal. 2:11-16 with Neh. 13:23-28); and there was neglect of the offerings of God (Mal. 3:8-12 with Neh. 13:10-13). Malachi's ministry would fit very well into the time just after Nehemiah or perhaps into the time when Nehemiah was absent for a short time from Jerusalem (cf. Neh. 13:6).

B. PURPOSE OF MALACHI

Malachi spoke to the priests, leaders, and people who lived in Jerusalem. Although they were his primary concern, there was probably a larger circle of people who were influenced by his message. A proper view of God was Malachi's great burden. If the people took God seriously, then their sinful ways would be corrected.

C. BASIC OUTLINE OF MALACHI

   I. The Declaration of God's Love (chap. 1:1-5)
  II. The Disapproval of Unfaithful Priests (chap. 1:6–2:9)
 III. The Denunciation of Backslidden People (chap. 2:10–4:3)
 IV. The Declaration of Final Warning (chap. 4:4-6)

D. IMPORTANT DATA ABOUT MALACHI

1. Key Word: The fear of the Lord
2. Key Chapter: 1—Exposure of irreverence
3. Key Verses: 1:6-13
4. Key Characters: The priests and people of Judah
5. Meaning of "Malachi": Derived from the author-prophet
6. Geography of Malachi: Judah

E. SPECIAL CONSIDERATIONS ON

The book was written in post-exilic times when Israel had been back in her land for about one hundred years. The people of Haggai's day and the people of Malachi's day were quite different spiritually. Haggai ministered to people who were far more responsive to the things of the Lord. During the one hundred years Israel had once again started to backslide. Outwardly Israel seemed to be doing well spiritually, but inwardly she was drifting away from her spiritual moorings. Malachi came as the last voice from God before the centuries of silence. His rebukes were specific and pointed.

A Summary of Malachi

Malachi's message began with the word "the oracle [burden] of the word of the Lord" (1:1). This title immediately reveals that this is a burdensome message and not a message of comfort. God did remind Israel that He loved them, and this love was seen in that He selected Israel for Himself. And it is seen in that He preserves Israel (1:1-5).

As the message continues, Malachi points out numerous sins that the priests and the people have become guilty of. For example, they bring blemished offerings to God (1:6-8 with Deut. 15:21); refuse to pay their tithe (3:8-10); and divorce their Jewish wives to marry foreigners (2:10-16). Other sins are also mentioned. But the key to understanding Malachi's message is to see the underlying cause for Israel's sinfulness. Israel's various sins were symptomatic of the fact that Israel had lost her fear of God. She no longer truly reverenced the Lord. The fear of the Lord involved an awe of the Lord and a commitment to Him. It included obedience, love, and loyalty.[1] This lack of fear was the key to her sinful attitudes and actions. *Fear* is used seven times in the book (1:6; 2:5; 3:5; 4:2).

Before Malachi concludes his message, he informs Israel that God will be sending His messenger to prepare for the coming of Messiah (cf. 3:1-3; 4:4-6). With the promise of a voice who would yet be heard, the Old Testament closes, and the voice of God becomes silent for four hundred years. The silence would be broken when the angel Gabriel would announce to an aged priest that he would be the father of a son—a son who would fulfill the promise of Malachi (cf. Luke 1:13-16).

1. Walter Kaiser Jr., *Toward an Old Testament Theology* (Grand Rapids: Zondervan, 1978), pp. 168-70.

Notes on Special Topics

Note A:

THE MOSAIC AUTHORSHIP
OF THE PENTATEUCH

For well over one hundred years there has been a debate on the authorship of the Pentateuch. Conservative scholars have consistently affirmed that Moses wrote it, whereas liberal scholars have denied Mosaic authorship.

Those who deny the Mosaic authorship of the Pentateuch today basically build their view on the theories of Jean Astruc (an eighteenth-century French writer) and Julius Wellhausen (a nineteenth-century liberal German theologian). Those who deny Mosaic authorship hold to the "documentary hypothesis" (known also as the JEDP Theory). This theory maintains that the Pentateuch was composed from a number of documents. These documents actually were written many centuries after the time of Moses, and Moses had nothing to do with their composition. His name was simply attached to them to give them greater value and acceptance. Some who held this theory declared that Moses could not have written the Pentateuch since he could not write, assuming that writing was not a part of life in the times of Moses. Since Wellhausen's day, however, archaeological finds have totally debunked this idea, showing that writing and literary interests were very much a part of life in Egypt and elsewhere in the ancient near east fifteen hundred years before the days of Moses.[1]

1. Howard Vos, *Genesis* (Chicago: Moody, 1982), pp. 15-16; John J. Davis, *Moses and the Gods of Egypt* (Winona Lake: BMH, 1971), p. 56.

Liberal scholars teach that the documents were actually written between 850 and 500 B.C. At that time, some unknown man (or men) known as a redactor, then put these documents together in the order and arrangement of our Pentateuch. These various documents were known by the letters JEDP.

> J represented the document composed by the school of writers who preferred the Divine name Jehovah, E the writers preferring Elohim, D the writer of the Book of Deuteronomy, and P the writer of those sections of the Pentateuch having to do especially with priestly liturgy, sacrifice, and genealogical and chronological sections.[2]

This "documentary hypothesis" has been effectively answered by conservative scholars. They have pointed out not only the basic invalidity of the major points of the theory and the evolutionary philosophy behind the theory, but also the terrible bias against the supernatural nature of the Scriptures.[3]

Several lines of evidence support the Mosaic authorship of the Pentateuch. First, the Pentateuch itself claims that Moses wrote many important parts (Ex. 17:14; 24:4; 34:27; Lev. 1:1; 4:1; 6:1, 8; Num. 1:1, 19; 33:2; Deut. 1:1; 17:18; 31:9, 24-26). Second, other Old Testament books declare that Moses wrote the Pentateuch (e.g., Josh. 1:7-8; 8:31-34; 22:5; 1 Kings 2:3; 2 Chron. 23:18; 34:14; Dan. 9:11, 13; Ezra 3:2; Neh. 8:1; 13:1-3). Third, Christ believed that Moses wrote the first five books of the Old Testament. The Lord Jesus spoke of certain truths that Moses wrote or spoke of the Old Testament scriptures in terms as "Moses and the prophets" and "Moses, the Psalms and the prophets" (Matt. 8:4; 19:7-8; Mark 7:10; 12:26; Luke 16:29, 31; 24:44; John 1:45; 5:46; 7:19). Fourth, the writers of the New Testament attribute the Pentateuch to Moses (Acts 3:22; 26:22; 28:23; Rom. 10:5, 19). Fifth, the testimony of tradition has been unanimous in

2. Eugene Merrill, *An Historical Survey of the Old Testament* (Grand Rapids: Baker, 1980), p. 15.
3. Merrill F. Unger, *Introductory Guide to the Old Testament* (Grand Rapids: Zondervan, 1956); Oswald T. Allis, *The Five Books of Moses* (Philadelphia: Presbyterian and Reformed, 1949); E. J. Young, *An Introduction to the Old Testament* (Grand Rapids: Eerdmans, 1969).

support of Mosaic authorship. Literature from the intertestamental period, from the early church, and from the church of later centuries have agreed on Moses as the writer of Genesis-Deuteronomy. Only recently has there been an unfounded challenge to Mosaic authorship by liberal critics.

It should be noted that the Pentateuch is fully inspired by God. But the truth of inspiration does not eliminate a variety of sources being used by Moses. (Luke used a number of different sources in putting his gospel together according to Luke 1:1-4.) Moses received some information directly from God (e.g. the law at Mount Sinai). Some truth was written down because Moses himself was an eyewitness of some events (e.g. the plagues on Egypt and the wilderness wanderings). Other information may have come from very ordinary means such as written documents or oral tradition (e.g. the account of the Flood of Noah or the many stories of the patriarchs). Inspiration has to do with the accurate recording of the truth. God guided this man Moses, using Moses' personality, vocabulary, and experiences, keeping him from error of any kind. "Inspiration argues only for accuracy of the written record; it does not stipulate that the writer had a mind that functioned as a blank tablet to be written on by the Holy Spirit."[4]

The Pentateuch, therefore, is an inspired, inerrant, authoritative document written by the man Moses.

4. Vos, *Genesis*, p. 7.

Note B:

VARIOUS VIEWS OF ORIGINS

A variety of views has been proposed to answer the question of the origin of the earth and the universe. Great amounts of material have been written in defending and promoting various views. It is simply impossible to reproduce the argumentation of the various positions. A brief summary is given of these views, recognizing the fact that within each perspective there may be many different variations.

EVOLUTION

The word *evolution* simply means "change," "development," or "progress." When applied to earth origins it stands for the view that the world and that which is in it began and developed by means of natural processes. Starting with simple, single-celled organisms, new species of more complex and intricate forms have developed over a period of billions of years. Mutations, natural selection, and vast amounts of time are the basic elements of this view. A personal Creator God is not needed or wanted in this theory. For the Christian, this theory must be rejected.

THEISTIC EVOLUTION

This view attempts to bring together the basic components of the theory of evolution with the Creator God of the Bible. The basic idea is that God created life but used the process of evolution to bring about the earth and the universe as we observe it today. This view holds that Adam's body was simply that of an animal that was the result of millions of years of evolutionary development. Several hundred thousand years ago, God placed an eternal soul into this ape-like biped. This act is that which sets animals and man apart.

But in trying to combine these opposite views, "theistic evolution" has compromised the clear teaching of Scripture on such subjects as the direct creation of man, the nature of man, and the origin of sin and death. It has been careless with the words and text of Scripture.[1] This theory will be unacceptable to those who have a high view of Scripture and believe in careful exegesis.

CREATIONISM

Creationism believes that almighty God supernaturally created the heavens and the earth by specific acts. Creation was out of nothing and was instantaneous. God did not use an evolutionary process to bring things into existence. Within creationism there are several basic viewpoints.

A. THE DAY-AGE VIEW

This view, also known as the Geologic Day View, generally holds that the days of creation in Genesis 1 were not literal twenty-four-hour days, but rather long periods of time. Thus, the earth is old, but man created on the sixth day is relatively young. Some have held that the days of Genesis 1 are literal twenty-four-hour days, but that there are great amounts of time separating the days. This view is held by several authors.[2]

B. THE RUIN-RECONSTRUCTION VIEW

This view, also known as the Gap Theory, proposes a large gap in time between an original creation (found in Genesis 1:1) and a re-creation (found in Genesis 1:3-31). The basic idea is that in the dateless past, God created a heaven and an earth that were perfect.

1. John C. Whitcomb, *The Early Earth,* rev. ed. (Grand Rapids: Baker, 1986), pp. 118-40.
2. Davis A. Young, *Christianity and the Age of the Earth* (Grand Rapids: Zondervan, 1982).

But then Satan fell into sin, and with him many other angelic beings also fell. Sin, therefore, entered the universe, and God destroyed the original earth, leaving it "waste and void." After vast amounts of time, God re-created the heavens and the earth. The days of Genesis 1 are literal twenty-four-hour days, but they describe the re-creation and not the original creation.[3]

C. THE LITERAL DAY VIEW

This view holds that the days of creation in Genesis 1 are literal twenty-four-hour days and that they are the days of the original creation. The heavens and the earth that we observe today, though marred by sin, are those created in Genesis 1. This view also believes in a young earth (that the earth is tens of thousands of years old and not millions or billions).[4] The author of this book holds to this view.

3. Arthur Custance, *Without Form and Void* (Brockville, Ont.: Arthur Custance, 1970).
4. John C. Whitcomb, *The Early Earth*, rev. ed. (Grand Rapids: Baker, 1986); Henry Morris, *Scientific Creationism* (San Diego: Creation-Life, 1981).

Note C:

THE NAMES OF GOD IN THE OLD TESTAMENT

Names in the Scriptures are not arbitrarily given. It was highly significant when God changed the name of a man, for it might indicate a new relationship or perhaps something new about the character of that man. Likewise, the names by which God identified Himself revealed a great deal about His character and relationships. It must always be remembered that man did not give these names to God, but they are self-revealed. They are, therefore, important sources of truth about God. It should be noted also that all the names of God combined still do not tell us everything about our God. He even has names He has chosen not to reveal (cf. Rev. 19:12).

There were three primary names of Deity in the Old Testament Scriptures: Elohim, Jehovah, and Adonai.

PRIMARY NAMES

A. ELOHIM

This is the most general and the most frequently used name of God in the Old Testament. The root of the word carries with it the idea of being strong and mighty. The word *elohim* is plural and is probably to be regarded as intensive. It therefore communicates the idea of a "fulness of power."[1] (Note: Although the truth of the Trinity cannot be proved from this plural name for God, it

1. Louis Berkhof, *Systematic Theology* (London: Banner of Truth, 1941), p. 48.

does allow for this doctrine in its later New Testament revelation.) This name is simply translated "God," but carries with it the concept of might and strength. The awesome power of Elohim is seen from the very beginning of the Old Testament, where He creates man and the universe (Gen. 1:1, 2, 26, 27). The name is used thousands of times by the writers of the Old Testament.

B. JEHOVAH

This name for God comes from four Hebrew consonants YHWH. It is uncertain how the name was actually pronounced, but most believe that "Yahweh" would be a better pronunciation that "Jehovah." Exodus 3:13-14 connects this name with the Hebrew verb "to be" (*hayah*). Fundamentally, the idea is that God is the "self-existent One" ("I AM that I AM").[2] In Exodus 6:6-8 the name is used three times to present God as the self-existent One who would save Israel and meet their needs.[3]

> His name was "I am the God who will be there" (Exod. 3:14). It was not so much an ontological designation or a static notion of being (e.g., "I am that I am"); it was rather a promise of a dynamic, active presence. . . . Israel would know His presence in a day-by-day experience as it never was known before. . . . The name came to represent the presence of God Himself instead of merely experiencing the effects of His presence on nature.[4]

C. ADONAI

This name is derived from a word meaning "to judge" or "to rule" and thus points to God as the Lord to whom everything is subject. He is the sovereign Master who has absolute authority over all creation (Ex. 4:10; Isa. 6:8-11; Josh. 5:14, 7:8).

2. Ibid., p. 49.
3. Charles R. Gianotti, "The Meaning of the Divine Name YHWH," *Bibliotheca Sacra* 142 (January-March 1985): 38-51.
4. Walter C. Kaiser, Jr., *Toward an Old Testament Theology* (Grand Rapids: Zondervan, 1981), p.107.

Along with these three primary names for God, the Old Testament has a large number of compound names that reveal more of the Person and work of God.

COMPOUND NAMES

A. EL SHADDAI

This name for God is used about forty-five times in the Old Testament, with the greatest frequency of usage in the era of the patriarchs. The name is usually translated "Almighty God."

> El Shaddai emphasized the supernatural work of His grace. As He overpowered nature and forced her to forward His plan of salvation, El Shaddai indicated God's ability to master nature. Thereby it linked together His work in Creation and now His overpowering work in history to effect His plan. . . . God is omnipotent and a great Sovereign who can and will act on behalf of those whom He loves and who are called according to His purpose and plan.[5]

The emphasis of this name is not only on His great power, but on His great power controlling all forces on behalf of His people (e.g., Gen. 17:1; 28:3; 43:14; Ex. 6:3; Num. 24:4, 16; Job 5:17).

B. JEHOVAH SABBAOTH

This compound name is translated "the Lord of Hosts" (e.g., 1 Sam. 4:4; 2 Sam. 6:2; Isa. 37:16; Pss. 80:4; 89:6-8). The "host" referred to is probably not Israel's army, but rather the angelic hosts who surround the throne of God. This name was a reminder to Israel of the awesome force available for their defense.

C. EL ELYON

The word *elyon* comes from a word that means "to go up" or "to be elevated." The name, therefore, is translated as "the Most High God." God is to be lifted up and exalted (e.g., Gen. 14:19-20; Num. 24:16; Isa. 14:14).

5. Ibid., p. 98.

D. OTHER COMPOUNDS

There are many other compound names in the Old Testament, including the following: *El Olam*, "the everlasting God" (Gen. 21:33); *Jehovah Tsidkenu*, "the Lord our Righteousness" (Jer. 23:6); *Qadosh Israel*, "the Holy One of Israel" (Isa. 1:4); *Jehovah Elohim Israel*, "the Lord God of Israel" (Judg. 5:3); and *Jehovah Shalom*, "the Lord is peace" (Judg. 6:24).[6]

6. Charles Ryrie, *A Survey of Bible Doctrine* (Chicago: Moody, 1977), pp. 28-29.

Note D:

THE DATE OF THE EXODUS

Although a number of dates for Israel's exodus from Egypt have been proposed, two views dominate. The view held in this book is the "early date" for the Exodus, which places Israel's departure from Egypt at about 1445 B.C. The second major position is the "late date" and puts the Exodus at about 1290 B.C.

The "early date" is built upon the normal interpretation of two key scriptures: 1 Kings 6:1 and Judges 11:26. First Kings 6:1 states that Solomon began to build the Temple in the fourth year of his reign (967/66 B.C.). The verse declares that the building of the Temple began 480 years after the Exodus, thus fixing the date for the Exodus at about 1446/45 B.C. Some have tried to challenge the validity of the text, but the number 480 is attested in the major manuscripts and can be maintained with certainty. Others have tried to argue that the 480 years actually represent twelve generations (12 x 40 = 480). It is said that 12 and 40 are representative numbers, and that a generation is actually closer to 25 years; thus the text is to be viewed as an approximation (of about 300 years).[1] But this attempt to explain away this key text by reducing the length of time involved is answered by pointing out that the text is not dealing with approximations but rather with specifics; specific historical events and specific months and years of a king's reign.[2]

---

1. J. N. Oswalt, "Chronology of the Old Testament," in *International Standard Bible Encyclopedia* (Grand Rapids: Eerdmans, 1949) 1:677.
2. Charles H. Dyer, "The Date of the Exodus Reexamined," *Bibliotheca Sacra* 140 (July-September 1983): 559:235.

Of particular importance to this discussion is the fact that the text under question does not appear in a poetic section of Scripture, nor is it poetically oriented. It represents sober historiography and points to two specific events in history with a numerically described time gap between them. Such a statement on the part of a historian is obviously oriented toward a specific chronological idea. While the number itself might represent a rounded figure, it nonetheless points to a specific period of time between two points in history. There is no indication in the text itself or in the context that the writer is using the number symbolically. On the contrary, the fact that the number takes in several eras of Israelite history indicates that a genealogy is not in view but the number of years between two great events in Israel's history.[3]

Judges 11:26 provides equally significant data for an early date of 1445 B.C. In this verse, Jephthah (one of Israel's judges) declares that Israel had occupied the city of Heshbon in the land of Moab for 300 years.

These cities were taken by Israel just before their invasion of Canaan (cf. Num. 21:25-35). The possession of Heshbon occurred approximately 340 years before Jephthah. The problem for those who hold the late Exodus date is obvious. If the Exodus took place in 1280 B.C., then Jephthah would have been a judge in 940 B.C.—during the reign of King Solomon! However, if the Exodus took place in 1445 B.C., then Jephthah judged in 1105 B.C., well within the period of the Judges.[4]

Once again those who hold to a "late date" attempt to neutralize the normal reading of the verse by suggesting that this is a broad generalization by one who did not have accurate records. It is said that Jephthah's statement to the king of Ammon is not to be taken as a rigid historical fact but as a rough guess.

3. John J. Davis, *Moses and the Gods of Egypt* (Winona Lake, Ind.: BMH, 1971), p. 30.
4. Dyer, "The Date of the Exodus Reexamined."

> It is scarcely possible, however, that Jephthah should make
> such a blunder in the midst of important international negotia-
> tions. . . . It is doubtful that Jephthah could have exaggerated
> this number as it was used in the argument to the king and have
> gotten away with it. The King of Ammon had some knowledge
> of the historical precedence involved in Israel's occupation of
> the territory of Transjordan (cf. Judg. 11:13). Again it would
> be well to point out that numerical information given in the pas-
> sage under question does not appear in a poetic section and
> therefore probably reflects sober historical fact.[5]

The Judges passage when coupled with the statement in 1 Kings
presents a strong case for the 1445 B.C. date for the Exodus.

The scriptural evidence for the "late date" rests quite heavily
on Exodus 1:11. This verse states that the enslaved Israelites built
the storehouse cities of Pithom and Rameses. The point is that
since the city of Rameses was built just before the Exodus and
since the city was named after Pharoah Rameses II who lived in
the thirteenth century, the Exodus must have occurred during the
reign of this thirteenth-century pharaoh. But this position has several problems with it. First, the city may not have been named after Pharaoh Rameses II at all, since there was evidently a land
area by that name long before him (Gen. 47:11). There was possibly a Ramesside dynasty, ages before Rameses II, from which the
land (and thus the city) got its name.[6] Second, the actual chronology of the period makes clear that Rameses II could not have been
the one who ordered the building of these cities. The construction
work began decades before Rameses II and the Exodus.[7]

The "late date" position has rested primarily on the evidence
of archaeology. But all of the evidence that is used to point to the
late date view can be interpreted with equal force for an early
date. Although archaeology is valuable and has proved helpful
time and again in illustrating the Bible's validity, it cannot be

5. Davis, *Moses and the Gods of Egypt,* p. 31.
6. Eugene Merrill, *An Historical Survey of the Old Testament* (Grand Rapids:
   Baker, 1980), p. 107.
7. Davis, *Moses and the Gods of Egypt,* p. 19.

called upon to settle this question. The declarations of Scripture must provide the primary evidence in determining the date of the Exodus. A high view of the Scriptures, coupled with normal interpretation of the Bible passages, points to a date of 1445 B.C. If this is the correct date, then there is the possibility of identifying the pharaohs of Egypt who appear in the text of Scripture.

ISRAEL AND THE PHARAOHS

PHARAOH	EVENT/PERSON IN BIBLE
Sesostris III (1878-1841)	Jacob and his family entered Egypt to avoid the famine
Amenemhet III (1841-1797)	Joseph died during his reign
Ahmose I (1570-1548)	The pharaoh who "knew not Joseph"—Exodus 1:5
Amenhotep I (1548-1528)	Possibly the pharaoh of Exodus 1:15, who attempted to reduce Israel's population
Thutmose I (1528-1508)	Moses born in 1525; possibly the pharaoh of Exodus 1:15
Thutmose II (1508-1504)	
Thutmose III (1504-1448)	The pharaoh who severely oppressed Israel—Exodus 2:25
Amenhotep II (1448-1423)	The Exodus was in 1445; the pharaoh of the Exodus

Note E:

ISRAEL AND THE NATIONS

The Amalekites

Amalek was a great-grandson of Abraham. He was the son of Eliphaz, who was the firstborn of Esau (Gen. 36:10, 12, 16; 1 Chron. 1:36). The descendants of Amalek settled in the desert area southwest of the Dead Sea and down into the Sinai Peninsula.

The first mention of the Amalekites was in connection with their attack on Moses and the Israelites at the time of the Exodus (Ex. 17:14; Deut. 25:17-19). Even though they were related to Israel (see chart "Nations Related to Israel," p. 253), the Amalekites are always seen as bitter enemies of God's people (Num. 14:45; 1 Sam. 30:1-2). God executed judgment on these people especially at the hands of Saul and David (1 Sam. 15:1-9; 30:16-20). They are last heard of in the days of King Hezekiah (1 Chron. 4:43). It should be noted that Moses does mention the Amalekites long before Amalek was born (Gen. 14:7). But this reference is best interpreted as Moses speaking of the land area that afterward would become known as the country of the Amalekites.

The Ammonites

The Ammonites came from Ammon, who had been born as a result of an incestuous relation between Lot and his younger daughter (Gen. 19:33-38). These peoples were, therefore, related to Israel. They lived east of the Jordan River, between the rivers

NATIONS RELATED TO ISRAEL

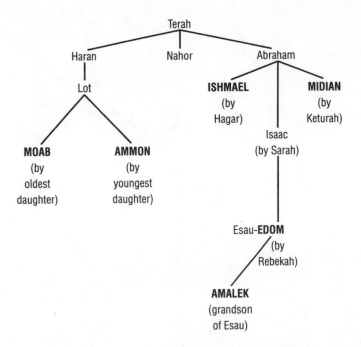

Jabbok and Arnon (see map "Israel's Near Neighbors," p. 254), until they were pushed farther east into the desert by Sihon, king of the Amorites.

Though related to Israel by ancestry, the Ammonites are invariably seen as hostile to them. Moses and the Israelites were careful to respect their land and to avoid taking anything that belonged to them, as Israel headed for the land of Canaan (Deut. 23:3-4).

The Ammonites oppressed Israel in the days of the judges (Judg. 10:7; 11:4-11) and were a problem to Israel in the time of the monarchy (1 Sam. 11:1-13; 2 Sam. 10:1-19) and the years after the monarchy (Jer. 40:14; 41:10; Neh. 4:3). Because of their wickedness, judgment was pronounced on them, and they have now disappeared from the earth (1 Kings 11:5, 7, 33; Ezek. 25:5; Zeph. 2:9).

ISRAEL'S NEAR NEIGHBORS

ARAM
(Syria)

PHOENICIA

The Great Sea

Sea of
Galilee

Yarmuk R.

ISRAEL

☆
Samaria

Jabbok R.

Jordan R.

AMMON

PHILISTIA

☆
Jerusalem

AMORITES

Dead
Sea

Arnon R.

JUDAH

MOAB

Zered R.

AMALEK

EDOM

THE ASSYRIANS

The Assyrians were Semites (descendants of Noah's son Shem). The bloodline and language of the Assyrians was originally quite close to that of the Babylonians. As the centuries went by, however, the Assyrians intermarried with other peoples very little, thus keeping some purity in their bloodline. These people originally settled in northern Mesopotamia on the Tigris River (see map "Israel's Distant Neighbors," p. 258).

The Assyrians were one of several nations used by the Lord to discipline His people Israel. It must be remembered, however, in reading Israel's history that none of these foreign nations could have become strong enough to conquer Israel's covenanted land area except by Divine permission and because of Israel's sin (Lev. 26:23-33).

The Assyrians began to build an empire around 1100 B.C. (the era of the monarchy in Israel began in 1043 B.C.). But for about two centuries the empire lay dormant. When King Ashurnasirpal II (883-859 B.C.) rose to power, he created a great Assyrian fighting machine and began conquering many areas. His son, Shalmaneser III (858-824 B.C.), inherited his father's war machine and conducted numerous campaigns against Syria and Palestine. Assyria then declined somewhat until the coming of Tiglath-Pileser III (745-727 B.C.), a mighty warrior and able statesman, who brought Assyria to a place of great power and glory. He overran Israel and took tribute from King Menahem of Israel (cf. 2 Kings 15:19) and also took some of the conquered peoples to distant sections of his empire. Hoshea of Israel attempted to revolt against Assyria and felt the crushing blow of Assyrian power. Shalmaneser V (726-722 B.C.) succeeded his father and besieged Israel's capital city of Samaria for three years (2 Kings 17:3-6). The next Assyrian king, Sargon II, finished the job of defeating Israel and taking captive the Northern Kingdom.

Under the kings that followed, Assyria's stranglehold on the ancient world began to ease. With the exception of one or two kings, the remaining Assyrian kings did not distinguish themselves. The capital city of Assyria, Nineveh, fell in 612 B.C. After experiencing defeats at Haran (609 B.C.) and Carchemish (605 B.C.), the empire of Assyria was gone.

It should be noted also that God sent two of His prophets to speak to the Assyrians. Jonah brought his message in about 780 B.C., and later Nahum directed a word of judgment against them in 650 B.C.

THE BABYLONIANS

The ancient city of Babylon is known to us through the biblical record ("Babel" in Gen. 10:10; 11:1-9). The city was eventually possessed by a semitic people. Babylon had an early period of strength (1800-1550 B.C.), but her most significant days of glory came about 600 B.C. and involved God's people.

As the power of Assyria began to wane, nations began to revolt successfully. In 626 B.C., Babylonia gained full independence from Assyria through the leadership of Nabopolassar. In 605 B.C., Nabopolasar (now in poor health) sent his son, Nebuchadnezzar, to fight the remnant of the Assyrian empire, which had been joined by the Egyptians under Pharaoh Neco II. In the battle of Carchemish, Nebuchadnezzar completely defeated the Assyrians and the Egyptians and established Babylon as the most powerful nation in the ancient Near East. Nebuchadnezzar pursued the Egyptians as they fled home to Egypt. But he stopped at Jerusalem and subjugated the Southern Kingdom of Judah. While there, he received word that his father had died, so he hurried back to Babylon to claim the throne (taking some Jews, like Daniel, with him as captives). In 568 B.C. he defeated Egypt, thus making complete his world conquests. He died in 562 B.C. None of his successors had his abilities. They were unable to keep this massive empire together for long. The kingdom of Babylon ended in the year 539 B.C., being taken over by the Medes and the Persians. But Babylon was raised up long enough to accomplish the purposes of God.

THE EDOMITES

The Edomites were the descendants of Esau, the brother of Jacob. They settled south of the Dead Sea (Gen. 25:30; 36:1-9; 31-43). In the Bible, the Edomites are also called "Seir" or "Mount

Seir'' after the geographic area where they settled (Gen. 36:9; Ezek. 35:1-15).

Esau's hatred for his brother, Jacob, seemed to continue through his descendants. Being a near relative apparently made no difference to them. The Edomites refused to allow Moses and the Israelites passage through their land, thus causing great discomfort for Israel (Num. 20:18-21). For some 400 years nothing is mentioned about the Edomites. But they reappear during the monarchy period as an adversary of Israel (e.g. 1 Sam. 14:47; 2 Sam. 8:13-14; 1 Kings 11:15-16; 2 Chron. 20:22; 21:8; 25:11-12; 28:17). Because of their terrible treatment of ''brother Jacob,'' the Edomites were severely denounced by the prophets (e.g., Obadiah, Isa. 34:5-8; Jer. 49:17; Amos 1:11-12).

THE EGYPTIANS

In many ways the most important foreign nation Israel dealt with was Egypt. The great importance of Egypt has been discussed in Genesis and Exodus (the first two foundational books). Egypt was used by God as the great protector of the infant nation of Israel (Gen. 42-50). Later Egypt became the great persecutor of Israel, thus bringing about the awesome display of God's power (Ex. 5-14). After the Exodus from Egypt, the nation of Egypt still affected Israel and Israel's foreign policy in the following centuries.

During the Old Testament times following the Exodus (1445-400 B.C.), Egypt never became a world power like Assyria and Babylon. They were, however, on several occasions a ''thorn in the side'' of the world powers. They joined with other nations to resist the Assyrians, then the Babylonians, and later on the Persians. On some occasions their actions directly affected Israel (e.g., 2 Kings 23:29, the killing of King Josiah).

THE MEDO-PERSIANS

Medo-Persia was a dual nation that dominated the ancient world from 539-330 B.C. It was composed of two similar peoples, the Medes and the Persians.

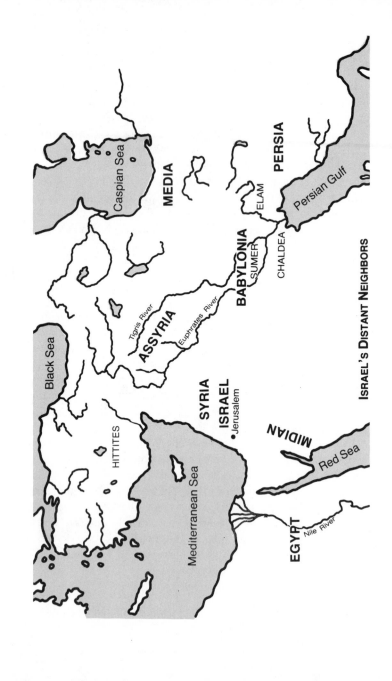

ISRAEL'S DISTANT NEIGHBORS

Media came under the rule of the Assyrians, as Assyrian documents testify. But Media began to rise to power, and in 614 B.C. they conquered the Assyrian city of Asshur. They then joined forces with the Babylonians to overthrow Nineveh in 612 B.C. Nebuchadnezzar of Babylon married the daughter of Cyaxares, the Median king, thus strengthening the alliance between those two nations.

The Persians came into the area east of the Tigris River about 1500 B.C. For most of the following centuries they were dominated by the Medes. However, with the rise of Cyrus II in 550 B.C., Persia subdued Media. Media remained an important province, which is seen in the use of the dual name "Medes and Persians" (e.g., Dan. 5:28; Esther 1:19). This great empire was able to last for more than two centuries until it finally fell before Alexander the Great.

THE MIDIANITES

After the death of Sarah, Abraham married Keturah and had six sons by her (Gen. 25:1-6). The fourth of these sons was Midian. In order to insure that Isaac alone would be the "covenant" son, Midian and his brothers were given gifts and sent to the east. The Midianites were found in an area south and east of Palestine.

The Midianites do not appear often in Scripture. They are the ones who took Joseph to Egypt and sold him (Gen. 37:13-28). Exodus 2:15-22 records that Moses fled to the land of Midian after killing an Egyptian and there married a Midianite girl. The Midianites figure in the story of Balaam and the resistance to Israel as they prepared to enter Canaan (Num. 25:6-17; 31:1-8; Josh. 13:21). And the Midianites were one of the nations that oppressed Israel during the time of the judges. Gideon brought Israel deliverance from the Midianites (Judg. 6:33; 7:1-14, 25).

In the Genesis narrative the terms *Midianite* and *Ishmaelite* are used interchangeably. Most likely this is because they became closely associated through intermarriage. It should be noted that with these nomadic peoples racial lines were not rigidly adhered to, and so some very close connections can be observed on occasion.

THE MOABITES

Moab was a son of Lot, resulting from Lot's incestuous relationship with his older daughter (Gen. 19:33-37). The Moabites lived on the eastern side of the Dead Sea, below the Arnon River.

Moab's relationship with Israel was evidently not quite as hostile as some other nations. They seemed to be a more peaceful people. Moab, however, did refuse passage to the Israelites, but showed no hostile action when Israel went along their border in order to arrive on the east side of the Jordan (Judg. 11:17, 25-26; Deut. 23:3-4). The Moabites lived in peace with Israel for three hundred years (Judg. 11:25-26). Over the centuries there were, however, times of war. The Moabites oppressed Israel in the days of the judges (Judg. 3:12-30) and were themselves defeated by Saul (1 Sam. 14:47) and David (2 Sam. 8:2). Moab at times paid tribute to Israel (e.g., 2 Kings 3:4-5), but at other times was independent and prosperous. Several Israelite prophets warned Moab of coming judgment (e.g., Isa. 15, 16; Jer. 48).

THE PHILISTINES

Unlike many of Israel's neighbors, the Philistines were genetically and culturally unrelated. According to the Scriptures, they came from a place called Caphtor (Jer. 47:4; Amos 9:7), which is apparently a reference to the island of Crete. Archaeology would suggest a broader geographic origin for the Philistines. They not only came from Crete, but probably from numerous islands of the Aegean Sea and perhaps coastlands as well. About 1200 B.C. the Philistines attempted to invade the delta region of Egypt. Unable to defeat the armies of Pharaoh Rameses III, they settled on the southwest coast of Palestine.

The Philistines established a city-state type of organization. There were five major cities (Gath, Gaza, Ashkelon, Ashdod, and Ekron) which formed this powerful Philistine federation.

The Philistines were a constant source of trouble for Israel. Philistine power was evidenced in Israel during the time of the judges (e.g., Judg. 14, 15; 1 Sam. 4). During the early days of Israel's monarchy the Philistines played an important role. Saul had limited success, but David was able to subdue them (1 Sam. 13;31; 2

Sam. 5). They were a problem for the kings of Israel at other times during the monarchy period. Their judgment was predicted by several of the prophets (e.g., Jer. 47:1-7; Ezek. 25:15-17). The Egyptians and Babylonians were able to crush the Philistines.

THE PHOENICIANS

The Phoenicians were a racial mixture of Canaanites and Semites. The earliest settlers of the area were Canaanite, but they became overwhelmed by the great Semitic empires of the Fertile Crescent. The Phoenicians were one result of the intermixing of these racial groups. They occupied the coastal regions between the Lebanon mountains and the Mediterranean Sea north of the city of Acco. Tyre and Sidon were the two most famous Phoenician cities.

The Phoenicians were not hostile toward Israel and did not seem to have the interest or the capacity to invade Israel. They were a commercially oriented people. With their two great seaports of Tyre and Sidon (and others) and with the availability of timber for shipbuilding, they became world famous for their commercial activities.

The Old Testament Scriptures do not use the term "Phoenicia" but speak instead of the principle cities of Tyre and Sidon (e.g., 2 Sam. 5:11; 24:7; 1 Kings 7:14; Isa. 23:17; Jer. 47:4; Judg. 1:31; 1 Kings 17:9; 16:31). Where there were contacts with these people, the relationship seemed good.

THE SYRIANS

The first settlers of the region commonly called Syria were evidently of Hamitic descent (cf. Gen. 10:6-20). These Canaanites were eventually invaded and taken over by a Semitic race, the Arameans. The tribes who lived in this region were not united in the early days of Old Testament history and, therefore, were not a significant political or military force. The ancient city of Damascus was the main city of this area.

The first hostile activity with Israel came in the days of King David as he extended the borders of Israel (2 Sam. 8:3-13). David was repeatedly successful against the Syrians (2 Sam. 10:6-19).

But after the division of Israel's kingdom (931 B.C.), the Syrians enjoyed their period of greatest power (from about 900 to 730 B.C.). During those years they were sometimes in alliance with Israel or Judah, whereas at other times they were vicious enemies (e.g., 1 Kings 15:18-20; 2 Kings 13:3-7). Syria acted as a natural buffer zone between Israel and the great powers of the north and east.

Note F:

THE EXTERMINATION OF THE CANAANITES

In Israel's first battle inside the boundaries of the Promised Land, they killed every human being except for Rahab and her family (Josh. 6:21). This total extermination of everyone in the city of Jericho was simply in obedience to a command of the Lord. The Lord had commanded that all Canaanites living within the designated land boundaries given to Israel were to be exterminated. ("Canaanite" is a general term used for the several different peoples who lived in that land.) No mercy was to be shown to them, and no treaties of any kind were to be made with them (Ex. 23:31-33; 34:11-17; Lev. 18:24-25; Deut. 7:1-2; 20:16-18). All of their religious images and artifacts were to be destroyed also. These people had been set apart for complete and utter destruction. Joshua and the Israelites were to carry out the Lord's command.

Some people have questioned the morality of God's command to exterminate the Canaanites. But the Scriptures and archaeology justify this command. The Canaanite society had become terribly degenerate. Their perverted religious practices had so polluted them that their iniquity was as great as it could be (cf. Gen. 15:16). They worshiped a large number of deities who were characterized by wicked behavior that in turn dictated the behavior of the Canaanites.

> The brutality, lust and abandon of Canaanite mythology is far worse than elsewhere in the Near East at the time. And the astounding characteristic of Canaanite deities, that they had no moral character whatever, must have brought out the worst traits in their devotees and entailed many of the most demoralizing practices of the time, such as sacred prostitution, child sacrifice and snake worship.[1]

Canaanite religion was basically a fertility religion. Since they were an agricultural society, the Canaanites were interested in fertility and production. Their gods (such as El and Baal) and their goddesses (such as Asherah, Anath, and Astarte) were fertility gods, whose activities affected the crops and the animals. It was believed that the perverted sexual relations among these gods and goddesses directly affected fertility on the earth. The gods themselves were supposedly stimulated to such relations by the perverted and depraved sexual activities of the Canaanites as they "worshiped" in the temples.[2]

Leviticus 18 is a key chapter in understanding the character of the Canaanites. This chapter details those sexual practices that were abhorrent to God, including adultery, incest, homosexuality, and bestiality. These practices characterized the people of Canaan (18:3, 24-28). Other evils, such as child sacrifice, were part of Canaanite life as well. The nations that inhabited the Promised Land were just as evil as the residents of Sodom and Gomorrah (Gen. 18, 19) or those people who lived in the days of Noah (Gen. 6:5, 11).

It was clear that Israel could have absolutely no contact with these people, or else Israel would become infected with the same moral and spiritual sickness. Israel was called repeatedly to be a holy people, different from the peoples who inhabited Canaan (Deut. 7:1-4). There was no room for compromise or coexistence. The Canaanites had evidently come to the place spiritually where they would never turn to the true God (like those mentioned in

1. Merrill F. Unger, *Archeology and the Old Testament* (Grand Rapids: Zondervan, 1960), p. 175.
2. Ibid., pp. 172-75.

Rom. 1:24-28). A few, like Rahab of Jericho (Josh. 6:17), may have come to the God of Israel, but they were rare exceptions. And too, it should be noted that any Canaanite wishing to avoid death could have easily fled outside the borders of the Promised Land and been safe. The taking of the land under Joshua lasted about six years. A person could flee outside of the boundaries from anywhere in the land in two or three days.

It must also be remembered that God is sovereign. He is the great Creator and can do what He wishes with His creation. He has the right and the power to deal with those who violate His holy laws.

> God is a holy God. He demands that sin be punished. The Lord reserves the right to punish sin wherever it is found, whether it be in the immediate destruction of a city or the condemnation of the sinner at final judgment. It is only by the mercy and the grace of God that any sinner is permitted to live his life completely.[3]

3. John J. Davis, *Conquest and Crisis* (Winona Lake, Ind.: BMH, 1969), p. 50.

SELECTED BIBLIOGRAPHY

Archer, Gleason. *A Survey of Old Testament Introduction*. Chicago: Moody, 1964.

Bruce, F. F. *Israel and the Nations*. Grand Rapids: Eerdmans, 1963.

Davis, John J. *Moses and the Gods of Egypt*. Winona Lake: BMH, 1971.

Freeman, Hobart. *An Introduction to the Old Testament Prophets*. Chicago: Moody, 1968.

Jensen, Irving. *Jensen's Survey of the Old Testament*. Chicago: Moody, 1978.

Kaiser, Walter C., Jr. *Toward an Old Testament Theology*. Grand Rapids: Zondervan, 1981.

Merrill, Eugene. *An Historical Survey of the Old Testament*. Grand Rapids: Baker, 1980.

Pusey, E. B. *The Minor Prophets*. Grand Rapids: Baker, 1965.

Schultz, Samuel. *The Old Testament Speaks*. New York: Harper, 1970.

Thiele, Edwin R. *A Chronology of the Hebrew Kings*. Grand Rapids: Zondervan, 1977.

Unger, Merrill F. *Archaeology and the Old Testament*. Grand Rapids: Zondervan, 1956.

Walton, John. *Chronological Charts of the Old Testament*. Grand Rapids: Zondervan, 1981.

Walvoord, John. *The Millennial Kingdom*. Findlay, Ohio: Dunham, 1963.

Whitcomb, John, and Morris, Henry. *The Genesis Flood*. Philadelphia: Presbyterian and Reformed, 1961.

Wood, Leon. *A Survey of Israel's History*. Grand Rapids: Zondervan, 1970.

Young, Edward J. *My Servants the Prophets*. Grand Rapids: Eerdmans, 1968.

Moody Press, a ministry of Moody Bible Institute, is designed for education, evangelization, and edification. If we may assist you in knowing more about Christ and the Christian life, please write us without obligation: Moody Press, c/o MLM, Chicago, IL 60610.